The World According to Fannie Davis

The World According to Fannie Davis

MY MOTHER'S LIFE IN THE DETROIT NUMBERS

BRIDGETT M. DAVIS

Little, Brown and Company

New York Boston London

Hachette Book Group supports the right to free expression and the value of copyright. The purpose of copyright is to encourage writers and artists to produce the creative works that enrich our culture.

The scanning, uploading, and distribution of this book without permission is a theft of the author's intellectual property. If you would like permission to use material from the book (other than for review purposes), please contact permissions@hbgusa.com. Thank you for your support of the author's rights.

Little, Brown and Company
Hachette Book Group
1290 Avenue of the Americas, New York, NY 10104
littlebrown.com

First United States Edition: January 2019

Little, Brown and Company is a division of Hachette Book Group, Inc. The Little, Brown name and logo are trademarks of Hachette Book Group, Inc.

The publisher is not responsible for websites (or their content) that are not owned by the publisher.

The Hachette Speakers Bureau provides a wide range of authors for speaking events. To find out more, go to hachettespeakersbureau.com or call (866) 376-6591.

All photographs and images courtesy of the author, with the exception of those on pages 17 and 254, courtesy of Michael Terrell.

ISBN 978-0-316-55873-0
Library of Congress Control Number: 2018949177

10 9 8 7 6 5 4 3 2 1

LSC-C

Printed in the United States of America

For my mother,
and
for Tyler and Abebitu, so they may know her.

Contents

Author's Note

Dear Reader,

Because of the many years that have passed, and the ephemeral nature of the Numbers themselves, the physical record that remains of my mother's business is scant. But my memory of her work is not; it is vivid. To edify and enhance my own memory, I've also relied on the recollections and knowledge of my mother's sister and brother, my nephew and cousins, and childhood friends. I've joined these interviews with extensive research, my own earlier writings and diary entries, as well as family documents and personal papers kept in my mother's brass trunk—to reconstruct the world of my childhood and young adulthood as the youngest daughter of my mother, Fannie Drumwright Davis Robinson, who ran Numbers in Detroit. This is her story. And mine.

...They did not dream the American Dream, they willed it into being by a definition of their own choosing.

—Isabel Wilkerson, *The Warmth of Other Suns*

My mission in life is not merely to survive but to thrive; and to do so with some passion, some compassion, some humor, and some style.

—Maya Angelou

The World According to
Fannie Davis

Prologue

On a morning like most, I sit beside Mama at the dining room table, eating my bowl of Sugar Frosted Flakes and watching her work. She's on the telephone, its receiver in the crook of her neck as she records her customer's three-digit bets in a spiral notebook, repeating each one. The crystal chandelier blazes above.

"Five-four-two for a quarter. Six-nine-three straight for fifty cents. Is this both races, Miss Queenie? Detroit and Pontiac? Okay. Three-eight-eight straight for a quarter. Uh-huh. Four-seven-five straight for fifty cents. One-ten boxed for a dollar." Mama writes the numbers 110, draws a box around them, hesitates. "You know, I got customers been playing one-ten all week. Yeah, it's a fancy number. Oh did you? What'd you dream? He was a hunchback? Is that what *The Red Devil* dream book say it play for? Now *that* I didn't

3

know. I know *theater* plays for one ten. Well, I can take it for a dollar, but since it's a fancy, I can't take it for more than that. You understand. What else, Miss Queenie? Six-eight-four for fifty cents boxed, uh-huh. Nine-seven-two straight for a dollar."

I find comfort in Mama's voice, in the familiar, rhythmic recitation of numbers. I bring the bowl to my lips and drink the last of the sweetened milk before I rise and kiss Mama's forehead. She mouths "Bye-bye" as I join my sister Rita, who's waiting on the porch; together we walk three long blocks to Winterhalter Elementary and Junior High School, passing by the lush Russell Woods Park. I'm a first grader.

In class, I wait in line to show my teacher, Miss Miller, my assignment. We've had to color paper petals, cut them out, and paste them onto a picture of a flower. I like mine, as I've glued each one just at the base, so that the petals now reach out, into a pop-up flower. Miss Miller looks over my work, gives it one star instead of two, and stops me before I can return to my seat.

"You sure do have a lot of shoes," she says. Last week, she asked what my father did for a living, and because I knew never to disclose the family business I said, "He doesn't work." She asked: "Well, what does your mother do?" I froze. "I'm not sure," I lied. I knew my mother was in the Numbers, but I also knew not to tell that to anyone. I worried that my vague answer was the wrong one, but I didn't know a better response. No one had told me yet what I *should* say.

Now with Miss Miller staring at me I look down at my feet, which are clad in—I still remember—light blue patent leather slip-ons with lace-trimmed buckles. A favorite pair bought to match a brocade ensemble I've just worn for Easter. I nod, not knowing what else to do.

"Before you sit down, I want you to name every pair of shoes you have," she insists. "Go ahead." There's no lightness in her voice.

Anxious, I go through a mental inventory of the shoes that line the built-in rack in my bedroom closet. I manage to recall ten pairs in various colors and styles: the black-and-white polka-dotted ones with a bow tie; the buckled ruby-red ones, the salmon-pink lace-ups...

"Ten pairs is an awful lot," says Miss Miller. Her blue eyes fix on me with something I can't name, but which I'd now call disdain, and she orders me to take my seat.

I can feel my classmates staring at me as I return to my table. Is it wrong to have so many pairs of shoes? Did my mother get them in a bad way?

The next day in class, Miss Miller calls me back to her desk. I can smell the hairspray in her teased blond bouffant. "You didn't mention you had white shoes," she snaps.

Indeed, I'm wearing a white version of the same pair I wore the previous day. I feel as though I've been caught in a lie, and I know I've disappointed my teacher. I worry that I'll get in trouble. At school, or worse, at home.

"I'm sorry," I whisper.

Miss Miller shakes her head in disgust and dismisses me with a wave of her hand.

I return to my desk, trying hard not to look down at my shoes. I am ashamed of them.

That evening, I tell Mama what happened. But I wait until after she's finished taking her customers' bets and before the day's winning numbers come out. I've already learned that the best time to tell Mama difficult news, something that could get you in trouble, is during that brief, expectant pause in the day. That's when Mama is least distracted, and still in a good mood.

She listens, and when I confess I forgot to tell Miss Miller about the eleventh pair of shoes, her dark eyes flash with anger. I fear a spanking.

"That's none of her damn business!" she says. "Who does she think she is?"

Before I can feel relief that she's not mad at me, Mama says, "Get your coat and let's go."

I do as I'm told. Mama throws on her soft blue leather coat, the color of the Periwinkle crayon in my Crayola box, and together we slide into her new Buick Riviera; are we headed back to school to confront Miss Miller? Thank God no, as Mama heads south, away from Winterhalter Elementary; she soon turns onto Second Avenue, drives to the corner of Lothrop, and parks in front of the New Center building. There sits Saks Fifth Avenue.

We enter through regal double doors and I instantly fall in love with the store's marble floors, brass elevators, and bright chandeliers. I feel lucky just being here. Mama takes my hand and leads me to the children's shoe department, where an array of options spreads before us. She points to a pair of yellow patent leather shoes. "Those are pretty," she says.

Perhaps the saleswoman looks at us askance, given how rare it must have been to see black people inside Detroit's upscale shops in the sixties, but I don't remember. What I do remember is how nonchalantly Mama opens her wallet, pulls out a hundred-dollar bill, and pays for the shoes, while the saleswoman looks at her the way Miss Miller looked at me.

When we get home, Mama says, "You're going to wear these to school tomorrow. And you better tell that damn teacher of yours that you actually have a dozen pairs of shoes, you hear me?"

The next day, I wear my brand-new shoes with a matching yellow knit dress. Nervous as I walk up to my teacher's desk, I announce: "Miss Miller, I have twelve pairs of shoes." She looks down at my feet and then levels those blue eyes at my face. "Sit down."

Miss Miller never says another word to me. I feel her rejection but I'm also relieved; I no longer have to worry about what I wear to school, or feel bad about my nice things. I feel both protected and indulged by Mama. Growing up, that's how it was for me, and my three older sisters and brother. We lived well thanks to Mama and her Numbers, which inured us from judgment. My mother's message to black and white folks alike was clear: *It's nobody's business what I do for my children, nor how I manage to do it.*

The fact that Mama gave us an unapologetically good life by taking others' bets on three-digit numbers, collecting their money when they didn't win, paying their hits when they did, and profiting from the difference, is the secret I've carried with me throughout my life. I've come to see it as her triumphant Great Migration tale: Fannie Davis left Jim Crow Nashville for Detroit in the midfifties with an ailing husband and three small children, and figured out how to "make a way out of no way" by building a thriving lottery business that gave her a shot at the American dream. Her ingenuity and talent and dogged pursuit of happiness made possible our beautiful home, brimming refrigerator, and quality education. Our job as her children was twofold: to take advantage of every opportunity she created, and to keep safe the family secret. The word *illegal* was never spoken, but the Numbers were by their nature and design an underground enterprise. We understood this. So my siblings and I followed her edict: Keep your head up and your mouth shut. Be proud and be private.

But as I grew older, our family secret became the paradox of my life. I idolized my mother and loved being her daughter, was especially grateful for the example she'd set. As an adult, I wanted to share with the world her generous nature and keen parenting skills *and* sharp business know-how. But of course the bravest, badass part of her life had to be kept hush-hush. I considered writing a thinly veiled fictional story, but even that felt too risky. And writing about my mother without mentioning the Numbers would be fruitless. I know because I tried and it didn't work. Mama and her Numbers were inextricably intertwined. So, I kept quiet.

After Mama died in 1992, my sister Rita briefly took over running the business; but she eventually closed it down and our family's life in Numbers ended, and with it, the threat of exposure disappeared. For the next two decades, I told no one but my husband what my mother had done for a living. The family secret, a handed-down order, was well in place by the time I was born. It was all I'd known my entire life. I am hardwired *not* to tell. I can still hear Mama's voice, hear her warning: "No good can come from running your mouth."

I believed her. And I didn't want to betray Mama's trust, nor dishonor her legacy. I worried that people would judge her,

judge us, for her livelihood. Besides, as long as I kept her secret, abided by her rule, I kept her alive in my memory. Telling
would be odd, might trigger a betrayal that led to forgetting.
I grappled with that odd dissonance for a long time, proud of
my mother but unable to brag about her.

Over time, as I began to understand the depth of my loss,
my own feelings shifted, and I *wanted* to tell Mama's story;
this desire grew into a smoldering, yearning urge that got
harder and harder to suppress. I felt cheated. As dynamic
and trailblazing as she was, I couldn't brag about her the
way friends bragged about their own mothers going back to
school to get a PhD, or surviving as divorced single moms
or joining the Peace Corps at fifty. Now it was killing me to
keep her life's work a secret, and I compensated by talking
about her incessantly, quoting her pithy sayings whenever an
opportunity presented itself. I made sure those who hadn't
met her learned via my constant bragging how exceptional
she was. If asked, I told people my mother had been "in
real estate," that she managed properties she owned, that
her livelihood came from collecting rent—a half-truth. (Little did I know that "being in real estate" was code for being
a number runner.)

As more years passed, I began to feel remiss for *not*
telling, guilty of omitting such a crucial fact about my
mother's life. I talked about her less and less because of that
guilt, and *that* saddened me, as I knew that my mother's
work had transformed our family's lives, kept us going. It felt
disrespectful, really, to keep quiet, as though I was dishon-
oring Mama with my silence. I was who I was because my
mother chose to be a number runner, and my own children

didn't even know who their grandmother had been, what she'd accomplished with her life. A secret, good or bad, weighs on you.

And there was this new fear: If I didn't tell, would I forget what the Numbers were? Grappling with these mixed emotions, for years I topped my New Year's resolution list with the same goal: "Tell Mama's story." But I *still* couldn't get past the habit of withholding, or the fear of revelation.

Finally, in the way in which we draw from public figures' mythic lives for personal inspiration, I convinced myself that if patriarch Joseph P. Kennedy Sr. could allegedly use his early years as a bootlegger to launch his family's fortune, actions that brought him no recrimination since alcohol became legal anyway, then Mama's work was analogous. She too engaged in a business practice that eventually became legal.

And so I took a big, scary step: I flew to Detroit, sat at the dining room table across from my aunt Florence, my mother's remaining sister, who was celebrating her eightieth birthday that year, and nervously asked the one person whose permission I most needed: Would it be okay with her if I wrote about Fannie's life as a number runner? My aunt's answer surprised me.

"Honey, I'll help you tell it," she said. "'Cause what your mama did was unheard of, what she created was something else and folks *should* know." And then she smiled. "She made sure you didn't have to worry about no life in Numbers, so I know you don't really understand too much. I'll explain it to you."

I laughed with relief. She was right. I didn't understand the intricacies of the Numbers business. Having Aunt Florence's blessing *and* her know-how freed me. I started by digging through an old brass trunk filled with my mother's possessions that I'd kept in storage in Manhattan for many years. I hadn't looked through this trunk since Mama's death. Inside, I found a manila envelope filled with nearly a dozen letters that my sister Rita, four years older and the closest sibling to me in age, had written to God. They were composed on pages clearly ripped from the spiral notebooks once ubiquitous in our home, used to record customers' bets, bills, and payouts. In one letter, my then twelve-year-old sister wrote:

Dear God,

Please don't let 543 come out tonight. And please take away Mama's headaches.

Your loving servant, Rita

In another letter, she simply wrote:

Dear God,

Please stop me from worrying.

Thank you, Rita

I'd known that Rita wrote letters to God and stuffed them into the family Bible when we were growing up, but I'd never actually seen one. Reading those letters, all of equal plea, written in a child's hand, blew open the honed narrative about my mother that I'd burnished over the years. With her number running, she'd pulled off an amazing feat worthy of recognition. But the truth was more complicated, and stark: Mama's livelihood was risky business, and my sister articulated the stress we all felt from living with that risk. Rita also understood that given the secret nature of our lives, she could *only* confide in God.

Back then Rita understood what I did not. To maintain our comfort, Mama fought steadily against the threats of fierce competition and wipeouts, but also against exposure and police busts—and thanks to the cash business she was in, armed robberies and break-ins. Rita knew before I did that Mama carried a pistol in her pocketbook, kept another one in her bedroom. Still a child, and the baby of the family, I knew just enough to keep our secret safe; but my sister, a preteen, knew enough to worry about our safety.

And while it was important to keep our secret, it wasn't at the forefront of my young life. That word *secret* is so loaded, suggests its country cousin, *shame;* but I wasn't ashamed of anything because our family secret wasn't dark, and my mother acted neither apologetic nor embarrassed. Secrecy was my normal, part of what it meant to be the child of a particular kind of small business owner: you help out, you keep quiet and you either go into the family business one day, or vow to do something else with your life.

Also, while I knew to preserve our secret, I didn't fully appreciate what could happen if it got out. Yes, Mama could get busted, but I didn't process what that meant: that our good life would end. No one in our family ever talked about it, but we knew. Mama's was a cash business and plenty of money was always literally in our midst, yet my siblings and I understood viscerally that our middle-class prosperity was tenuous, always under threat, because Mama's livelihood was based on a win-or-lose daily gamble. Nowhere was that threat more evident than in our household's nightly ritual: as dusk fell and we all waited for the day's winning numbers to come out, a tense silence moved through our home like a nervous prayer. And once it was past 7 p.m. and we knew those three-digit combinations, we took our cues from Mama. Either she looked relieved, or she looked worried. Either she'd been lucky that day, or her customers had been. If she found a big hit by one of her customers, the energy in our household shifted to the solemn yet brisk activity of gathering and counting money, oftentimes large sums of it. Yet Mama never resented her customers' wins. "People play numbers to hit," she used to say. "So you can't be mad when they do. Business is business."

Each time my mother had a large payout, I didn't realize she could be wiped out. Despite the "good spell" versus "rough patch" nature of her work, Mama never conveyed a sense of fear or instability. She was a domestic magician with incredible sleight of hand. She made our family's life *appear* stable and secure. And so I might've been anxious beyond my own understanding, but in my day-to-day world, I believed there was nothing to worry about.

I now know that risks were everywhere, coming from different sources, reverberating inward. How hard it must have been to shield us from the vagaries of the business, all run from our home, in full view, where the phones and the doorbell rang constantly and the work of running the Numbers sometimes continued until bedtime. It was risky for Mama to send that "how dare you" message to my first-grade teacher. Doing so could've invited Miss Miller's wrath and retaliation. The year was 1967, mere weeks before Detroit's uprising, its infamous "race riot." Racial tensions ran high. Miss Miller could've reported to authorities her suspicions about our family's income. I now think of the risk Mama took that day as a small revolutionary act, just one of many.

My mother gave us a good life at great expense. I thought I knew her skills as a number runner, that she used her facility with numbers, good judge of character, winning personality, and dose of good luck to build and maintain her business for three decades. But I had no idea just how much of a gambler she was, or the kind of psychological work it took to keep our world afloat.

Scariest of all is this: the only way for me to tell Mama's story is to defy her, by running my mouth.

PART I

Hitsville, USA

Fannie, her brother John, and her sister Florence,
Detroit, 1970s

One

Broadstreet

The address listed on my birth certificate is *8878 North Clarendon*. That two-family flat must've felt like a lucky place for my mother, her nicest home yet in Detroit. It's easy to see why, as soon as we moved in, she got a hunch to play the first three digits of our address and adopted a version of that combination as her "pet" number. Soon enough, Mama hit on 788. I like that word *hit*, its imagery of striking back against a formidable force, of swinging bat against ball for the win, of landing on a great idea. It conjures up a hero's triumph, and my mother is the hero of this story. Her win is mythic in our family lore.

"How much did she hit for?" I once asked Aunt Florence.

"Hell, Fannie hit for big money!" said Florence. "She had fifty dollars or something on that number!"

I marvel at the grandeur of my aunt's claim, that with a 500-to-1 payout, Mama hit for $25,000 or more. This she did

17

in the city already known as Hitsville, USA, thanks to Berry Gordy and his winning Motown Records. That amount was easily more than a decade's salary for my father, a factory worker.

"Fannie was just lucky," says Aunt Florence. And then she explains her sister's big hit this way: "It was because she gave so freely. That's why Fannie had such good luck."

I'd heard this about my mother my entire life, that she was a lucky woman, and that her luck was a direct consequence of her generosity. The two are entwined in her sister's and others' minds, one explaining the other. I've come to believe my mom's luck was in fact preparation meeting opportunity. As for her big hit, no one is certain exactly how much money my mother played on 788 that day, because she never told anyone. I'm sure she was happy to let everyone believe she won many, many thousands of dollars, neither confirming nor denying the story. She would *love* that her good fortune all those years ago has now become a legend, one made more engaging because she hit with a man whose name was Wingate.

This I do know: She did give freely, and she did win big; and whatever the amount, it was enough to change the trajectory of our family's fortunes. With her winnings, Mama decided to buy a house.

She considered buying a home in Conant Gardens, the all-black, exclusive enclave of doctors, ministers, funeral parlor owners, and lawyers, i.e., the black bourgeoisie; but that wasn't her crowd. Besides, she had little use for separate but so-called equal. My mother understood from her Southern roots a basic principle that still holds true: where there's a white presence, there will be amenities. She wanted grocery stores with quality produce and roads that got repaired and streetlights that came on magically at dusk and garbage that got collected on time. She believed that as long as her children sat beside white classmates in a public school, we'd all receive a decent education. "I pay the same taxes," she used to say. "I should have the same benefits."

The year was 1961, and because a sweet irony was occurring, she had options: Detroit's black residents were finally winning their legal fight to live where they wanted, thanks to the efforts of the Detroit chapter of the NAACP, which was the largest in the nation, and interestingly, believed to be funded heavily by the city's number runners. Rather than live beside black neighbors, upper-middle-class residents who could afford to fled the city for the suburbs; that flutter of white flight meant they had to sell their houses to black buyers.

My mother fell in love with one of those houses, a three-story, four-bedroom New England–style Colonial red brick with a big backyard, on a tree-lined wide avenue appropriately named Broadstreet. The house was in an area on the city's west side called Russell Woods, where white clerks, engineers, accountants, midlevel white-collar workers, and businessmen all once lived. Other houses on the block were in a variety of architectural types, one a mock French château, another a Tudor style, and others replicas of formal Georgian estates. All of them were designed to be small-scale versions of the more elaborate houses of the auto execs and bankers and doctors and lawyers who lived in the tonier neighborhoods throughout the city. A pretty park was nearby. Winterhalter, a good elementary and junior high school, was just four blocks up the same street. Mackenzie High was not much farther.

The curb appeal was irresistible: The house's front porch was wide and generous, beneath a striped awning. Its front door was spectacularly curved at the top, with a heavy brass circular knocker, a molded animal head at its center. It could've been the door of a small castle. The tall, rectangular leaded-pane windows were each adorned with stained-glass designs etched across the top, and the front porch's iron balustrade had curving balusters both decorative and protective. Even its address was appealing, five whimsical dark digits tumbling across a white plaque: *12836.*

On April fifteenth, tax day, my mother carried me on her hip as she strode up the curvy walkway of our new home, crossing the threshold and stepping us into the middle class. She was just shy of thirty-three and had migrated north with my father six years before. I'd soon celebrate my first birthday. My sister Rita was days away from turning five, my brother, Anthony, was eight, my sister Selena Dianne was twelve, and my oldest sister, Deborah, was fourteen. Mama paid $16,700 for the house. The average cost of a home that year was $12,500. The sellers were a white businessman named Torkom Prince and his wife, Beatrice.

Here's what I didn't know until I was good and grown: Mama couldn't buy the house the way most people buy homes, because banks and other lenders wouldn't give her a mortgage. My mother was forced to enter into a deal with the seller and buy the house via a shaky type of land contract. But the seller, Mr. Prince, wouldn't sell the house directly to *her*, despite the fact that this land contract, which was essentially an installment plan, ensured no risk for him. He told my mother that since her husband's work wasn't steady—my father worked

on-again off-again for General Motors—and with her being a
Negro woman, he couldn't take the risk; this despite her hefty
down payment.

Mama quickly landed on an idea: she asked an older family
friend, a black man with good credit and a long work history
in the auto plants, to "buy" her dream house for her. He
agreed. When I recently found the original documents, I was
taken aback to see it in black and white: Wallace Colvin's
name on the contract as purchaser, not my mother's.

She had to trust the integrity of Mr. Colvin, a man whom I
only once heard about and never met in subsequent years, so
he couldn't have been a close friend. Turns out, many African-
Americans in the same predicament got swindled out of their
life savings, *and* their homes, by third-party, so-called friends.
I found out that the use of these land contracts, known as
buying on contract, was by its nature predatory. It meant that
the buyer entered into an agreement "that combined all the
responsibilities of homeownership with all the disadvantages
of renting, while offering the benefits of neither," as Ta-Nehisi
Coates put it in his seminal *Atlantic* article, "The Case for
Reparations." The seller essentially remained its owner until
the house was fully paid for. The buyer built no equity in the
property. The seller carried the homeowner's insurance. Not
only that, my mother had to trust that Mr. Prince was paying
the property taxes out of the money she paid him every month.
If he opted *not* to pay those taxes (or claimed he hadn't), she
had little recourse but to come up with the "owed" taxes; if
she didn't, the house remained his. Everything about it was
so risky that while Mr. Colvin could have initially cheated her
out of the house, Mr. Prince had long-term chances to do so.

What laws would've protected her? None. My mother knew this, and had to rely on Mr. Prince's so-called decency.

I somehow sensed this, even as a little girl. Every time Mr. Prince came to our house from his new suburban home in Orchard Lake to collect his money, in cash, I felt a twinge of fear. I'd sit on the steps and eye him through the banister; he was scary, so foreign, practically the only white person ever to enter our home, and I thought he was there to check up on us, deciding whether or not to let us stay in the house.

I now know that my child's worry wasn't completely unfounded: under the terms of the contract, Mr. Prince could've taken back the house if Mama missed one payment. I imagine that as my mother decorated rooms, as I played in the backyard, as my siblings invited their friends over to hang out in the basement lounge, as kin from down South came to visit, her awareness of this possibility, of losing our home, was right there, ever-present. I imagine too how much harder that made her work.

I came to learn that my mother was by no means alone in having to buy her house "on contract." Even African-Americans with stable employment and good, verifiable income couldn't get traditional financing. I was stunned to learn this fact: *federal policy ensured that banks denied loans to black home buyers.* I thought my mother's unorthodox vocation as a number runner prevented her from getting a traditional mortgage and that at least other working-class and professional blacks could acquire bank credit. Turns out, it didn't matter *who* those black home buyers were: Red lines were drawn around all black communities, or wherever a black family lived—even neighborhoods like Conant Gardens, the upscale African-American community of suburban-style ranch homes with manicured lawns—and they were deemed "high-risk"; thus the FHA refused to insure mortgages for those houses. That's why lenders could so easily get away with refusing home loans to Negroes. Redlining, as it was known, proliferated unabated for many years.

One month before my mother (via Mr. Colvin) purchased the house from Mr. Prince, President John F. Kennedy reduced the interest rate on FHA-insured home loans to 5.5 percent. Three months later, he lowered it again to 5.25 percent, because he felt the higher rate was "unrealistic." The White House also encouraged savings and loans associations to follow suit with conventional loans. Those great government-backed, low-interest loans were unavailable to enterprising and aspiring black Americans like my mother; while whites were rushing into the middle class, purchasing new homes at great rates for little money down, the interest rate on Mama's contract purchase, paid dutifully to Mr. Prince every month, was 13 percent.

Why didn't my mother just pay for the house in cash, since she had a lump sum thanks to her hit? First, Mr. Prince would've been suspicious, possibly resentful of that kind of money, and she couldn't afford those suspicions. She had a secret to keep; paying in cash was way too risky. Besides, she needed to save as much of her windfall as possible for big payouts, which all number runners have to anticipate.

So why didn't she—and other blacks—buy more affordable homes in Detroit's white, working-class areas, where appraisals were fair? Because in those neighborhoods, real estate agents enforced "covenants" to keep them "homogeneous," as in all white. And according to historian Thomas Sugrue, whites in those neighborhoods fought bitter battles to keep "the first black family" out, mounting organized grassroots campaigns that relied on everything from hysteria to intimidation to violent harassment, even riots. Essentially, they practiced terrorism. And so black residents were all but shut out of the private real estate market. That meant most were trapped in the city's poorer housing in strictly segregated areas, prey to unscrupulous white landlords. The most fundamental American hope, what Coates has called "that final badge of entry into the sacred order of the American middle class," to buy a home that increases in value and becomes your biggest asset, was effectively unavailable to the majority of African-Americans nationwide. "The FHA adopted a racial policy that could well have been culled from the Nuremberg laws," Charles Abrams, the urban studies expert, wrote in 1955, the year my parents arrived in Michigan from Tennessee.

Those few blacks in the vanguard, like my mother, who in the early sixties could manage a land contract's whopping 30 percent down payment and a high interest rate, could have nicer houses in *better* neighborhoods than the bigoted working-class whites who couldn't afford to flee the city. Imagine the resentment. In fact, my mother remained grateful to Mr. Prince for selling his house to her. "He didn't do me dirty," she used to say. To her mind, he didn't charge her an exorbitant price for the house, or use unscrupulous means to take it back, or tack on fake additional tax and insurance costs. Many black home buyers weren't so lucky, falling prey to plunderers' tactics and losing the homes they bought on contract, along with all the money they'd invested in them. "The seller could repossess the house as easily as a used car salesman repossessed a delinquent automobile," writes Beryl Satter in *Family Properties*, her scathing account of this widespread practice in Chicago.

On Broadstreet, white flight happened in stages. My first playmate was the little white girl next door named Suzy. I remember her, and I remember my mother later telling folks how "that child didn't care about color, and for a hot minute, seem like her parents didn't neither." Our briefly mixed-race neighborhood was lovely by anyone's measure. Four years after we moved there, Diana Ross and the Supremes, ascending to stardom, each chose to buy her own home around the corner from ours on a stately street with an enticing Spanish name: Buena Vista. Diana got the big corner house.

Within a few years came the hard-won Fair Housing Act—the 1968 legislation signed into law days after Dr. Martin Luther King Jr.'s assassination—legally ending redlining, and with it such a rush of white escape that block after block of the city's best housing stock eventually became 90 percent black-owned, including our block and those surrounding it. In fact, huge swaths of the white population of Detroit, having lost the open housing battle and convinced that a black presence lowered property values—confirmed by the fact that the FHA devalued homes in any neighborhood where African-Americans lived—abandoned Detroit, unwilling to live beside its black citizens. People like my mother, my father, my siblings, and me.

Yet when Mr. Prince bought the house in 1948, he paid *one dollar*. This I discovered after a title search. Who knows the backstory there? In 1948, Detroit's Negro population was at its height; black folks migrated there in droves after World War II; the auto industry was booming, thanks to its production of war materials, and many blacks could've afforded decent homes had they been easily allowed to buy them. (Interestingly, a lucky few were extended personal loans by big-time number runners.)

Meanwhile, Mr. Prince, by virtue of his white privilege, was amassing generational wealth, this one property paying off for him across decades. What kind of luck did he enjoy to buy a house for $1 and ultimately sell it, across time, for 39,000 times that? Not because he lived right or had great business acumen, but because the government set up everything in his favor? As Mama used to say, "Bootstraps? Hell, they do everything they can to keep us from having boots. Don't tell me a damn thing about some bootstraps."

Before he left, Mr. Prince took the doorbell chimes. Who rips out the doorbell when they sell a house? Mama was unfazed and promptly bought her own chiming bells, and those three golden stair-step columns sang out in domestic harmony each time a visitor rang our doorbell. I can still hear those distinct, elongated notes: *dingggg, dongggg, dingggg.*

To this day, I mentally walk through the interior of Broadstreet, what we lovingly called it, our Manderley, and remember everything about the house. The vestibule had tiled flooring and a hall closet with a full-length mirror on its door. "The first thing you saw when you entered was yourself, and the last thing you saw when you left was yourself," says my cousin Jewell, Aunt Florence's daughter. The house had what we now call original details: double French doors leading to the dining room (which Mama kept flung open), a single French door off the den, a working fireplace and mantel below a huge built-in mirror, stucco walls throughout the downstairs, waist-high built-in bookshelves with glass-fronted doors, windows that cranked outward and ran across the length of the living room and den, and cherubs and fruit molded into the plaster of the ceiling in the formal dining room. Meanwhile the eat-in kitchen with turquoise appliances had a newfangled dishwasher and a breakfast nook with its own sensuously curved turquoise leather banquette; the pink-and-black-tiled powder room with its black toilet is where I got my one and only spanking from my father—three slaps across my bottom for sneaking out of the yard and running across the back alley. The staircase leading to the second floor had both a wide landing and a swooping wooden banister with a thick, hand-carved curlicue post top; Jewell and I loved to slide down that banister. We also liked tossing clothes down the chute, ever marveling at how they tumbled through the walls of the house, landing in a pile on the basement's laundry room floor.

Upstairs were four bedrooms, each one shared except for my brother's; he had his own room. My and Rita's room had wide window seats and twin closets with those sloping shoe racks. Mama and Daddy's room had much larger twin, walk-in closets, each little rooms themselves with windows that looked down onto the street below. I spent many hours playing inside one of those closets, filled with my mother's myriad purses, hat-boxes, shoe boxes, and hanging clothes, some still with price tags. That's also where she kept her combination-lock safe, used to store cash, valuables, and that day's "business"—slips with her customers' bets. The creaky, cedar-smelling attic was where I spent rainy afternoons, peeking out its window like a fairy-tale princess in a tower, watching birds and studying treetops, and each year, joining Jewell in secretly opening our Christmas presents stored there.

The basement, remodeled by Mama, was a world unto itself, with a bar that wrapped across the entire back wall, complete with swiveling barstools, built-in bookshelves, and a separate playroom for me behind the furnace. That play-room was my haven, furnished with a turquoise rocking chair and matching toy chest purchased by Mama from an F.A.O. Schwarz catalog, and a Suzy Homemaker toy dishwasher, washer, dryer, and vacuum cleaner. With my Easy-Bake Oven, I made little cakes for my father, cooked by a lightbulb inside, and then invited him to my playhouse for tea parties. In that playhouse, I began to craft my first short stories about imaginary people, written with crayon on construction paper. Across the raw-wood door, I scrawled the word *Broadway*, and beneath it drew a large star.

But it was the backyard that I treasured most. From my child's perspective it was so huge, divided by a walkway that led to the back gate, which opened onto that back alley. If you crossed the alley you were on Buena Vista. On one side, the yard was filled with rich, green, cushy grass. On the other was my swing set, with its sinewy metal slide and swings that al-lowed me to jump off, onto that soft grass. Behind the swing set were a peach tree and encroaching limbs from the neigh-bor's apple tree. If I swung high enough, I could grab one of those apples, tart and delicious. Most of all, I remember my fa-ther watching me play in the yard from his perch on the back porch. He liked to lean on the back railing, arms folded as he looked out, his transistor radio tossing rhythm and blues into the air. I also spent hours in the garage, which had its panoply of tools and ornaments and discarded odds and ends. Inside, I played a solitary game I called Invention, making what seemed to me new and useful things. In bursts of artistic expression, I made junk sculptures. Sometimes Daddy would join me in the garage, but mostly he just liked knowing I was nearby.

When I saw the artist Mickalene Thomas's museum exhibition *Origin of the Universe* a few years ago, I immediately recognized the re-created living room of her childhood home, with its bold choices and pizazz. It reminded me of Mama's decorating style, the combination of French Provincial and sixties modern. In our home, plush and daring red carpet snaked through the entire downstairs; crystal teardrop side lamps captured the light pouring through the custom drapes, a conservative paisley in the living and dining rooms and a mod geometric design in the den. Fine china from Bavaria (Briar Rose pattern on white) filled the dining room's china cabinet. Mama's bed stayed dressed in gorgeous linens trimmed in white eyelet. My bedroom and Rita's was painted a shade of magenta that I've yet to see again, with coordinated pink-and-white-striped shades on the windows, and a double bed with an actual fluffy white canopy on top. Too, Mama liked unusual accent pieces, a playful disruption of the expected. My favorite was a three-piece coffee table with bronze legs and smoked-glass tops, each etched with a gold design, and fitting together like tic-tac-toe pieces—two Xs, one O.

People who visited often oohed and aahed when they entered the house, reacting to its decidedly nonconservative, nonpractical décor. Many of those people did business with Mama, playing their numbers with her, and she understood what all entrepreneurs understand: customers want to do business with people who look prosperous. Especially in the world of the Numbers, where luck and superstition run side by side, customers believed that good luck rubbed off, so they wanted to play their numbers with my mother, who certainly appeared to be doing well. Fannie Davis looked like a lucky woman.

Best of all, our chic home was child-friendly. Despite the upscale décor, there were no rooms we couldn't enter. Mama also had a cardinal rule: use everything. The china got eaten on. We didn't have "guest towels." The off-white brocade sofa was briefly covered in fitted plastic, as was *de rigueur*, but Mama eventually removed it, deciding nothing was that precious. When the sofa got dingy, she had it professionally cleaned. When dishes got chipped or broken, she replaced them. When the walls got scuffed, Daddy, who had learned to paint like a pro from my grandfather, repainted them. The house could get messy too. After all, seven people lived in it. On Saturday mornings, everyone had a chore, and Mama would announce that when she returned from "my collecting," as she called it, i.e., collecting money owed from customers, she wanted the house spotless. It was. (My job was to sweep my bedroom floor.) And then it got messy again. And then we all cleaned it again the following Saturday.

In my memory the front, side and back doors of Broadstreet were always opening and closing. People were forever going into and coming out of our house. Those chiming bells rang out a lot. Some visitors were Mama's customers, who preferred to pay their bills and collect their money in person. Some were family friends. Some were neighbors. Some were relatives from down South, who came to see for themselves how "Fannie and John T. had made it" up North. We used to call it Grand Central Station; it was years before I learned that was a real place in New York.

The house also fulfilled one of my mother's ardent desires: to have a regal place from which she could reign as a *grande dame* of benevolence. I've heard legions of stories about my mother's generosity that go as far back as her youth in Nashville, but her reputation for helping others grew exponentially once the family moved to Broadstreet. The Numbers gave her the means to give, but our house gave her a headquarters from which to do it: Neighborhood kids who weren't doing so well got new clothes alongside advice to stay in school. Teens whose home lives were chaotic got a place to crash for a few days, young women in troubled marriages got to sleep on the basement sofa until it was safe to go home. Mama had a standard, short response whenever someone thanked her for her generosity: "I'm just glad I have it to give," she'd say.

Everyone from her children's friends to her own friends to her customers came through Broadstreet to seek my mother's counsel. "Fannie knew what to do in any situation," her best friend, Lula, once told me. "She was a wise woman, you know, she had a gift. And she wouldn't tell you what you wanted to hear, nah. She'd just give it to you straight."

My mother, with my father's support, even let others borrow the house for social events. "Somebody was always asking to have something over there," recalls Elaine, a lifetime family friend. "I know our family had two baby showers on Broadstreet. Then there were people who had birthday parties, engagement parties, and graduation parties. Fannie and John T. always welcomed everybody that came through. They were both like, 'Yeah, sure, have yourself a nice time, make yourself at home.'"

Food was ubiquitous. "I remember you-all had one of those new refrigerators," says Elaine. "We'd never seen one with doors side by side, so we were truly impressed. And it was just always full." Whether it was a huge pot of spaghetti with ground beef or T-bone and Delmonico steaks or rump roast or fried catfish, something was always simmering on the stove or cooking in the oven. If you were at our house, whoever you were, you got fed. "If we wanted anything from hot sausages to egg salad sandwiches, we could have it," recalls Elaine. "Fannie would offer you food and tell you, 'You don't have to say you're not hungry if you're hungry.' She would always be matter-of-fact, so you never ever felt like you were imposing, or taking a handout."

The kitchen was the heart of the house. It was big enough for me to do cartwheels in, and the turquoise leather banquette, which Mama designed and had custom-made, could seat seven or eight people as they slid around the Formica-top table. That banquette stayed full with folks squished around it.

Linda, who spent many school days coming over as my sister Rita's elementary school buddy, explains: "Your mother just had that gift of hospitality. People were always there, so it was very lively, and so you wanted to be there too."

That was my mother's policy: Feel free, feel welcome. Be happy.

Because three of my siblings grew into their teenage years on Broadstreet, the lounge-style basement became *the spot* for them and their friends. Even though it couldn't possibly have been the case, in my memory there were parties down there every night. Certainly I can remember folks coming through in a steady stream, lots of laughter and loud Motown music, the sounds of bid whist (that complex card game played passionately by black folks) and the smell of cigarette smoke. "Everybody who was anybody would come into your house because your brother, Anthony, had a lot of friends," Linda tells me. "I used to see his girlfriend, Renita, pass by my house to go over there."

That girlfriend later became my brother's wife, and she remembers good times in the basement. "Anthony would stuff so many people in there, all coming through that side door. We'd drink—maybe a little wine for me, that's it—and laugh and play cards," she tells me. "And he'd keep going upstairs and coming down with something for us to eat." She smiles at the memory. "That was the place to be."

"I loved that house," my cousin Jewell says simply. She voices this love while sitting in the dining room of her own three-story gray brick house in Oak Park, two miles from Detroit's city limits. "Broadstreet was the ideal home; it was so huge, and it held so much love," she explains. "In my quest for the perfect home, it had to have some elements of Broadstreet."

More than forty-five years later, when Jewell did finally buy her dream house, she kept her word and chose one that reminded her of our home, one that had a similar living room fireplace, window seat, and marble-floored vestibule. "Whenever I hear my front door close, I think of Broadstreet," she says. "It has that same echoing slam."

It wasn't just the comfort of the house, nor its open-door policy, nor the abundance that flowed within its walls that made 12836 so special. Broadstreet was our armor against a world designed to convince us, black working-class children of migrants, that we didn't deserve a good life. Our nice big house made a lie of such claims, and even our extended family and friends felt its reverberating impact. Ours was a communal triumph. The pride my parents felt trickled out, and trickled down. Of course, I wasn't consciously aware of these things as a little girl. I only knew that I had the freedom to lie on the backyard's tickly grass, staring up at the sky, secure behind my family's protective fence, and imagine myself going to faraway places in airplanes like those that roared over the clouds. (Eventually, I did.) I could afford the indulgence of daydreams. There was something about the physical space of the house—the different floors, the many rooms, the sprawling front and back yards, the secret nooks and crannies—that gave me, as a child, a sense of possibility. I know you can dream from small, crowded spaces. But it's harder.

The house's spaciousness was also important to my mother's Numbers. From the privacy of her own home, no longer living in a rented flat of a two-family house, she had a new, roomy base from which to run her business. Where before she'd kept her activity behind closed doors, she now expanded to taking numbers both in her upstairs bedroom and at the dining room table. Sitting beneath that crystal chandelier, Mama accepted customers' bets—any three-digit combination from 000 to 999—and then turned those in to one of the biggest Numbers men in Detroit: Eddie Wingate, a larger-than-life figure who used his wealth to purchase racehorses, launch a record company that once rivaled Motown and open a hot-spot motel and nightclub called the Twenty Grand. Wingate, as everyone called him, was the very man with whom Mama had hit big; now he was her banker, paying off all hits and giving Mama, as a bookie who turned in all bets to him, a percentage of the weekly proceeds from her customers' plays. It was a steady income, enough to pay the monthly mortgage and then some.

As the ever-present possibility of Mr. Prince confiscating our home hummed beneath the surface of our good lives, Mama soon faced a new threat. One day, less than a year into life on Broadstreet, she somehow overlooked a customer's number and forgot to turn it in to Wingate. That number came out, which meant she suddenly owed her boss a massive amount of cash to pay off the hit. Mama knew not to cross Wingate, who was notorious for being a cold, ruthless man. But she didn't have it, even after including the money left from her big hit. And it wasn't like she could use our house as collateral. Her name wasn't on the deed.

Two

Fannie, age 18

For as long as I can remember, my mother collected loose silver change in myriad vessels around the house, in mason jars and clear glass bowls and plastic jugs. I used to enjoy seeing those silver coins pile up, glittering from the china cabinet or her nightstand or the den shelf. Sometimes I'd dip my hand into one, scooping up enough quarters to treat myself to McDonald's French fries after school.

So I can imagine her back in 1962, working to pull together the money she owed Wingate, emptying out all those vessels as I lay napping in my new French Provincial baby bed, her first major purchase since arriving in Detroit. My older siblings would've sat cross-legged on the brand-new, plush red carpet surrounded by multicolored coin wrappers, helping Mama wrap piles of quarters and dimes and nickels to take to the bank to exchange for dollars. To that, Mama scrambled to add whatever money she'd saved, whatever money she could borrow, and somehow she pulled together the cash.

"She had to really scuffle to pay that money," recalls my aunt Florence.

The effort to pay off that hit left Mama broke but empowered. She decided that since she had to start over anyway, this time she'd hold her customers' bets herself, be no one's bookie, be her own banker. "She said, 'If I could pay out all that, I can hold the rest of this shit,'" says Aunt Florence.

It was a big risk. With Mr. Prince's house note to pay every month, and Daddy's work unsteady, the last thing Mama wanted was for us to fall back into the poverty she and the family had faced in their early years in Detroit. By then, in 1955, the Motor City was the fourth-largest US city and everyone had said it was "the place to be." But my mother, father, sisters and brother, having traveled north from Nashville by train, ended up living on a mean, narrow street called Delaware. Throughout the rest of her life, Mama refused to even drive past Delaware, let alone down the street itself. "The memories are too painful" was all she'd say to me about that street, but really about life in the city before I was born.

It was my uncle John, Mama's brother, who later provided the details. "They were catching hell," he says. The apartment on Delaware was in a rough colored section of the city, just off Twelfth, a street that would become infamous a decade later. Back then in the fifties, according to the historian Thomas Sugrue, my parents were like most blacks, relegated to just a few areas in the city with old, ramshackle tenements owned by absentee landlords, complete with rashes of crime and rampant disease. Fire was an ever-present danger.

"I went by to bring them some coal to heat the furnace, and I was shocked," says Uncle John. He found them living in a cold-water flat in an overcrowded building. There were rats and roaches. "I told her to go back home; she didn't have to live like that," he recalls. "Our people had property."

No one would have blamed my parents for returning to Nashville. They rented from a white-flight landlord who took advantage of the shortage of available housing for newly arrived Negroes and charged them an exorbitant rent, causing my parents to spend most of their meager income on housing. Eviction was a constant threat.

But while her big brother was telling her to go home, Fannie's baby sister was encouraging her to stay. Aunt Florence would send her money every week. Sometimes it was ten dollars, sometimes fifteen or twenty. She was playing the Numbers herself in Nashville. "And if I hit the number, I'd sweeten the pot and maybe send thirty dollars," recalls Aunt Florence. "I'd say, 'I had a little luck.'" My aunt had her own migration plans and she didn't want her favorite sister to return home, so sending money was a kind of insurance premium. "She wanted to go home," says Aunt Florence. "She used to call me and say, 'I wanna come back, I'm coming back.' She would cry. I'd say, 'Don't come back, stay there,' 'cause I knew I was on my way. I'd say, 'Just stay there. Things gonna get better.' And honey, I made sure I sent her that money every Friday."

But things weren't getting better. My father, like most Negro men, was placed in one of the poorer-paying, less secure jobs at GM's auto plant; listed in a 1950s city directory as a "heat treater," he tended a furnace that heated and hardened metals for use in building the cars, often a dangerous and hard job. He was also part of a wave of black migrants last hired, first fired. Wages were good in the factories compared to what my father had left behind, working with my grandfather as a plasterer (Henry Ford initiated the trend of paying factory workers better wages to keep them at mind-numbing assembly-line work), but the fifties were a rough time for a black man in Detroit seeking an entry-level job. The auto industry had already begun reducing employment in the Rust Belt cities, replacing workers with automated technology and constructing new facilities in other areas of the country and abroad, all of which would devastate Detroit in the years to come. African-Americans had the least seniority on these jobs and so were often the first to be let go. And this occurred just when the city's population of working-age black adults was on the rise.

"Too many Negro families who have moved here to work in the auto plants are now unemployed," the *Detroit News* proclaimed by 1959. "For most there are no prospects of jobs." Indeed, Daddy got hired, laid off, rehired, and laid off repeatedly at the city's GM plant, located on the border of Hamtramck. He later confessed to me that he hated factory work. I'm sure the racially hostile environment in the plants made it even worse.

In the spring of 1956, my parents had another baby, their fourth, a girl they named Rita. She was born at Trumbull General Hospital, where my mother delivered her breech in the communal maternity ward, an experience that she later attested "no woman deserves."

For the next two years, poverty gripped the family. Sadly, the Motor City was *not* the place to be.

Thank God for the Drumwrights' foothold in the world. What saved my parents from the catch-22 cycle of endless poverty that gripped so many African-Americans was my grandparents' generosity. One desperate day in early 1958, my mother called her own mother in Nashville. "Kine, I need help," she said, calling her mother by her nickname, a moniker that matched my grandmother's kind nature. "How much, Fannie?" her mother asked. "As much as you can spare." My grandparents sent their daughter $900, an astonishing amount of money at the time, and possibly their life savings. Fannie was their first daughter to leave home and migrate north. They wanted her to make it.

When I learned this story, I wondered how my grandparents had that much money to loan their daughter. I'd been told the broad strokes about my grandfather, that he'd "run his own plastering business," but little else. Inspired anew, I decided to visit Mama's hometown and, with the help of my cousin Ava, find out more. What I discovered was that my mother's father, Ezra Drumwright, born in 1885, just twenty years after slavery's end and eight years after Reconstruction, became both a businessman and a property owner in the early decades of the twentieth century; this was at a time when most colored men in the South were sharecroppers, and those with land had their property routinely confiscated by whites.

As a young man, my grandfather had myriad jobs; Nashville's City Directory lists him as a "driver" in 1918, and a "laborer" in 1922; for some years he worked at a paper mill, but by the time he was in his thirties, he'd learned to plaster walls and do construction work on the advice of his brother, John Henry. ("You can't raise no family working here at the mill," his brother told him.) That not only got him out of doing menial labor, it gave him a skill that he could turn into a livelihood. He worked for his own uncle initially and later built government housing, going on to enlist other colored men to work under him, including his uncle. The story most told about my grandfather is that he was an exacting boss, very strict, and a perfectionist. He'd make his men tear down a wall and rebuild it if he thought it wasn't plastered properly.

My grandmother was his bookkeeper. My cousin Bill recalls that my grandfather often loaned his workers money. "He'd tell his wife, 'Caroline, I lent such-and-such some money. Deduct that from what they get at the end of the week.'" Another anecdote that has traveled down through the years is that despite being self-employed, my grandfather wasn't allowed to wear a white collar shirt to his white customers' homes or businesses. White folks didn't like what it implied. "He had to wear a simple shirt, like he didn't have nothing," explains Aunt Florence.

He also hid the fact that he owned a new car. "He bought a car for the boys," Aunt Florence tells me. The family lived near a hill, and over it was a white high school. My grandparents had two boys still living at home, including Uncle John. "Them white kids would walk up and down that hill all during the night," Aunt Florence recalls. "And my daddy felt like if the boys would be coming home at night and meet them and one girl hollered rape, they're gone. And he bought a car for that, to keep them safe."

Throughout his working life, my grandfather supported his wife and nine surviving children (one baby girl died after falling into a fireplace's burning embers), and remained staunchly proud that my grandmother never had to clean white folks' homes or, as she'd done before they married, wash white folks' clothes. (The 1910 Census lists my grand-mother's occupation as "laundress.") Pap, as they called him, was a smart, dark-skinned, no-nonsense man who was "damn good" at what he did, according to my aunt Florence; he had equal doses of drive, gravitas, and vision: exceptional among colored men of that era, he managed to save his hard-earned money, buy property, and *hold on to it*. African-Americans owned as much as 19 million acres of Southern land by 1910, according to the US Department of Agriculture, but the white backlash was so virulent that a decade later, those numbers had dropped precipitously. The backlash, often led by a newly resurgent Ku Klux Klan, was spawned by resentment that blacks were buying and profiting from land, and it led to "land takings" through exploitative so-called legal means, but also through intimidation, violent mob attacks, and murder. Of course, losing their land meant most blacks couldn't transfer wealth from one generation to the next, which helps explain the hundred-year decline in black land ownership.

Somehow my grandfather escaped that fate. Among my mother's possessions I found original deeds and contracts, yellowed and falling apart, written in fountain-pen ink, for property my grandfather bought from an E. S. Newson and her husband, A. W. Newson, real estate agents based in Huntsville, Alabama. He bought the first parcel of land, "Lot 7," on July 23, 1919, just months after the end of World War I, for $375 "cash in hand," when he was thirty-four years old, with four children. What makes his purchase astonishing is that, that very same summer, African-American soldiers returning from fighting for freedom in Europe, and expecting the same freedoms back home, were met with anger over their supposed competition with whites for jobs, resulting in the worst-ever spate of lynching in US history. In states throughout the country, including Tennessee, at least twenty-six full-fledged racial massacres took place; the violence was so virulent that civil rights activist and author James Weldon Johnson dubbed it the Red Summer of 1919. Turns out, many of those lynched were property owners. Quoted in 2006 by the Associated Press, Ray Winbush, as director of Fisk University's Race Relations Institute, said, "If you're looking for stolen black land, just follow the lynching trail."

The deed my grandfather received reads like the launch of matrimonial vows: "TO HAVE AND TO HOLD said Tract or Parcel of Land, with the appurtenances, estate, title and interest thereto belonging, to the said Ezra Drumwright and wife, Caroline Drumwright, their heirs and assigns, forever." Part of that land adjoined the Tennessee State Fair Grounds, and that's where my grandfather built the family home. That same home, 410 Wingrove, is where my own parents lived when they were a young married couple with children of their own in the late forties and early fifties. The family home on Wingrove is also where I'd later join my mother on visits back to Nashville. I'd sit on my grandmother's front porch, watching the lights glow on the State Fairgrounds' white wooden roller coaster and listening to the riders' delighted screams as they plunged downward. That same house is where Kine, my pretty, soft-spoken and gentle grandmother, was laid out for viewing after her death in 1970, at age eighty-one.

In 1925, my grandfather bought the land next door to his family home, Lot 6, for $150 cash, and it became 412 Wingrove; he later purchased another tract beside that, Lot 5, which became 414 Wingrove and is now part of a family compound. By 1999, those three lots were appraised at a total of $51,000.

The documents show that my grandfather bought a fourth tract of land on November 5, 1927, when his wife was pregnant with their ninth child, my mother. That property, 1005 First Avenue South, eventually became a boardinghouse where my aunt Ella, or Big Sis as everyone called her, lived and rented out rooms. She was, like her father, entrepreneurial. That boardinghouse, which I visited many times, with its linoleum floors and gigantic, king-sized bed in Big Sis's room, gave her a livelihood until her death in 1987. It remains in the family.

Yet another property that my grandfather purchased was 1267 Lewis Street. My grandmother "sold" that property to my mother in 1968 for ten dollars. I inherited that same property after my mother's death, and eventually sold it, investing most of the money for my children's college education. I also shared some of the proceeds with my nephew, Tony, who later told me that he'd been broke and that windfall allowed him to attend a weekend "singles' retreat" sponsored by his church; he was able not only to pay the retreat fees but to buy new outfits for the weekend as well. He said he felt good about himself that weekend, confident. The retreat is where he met his wife, Angelita. He's convinced that his great-grandfather's vision, alongside his grandmother's foresight, led to the life he lives now. I could say the same for myself.

"We have all been used to plenty," explains Aunt Florence.

"People used to call us Drumwrights the rich kids, but we wasn't. We just lived very well. We were the only ones in the neighborhood that had a phone; and when it was zero weather we could walk around butt naked 'cause we had a furnace in our basement." She goes on: "We had running water. We had a toilet on the inside...we had plenty of food, all kinds of lunch-meat in our refrigerator, like bologna, hog-head cheese. And Honey, plenty of fruit. When Fannie was pregnant, my papa made sure watermelon was at the house at all times 'cause she craved it." Aunt Florence shrugs. "We just had a good living."

My grandfather's decision not to migrate north and his good fortune not to have his land seized by white men—a fate hundreds of Southern blacks suffered as far back as the antebellum period—enabled his descendants to do better than they might have otherwise, have a step up in life. Indeed, most of his children's children went to college, own property themselves; all live middle-class lives. My grandfather died at age seventy-five the year I was born—most likely from prostate cancer, although no doctor diagnosed his condition. Strangely, no one seems to have a photograph of him but everyone tells me he was a handsome man; at his death, he still had thick wavy black hair with just a bit of gray around his temples. "My daddy was jazzy," says Aunt Florence. "But he took care of home."

I can see Pap clearly in my mind's eye: black, beautiful, and proud.

By the time my mother was born on May 9, 1928 (known as Christian Feast Day, which I find fitting), it was two months after Virginia became the first state to pass an antilynching law, something the US Congress never did. She was seventeen months old when the stock market crashed in 1929. But based on the stories handed down, there's no indication that her father lost work during those years. The 1930 census lists my grandfather as a forty-four-year-old man (he was actually forty-five) who can read and write, has a wife and seven children still living at home, and is by profession a "plasterer" for the city. The value of his home is listed as $2,000. You have to wonder how its value was determined. Regardless, by then, my grandfather owned five properties.

When she was a girl of just two or three, growing up in Nashville, my mother had such long, sandy-red hair that a doctor told my grandmother it was sapping the child's energy; and so her mother cut it all off. Left behind were short ringlets that covered her head, causing people to mistake her for a boy.

From that day forward, they say, Fannie Mae's energy was boundless; I like to think that she was left alone until her hair grew back, to have the freedom usually afforded boys to explore, and to daydream. In any event, *something* instilled in her a desire for more. As she grew, she became a voracious learner, an avid reader and a lover of history. She was smart and honest, so people were drawn to her. Often folks came to Fannie for advice, ideas, tips, and ways to help them out of precarious situations. She just seemed to *know* things. She was already honing what would become her twin passions: helping others to improve their station in life, and figuring out ways to improve her own. This combination of charisma, generosity, and drive distinguished my mother from her siblings. Other qualities distinguished her: she loved books, liked expanding her vocabulary, was the prettiest of the Drumwright girls, had impeccable taste, and dressed stylishly. My most treasured photograph captures her at eighteen, in her prom dress, an elegant, scooped-neck frock trimmed in crinoline that shows off her tiny waist and womanly cleavage. She wears a jeweled bracelet with a delicate handkerchief attached to it, and gloves that travel from her wrists to above her elbows. She looks into the camera with dark intelligent eyes.

She also loved beautiful things, and seems to have embraced early a philosophy penned by the writer Toni Cade Bambara: "Beauty is care, just as ugly is carelessness."

My uncle John says another thing distinguished my mother:

"I never seen Fannie drink a bottle of beer in my life," he confesses. "I never seen Fannie with a cigarette in her mouth either. That's two things I can say for sure about her; she did not smoke, and she did not drink."

She wasn't particularly fond of partying either. When she was a teenager, her older brother Napoleon, whom everyone called Flapper, owned a nightclub called Club Zombie, where she worked as a hatcheck girl. Even though her baby sister Florence and their cousin Annie Pearl loved to hang out at the club dancing and socializing, even selling liquor, Fannie did not. It wasn't her scene. She was the quiet one.

"Fannie was *sidity*," my aunt Florence tells me, shaking her head and laughing. "Honey, she acted like she was too good for everybody. Me and Annie Pearl used to call her Miss Lady."

It was as though she already knew she had plans to "make something" of herself. I suspect a confluence of circumstances led to my mother's ambition. Although she was a child during the early, harsh 1930s, by the time Mama was a young teen the country had plunged itself into World War II. With the economic boom that sprang from that, black men and women had jobs that would've gone to white men had they not been serving in the war. As the second-youngest child of her parents, my mother experienced, if not prosperity, then certainly creature comforts. She already understood the rewards of upward mobility. Plus, she had an ideal role model right there in the home.

As the historian Herbert G. Gutman has proven, African-American families were, contrary to popular belief, intact supportive units in the first decades of the twentieth century, and my mother's home life was no exception. My grandfather, as a self-employed businessman and a property owner, was a powerful force in her life. Because of her birth order as his ninth of ten children, she only knew him as a self-made man (this is not unlike my own life: as my mother's fifth and last child, I only knew her as a thriving, entrepreneurial, and independent woman), and so the idea of working for yourself, creating your own path, was normal to her. Indeed, witnessing her father's livelihood, and the self-respect that came with it, was most likely the major factor in her own life choices. I only heard her speak of my grandfather in glowing, respectful ways; I'm sure that's why even in her most impoverished days in Detroit, she refused to work a menial job for low pay. To be clear, she always admired hard workers; she just didn't see the point of laboring to benefit someone else. "If you're going to work that hard," she used to say, "you might as well work hard for yourself."

Meanwhile, throughout the 1930s, the Numbers were all the rage in Harlem, and gaining a foothold in other Northern cities like Detroit. According to the authors of *Playing the Numbers*, the gangster Dutch Schultz's personal attorney testified that in 1931 the Numbers were "played only by the colored people" and the daily gross was $300,000, or $80 million a year. With that kind of money being generated by the business, of course whites wanted in. Schultz briefly took control of the lucrative enterprise in Harlem, and in Detroit, on the eve of the Great Depression, Jewish gangsters tried unsuccessfully to wrench the business away from blacks. Even still, whites were by then fully involved alongside blacks in running the Numbers in Detroit. Italian gangsters looking to diversify during the Prohibition era had moved from bootlegging to Numbers gambling operations, drawn by the huge profits. (This while whites already controlled policy, the illegal precursor to the Numbers.)

In fact, a scandalous and wide-reaching event that best illustrates how heavily involved whites were in Detroit's Numbers occurred in 1939, when my mother was eleven, long before her own migration to the Motor City. In August of that year, a typist for a major Numbers operation known as the Great Lakes Policy House, Janet McDonald, murdered her daughter Pearl and committed suicide when her boyfriend, a Numbers man, ended their affair. They were found in her car in a garage, dead from carbon monoxide poisoning. Found near her body were six letters she'd written and addressed to local newspapers, the governor, and the FBI, charging that her former boyfriend collected graft money for police protection. The one addressed to the *Detroit Free Press* read: *Dear Sirs: On this night a girl has ended her life because of the mental cruelty caused by Racketeer William McBride, ex-Great Lakes Numbers House operator.* She then provided McBride's address and added: *He glories in telling lies, so don't believe everything he tells you, as I did.* She also implicated law enforcement. In a blaring headline that read DEATH NOTES CHARGE POLICE BRIBERY, the *Free Press* described the spurned white woman as a thirty-three-year-old "comely" divorcée.

When it was all over in June 1942, Mayor Richard Reading, a former sheriff, the police superintendent, twenty police officers (eight of them black), and several "policy operators," who included boxer Joe Louis's manager, John Roxborough, were convicted of graft conspiracy in a numbers racket estimated at $10 million a year—the equivalent of $151 million today.

From their inception in Harlem, the Numbers made their way not just to Northern cities but to Southern cities too, including Nashville; and so by the 1940s, my mother and her siblings were familiar with the Numbers. Surely, Mama occasionally played some numbers as a young woman, even as she soaked up can-do lessons from her father. Family members recall that her older brother Napoleon was briefly a runner. But no one remembers my mother taking any keen interest in the business back then. "I don't think Fannie fooled with the Numbers down South," recalls Aunt Florence. "She got in it here, in Detroit."

That makes sense. Fannie was a colored girl from a good, working-class family of brown-skinned folks, coming of age in the thirties and forties. As was the norm, she married her childhood sweetheart, John Thomas Mathew Davis, when she was eighteen, and within seven months, their first child, a girl, was born. I wonder what my mother's life choices might have been had she not gotten pregnant, had held off marriage, had been able to do the thing she'd desperately longed to do—attend Vanderbilt University, major in history.

Anyway, two years later, another daughter was born, and four years after that, on their sixth anniversary in 1952, my parents had a son. Fannie was twenty-four, with three children under the age of six. John T., as everyone called him, was twenty-six. Given that my grandfather had taught his son-in-law how to plaster and paint, he had decent, honest work that mostly sustained the young family for several years; but my father wasn't entrepreneurial, and working for my grandfather didn't allow him to fully support his own growing family. Nor could he count on the low-paying, menial work available to a black man in the South with no more than a high school education.

Besides, Fannie wanted more. When exactly did the idea to migrate north first take hold in her? Maybe it came shortly after Brown v. Board of Education in 1954, when the Supreme Court got rid of separate but equal education. Maybe that spurred Mama to aspire to more, to trust that certain parts of this country were inching toward making good on its Constitutional promise. Interestingly, the Confederate flag started popping up everywhere in the South after that landmark decision, and schools remained stubbornly segregated in Nashville despite the Supreme Court ruling. I found online a photo of a woman, Grace McKinley, holding her young daughter's hand as she walked her to Nashville's newly desegregated Fehr Elementary School in 1957; she was followed by a white mob, one member holding a sign that read GOD IS THE AUTHOR OF SEGREGATION. A look of terror is frozen on the face of that little girl, a fate wished upon no child. She appears to be about the same age as my sister Selena Dianne was at that time.

Maybe the idea to leave home came as word spread about good-paying jobs on the assembly lines in Michigan's auto plants. And the North appeared to be a little bit better, a place where you weren't forced to live under the mean vestige of "Southern ways" designed to strip you of your humanity. My parents, in their lives in Tennessee, had to speak to all white folks with "yes ma'am" and "yes sir," and had to withstand being called "gal" and "boy" even as adults. (When we were growing up, one of my mother's cardinal rules was that we should *not* call adults "ma'am" or "sir." "Call folks by their God-given name," she'd snap. "This ain't the South.")

I wonder too if they migrated in part because of incidents of violence against blacks attempting to vote, like that of Rev. George Lee, co-founder of Belzoni, Mississippi's NAACP chapter, who was murdered by whites in May 1955 for registering African-American voters; Lee was the first martyr of the Civil Rights Movement and my mother and father surely read about his murder in the newspaper, heard about it on the radio, joined in conversations about it with family and neighbors. Did it make them speed up their migration plans, or confirm the rightness of their choice to leave their birthplace, to join others and get the hell out of the South?

As Isabel Wilkerson lays out evocatively in her extraordinary book *The Warmth of Other Suns,* millions of Southern blacks (my parents among them) were subjected to the indignity of Jim Crow's "colored only" facilities: elevators; train platforms; ambulances; hearses; waiting rooms in everything from bus depots to doctors' offices; bathrooms; post office windows; telephone booths; bank tellers' windows; taxicabs; even betting windows at the racetrack. Colored drivers had to let a white person go first at an intersection, could not pass a white motorist on the road, were always at fault in an accident; my mother and father could not speak to a white person unless spoken to, or attempt to shake a white person's hand. Indeed, my parents understood that "the consequences for the slightest misstep were swift and brutal," as Wilkerson writes.

Given the micro- and macro-aggressions of Southern life, coupled with their own aspirations, they saved hard, and Fannie and John T. left the only home they'd known, the place both their families had lived for generations—my maternal great-grandfather Phile Thompson was born into slavery in Nashville in 1861—and became the first ones to migrate north, after my uncle John. They boarded a train and went where the Tennessee Valley Railroad line took them, more than 560 miles away, to Michigan.

My parents were, as Wilkerson eloquently notes, part of "a human rivulet, and then a flood of six million black refugees fleeing the terrors of the Jim Crow South...to an uncertain existence in the North" in what became known as the second, postwar wave of the Great Migration.

Mama and Daddy came to Michigan without the children, whom they left with my mother's parents in Nashville. They initially migrated to Pontiac, where my father worked on the assembly line for General Motors' Pontiac Metal Center. Once they had a place to live, my father went back to Nashville to get the children, deciding to leave their second-oldest, six-year-old daughter, Selena Dianne—everyone just called her Dianne—with my aunt Florence. My mother was upset when she arrived at the train station to pick up her family and her baby girl wasn't there. But she also knew that her daughter would be well cared for by her own sister. After escaping the racist South, they were totally unprepared for the racist life awaiting them in the North. That life would be hard enough with two children, the oldest just eight and the boy still a toddler. And by that summer, Mama was pregnant again.

Before the baby was born they moved to Detroit, whose population of nearly two million was at its peak. Yet, while I suspect housing conditions for African-Americans in Pontiac were abysmal, finding a decent place to live in Detroit proved to be its own challenge. Few options existed: you could choose between a small Lower East Side neighborhood just east of downtown called Black Bottom, or the Bottom, where blacks had lived since the turn of the century; or, just to the north, a densely populated area which migrants optimistically named Paradise Valley. It was anything but. My parents opted to forgo both the Bottom and Paradise Valley, and found the meager place on Delaware.

I wonder what that must've felt like for Mama and Daddy, to have essentially fled a terrorist state, escaping what Wilkerson calls "a man-made pestilence," to have endured hardship, risked their lives, and stared down poverty in an unsafe, unknown world simply so they could give their children greater opportunity, a little dignity. And would the risk be worth it? Fannie's own father's example of enterprising uplift wasn't much help in the unfamiliar North, with its own kind of pestilence. Indeed, my parents' migration all but nixed the secure family life they'd known back home.

And yet, who could think of returning to the South? In August of 1955, a fourteen-year-old black boy's badly mutilated body was found in the Tallahatchie River in Money, Mississippi. After his mother bravely insisted that he be buried in an open casket, black America saw how white men had shot, beaten, and tortured him for allegedly whistling at a white woman. (That woman admitted decades later that she'd lied.) "There was no way I could describe what was in that box," said the boy's mother, Mamie Till Bradley. "No way. And I just wanted the world to see." My mother told us that when she saw the photo of Emmett Till's mutilated corpse in *Jet* magazine, she almost had a miscarriage.

Luckily, the hundreds of dollars my grandparents sent helped my parents "get on their feet," as they say, and after two long years they moved away from the destitution of Delaware to a flat in a four-family house on North Clarendon Avenue, in a cleaner working-class colored neighborhood. That infusion of cash also gave Mama the resources to go back to Nashville and retrieve my nine-year-old sister, Dianne, where she'd lived with my aunt Florence and my uncle Gene for what was only supposed to be one year but stretched to three, so she could finally join the rest of the family. What was left of the money was likely the equivalent of several months' earnings for my father, as the average yearly salary for white Americans that year was under $3,000, much less for Negroes. Most of all, the financial gift was a godsend because it gave my mother what poverty did not: time to think. She knew that given my father's unstable job, exacerbated by his chronic hypertension, the money would quickly evaporate. And it did.

That summer, my cousin Bill came up North. He was fifteen and spent those three months working with my father, repairing and painting the interiors of private businesses. "Fannie just treated me like I was one of her kids," he recalls. "I loved being there. I really hated to go back to Nashville. And when I did, I told everybody the family was doing all right." But the truth was no secret to Bill: "They were struggling a little bit."

Fannie and John T. now had four children between the ages of two and twelve. She figured she had to do something. What she refused to do was one of the three jobs employing 75 percent of Detroit's black women at the time: "day work" as a maid in white homes, cleaning offices, or low-rung factory work. All those would require her to leave her children to raise one another while she did menial labor for too little money. Mama was clear that the only way she'd have more than what this country intended for her was to work for herself in a business she controlled that depended on a black clientele. Determined to find a better way, she didn't have to look that far.

The Numbers business in Detroit was still thriving in the 1950s. In fact, the Numbers were by then ubiquitous in black communities throughout the country. I'd venture to say that nearly every black person over forty is familiar with the Numbers—played them, knows people who played them, and knows about someone who ran them. Or still runs them. It is impossible to overstate the role of the Numbers in black culture. Just as Aunt Florence was playing numbers back in Nashville and sending "a little piece of change" to her sister up North, black folks in cities across the country were doing likewise. August Wilson's play *Fences*, set in 1950s Pittsburgh, includes an exchange between Rose and Troy about the Numbers: "That 651 hit yesterday," says Rose. "That's the second time this month. Miss Pearl hit for a dollar...seem like those that need the least always get lucky. Poor folks can't get nothing." Troy retorts: "Them numbers don't know nobody. I don't know why you fool with them." Rose reminds Troy, "Now I hit sometimes....It always comes in handy....I don't hear you complaining then."

Lotteries date back to the beginning of this country. All thirteen original colonies operated legal lottery businesses that were precursors to the country's stock market and thrived well into the nineteenth century; they soon became a huge, professional business, in fact the "genesis of American big business," according to the authors of *Playing the Numbers*. Indeed, proceeds from lotteries were used to finance all kinds of capital improvements, like roads and bridges, for the cash-starved Colonies.

At the same time, it's part of the African-American tradition to use lottery playing to better one's conditions in a society that has systematically subjugated its black population. That tradition includes Denmark Vesey, a Charleston slave, who later was executed for planning a revolt against slave owners. Vesey used $1500 he won from the city lottery in 1799 to *buy his freedom*. Vesey also helped found the African Methodist Episcopal Church in Charleston, where over two hundred years later a white supremacist shot dead nine African-Americans during a Bible class.

From the early days, African-Americans didn't just wager as part of the legal lottery system. Rather, they engaged—along with poorer whites—in an ingenious game played alongside these legal lotteries. For a fraction of the cost of a lottery ticket, a person could "insure" or "take a policy on" a number with an agent, effectively betting that a particular number would be drawn in a lottery on a given day. This game was called "insuring the lottery," or "policy," and was a way to make a side wager on the official state lotteries.

Antilottery laws were enacted in all but three states by 1860, similar in large measure to so many laws in America that were designed to thwart the efforts of free blacks to acquire wealth-based equality. The abolition of lotteries had the unintended but unsurprising consequence of huge increases in the amount of money gambled on policy. Winning numbers apparently came from drawings in the states that still had legal lotteries (Kentucky, Missouri, and Delaware), and those winning digits were chosen via a large barrel with slips of paper in it, each with a number from one to 78; twelve numbers were drawn in the morning, and thirteen numbers were drawn at night. The winning numbers were then telegraphed "in cipher" to the policy headquarters in other states. One press report claims the winning numbers were picked out of a barrel in Louisville, Kentucky, by a blind Negro. Policy kings most certainly fixed numbers and made it even harder for folks to win. If the policy game was played fairly, the estimated odds of winning were a staggering one in 70,000. Still, people played policy in droves. And from the start, blacks indulged disproportionately. Indeed, in those early decades of freedom from slavery, during Reconstruction, many blacks were free in theory only, facing such grim financial lives that it's easy to see the lure of indulging in a practice that could transform small amounts of money into large sums.

Policy shops, as they were called, were run almost exclusively by whites and proliferated throughout the country. These big businesses were run in full view of and with the cooperation of police. Their owners often employed black men as agents in order to lure black customers. Unsurprisingly, the business was rife with cheating and exploitation, as well as payoffs to police and politicians. So too began the denigration of lottery players, and the correlation among bettors, African-Americans, the poor, and fools. The press especially equated a defective character with betting on numbers. As early as 1887, two years after my mother's father was born, a *Detroit Free Press* headline blared: THE DEADLY POLICY SHOP AND ITS "COON ROW" GIG. The story's lede proclaimed, "Policy is generally the poor man's game and is played mostly by colored men, cheap waiters and 'tin-horn' gamblers."

In 1890 Congress passed an antilottery bill, and by 1894 all states had abolished lotteries. But that stopped nothing. Apparently still using numbers based on surreptitious drawings in Kentucky, the illegal lottery business thrived. At the outset of the twentieth century, the *Detroit Free Press* was hysterically and repeatedly reporting on the ways in which policy was ruining Detroit society, noting that the police force accepted bribes and payoffs so gambling could flourish.

In an article in the *Detroit Free Press* on March 30, 1903, the reporter made clear the disdain with which the newspaper viewed policy players:

> It is largely the gambling field of the ignorant, superstitious and poor, though more than one man having a prosperous little business has lost his all because infatuated with this lightly veneered form of robbery. It is responsible for no end of suffering, promotes crime and adds to the public expense in the support of the dependent.... The main thing is to have the evil eternally

wiped out, which the police authorities can do if they want to.

According to the newspaper, by 1906, policy had been "stamped out" by police. But by 1908 a brief resurgence occurred, as "energetic colored agents" apparently attempted to revive the "industry" and "policy bids fair again to monopolize much of the attention, as well as the money of the colored gamesters." And as late as 1915, the paper reported on a police raid of "Negro gambling houses" on St. Antoine Street and Hastings Street on the city's east side, resulting in "10 Negroes being locked up"; on the same day, police raided a pool hall on Grand River, where twelve more men were locked up, along with four Negro women, for larceny.

Policy seems to have died down considerably, if not completely, by the onset of World War I; yet its negative association with African-Americans was solidified, no matter that whites bet heavily alongside them. Numbers gambling as we know it today—the mother of today's state lotteries—was invented in Harlem in the early 1920s. And while there's speculation that versions of the Numbers game were introduced in the first decades of the 1900s, brought to Harlem by migrants from Cuba, the British West Indies, and Puerto Rico, historians say the widely held belief is that a black man named Casper Holstein invented the scheme as it is still played today.

Holstein, born in the Danish West Indies, was a Brooklyn high school graduate who, like the majority of colored men and women in America, was barred from using his talents in a chosen field, so he worked as a porter for a Fifth Avenue store. As the legend goes, in 1920 or 1921, he was sitting in a janitor's room for hours, deeply studying the "Clearing House" totals printed each day in a year's worth of newspapers that he'd saved. The Clearing House was a financial institution that facilitated the daily exchanges and settlements of money among New York City's banks. It occurred to Holstein that the numbers printed in the paper were different every day. Within months he came up with his scheme—he'd take the first two digits from the first total published by the Clearing House and one digit from the second total and create a daily three-digit winning number. If a player hit, he or she would be paid 600 to 1. It was an elegant system for many reasons. It didn't rely on dubious drawings in other states, or on complicated calculations; everyone could have access to the winning numbers at the same time, and the source was unimpeachable. But the most important reason for its beauty was this: unlike the policy, Numbers was a black-owned and black-controlled business.

The Numbers blossomed into a lucrative shadow economy in the early 1920s, and moved into black communities across America, thanks in large part to the Great Migration. From 1915 to 1930, well over a million black Southerners moved to the North. Given its role as a viable economic base— in Harlem alone the *New York Age* estimated that in 1926 the daily turnover on numbers was $75,000, with an annual turnover of $20 million—many saw it as black folks' own stock market. While some still referred to the business as "policy" for a few years, it was the newer, wondrous system known as the Numbers that had free rein over the lottery-playing market for seventy years—until the first legal state lottery was reintroduced in 1964.

Once the game as we know it today was introduced to Detroit, it quickly became a de facto informal economy, filling the void left by a formal economy that largely excluded African-Americans. Pushing against rampant discrimination, local Numbers operators used their profits to found legitimate businesses, providing migrant blacks with all kinds of access they wouldn't otherwise have had. They launched insurance companies, newspapers, loan offices, real estate firms, scholarships for college, and more. As such, these big Numbers men used their own wealth not only to enrich themselves, but also to combat racism *and* uplift the race. The Numbers quickly morphed into a thriving, sprawling underground enterprise, so intertwined with the city's lifeblood that it helped shape Detroit's twentieth-century identity. No better example exists than that of John Roxborough, the educated, upper-class black man who brought the Numbers to Detroit; as the city's biggest Numbers man in the 1930s, he used his largesse and business acumen to manage and invest heavily in boxer Joe Louis. Nicknamed the Brown Bomber, Louis became heavyweight champion of the world, knocking down racial stereotypes as both a hometown champ and an American hero. Today, the iconic memorial sculpture of the Brown Bomber's fist is what greets you at the epicenter of downtown Detroit. *The Fist* represents his punch against Jim Crow laws as well as his opponents, and has become synonymous with black Detroiters' fight for racial justice. And the Numbers made it all possible.

The Numbers also became inextricably tied to the auto industry. In fact, the plants unwittingly abetted the Numbers' rise. Factory workers functioned as runners, collecting bets and money from other workers, then turning it all in to bookies and bankers. Ford Motor Co.'s River Rouge plant, one of the largest industrial complexes in the world, which employed 85,000 workers by the end of World War II, had for decades a flourishing Numbers business. Between 1947 and 1951, the *Washington Post*, the *New York Times,* and the *Los Angeles Times* all reported on this phenomenon as national news. One report claimed that the Numbers were a $15,000-a-day business within the Rouge plant, while another estimated them to be a $5-million-a-year enterprise. The *Times* lamented in an editorial that Detroit's "numbers game" threatened plant discipline and claimed that "this evil has been linked to underworld elements that permeate the workplace." My parents weren't part of that so-called underworld, but they were well aware of it. Mama and Daddy had both played numbers for a few coins and had seen their neighbors and friends play them too, regularly. Mama took notice.

On a frigid winter night, my mother showed up at her brother's home and banged on his door. "Woke me up and everything," Uncle John recalls. She stepped inside and stood before him, not even bothering to take off her coat.

"I want to try to bank the Numbers," she announced.

She knew the allure of playing the Numbers, and she also knew real money could be made.

"All I need is a hundred dollars to get started," she told John.

My mother was hoping that her big brother could loan her the money. He was an exercise "boy" for Detroit's racetrack, a gifted horseman who'd go on to be one of the first African-American horse trainers in the country. He'd been on his own since he was fourteen, working at racetracks, and had been in Detroit for several years longer than Fannie. His work was steady, and he made a decent living. "She explained it to me and everything," he recalls.

She told him her plan was to start taking the neighborhood's "penny" bets, collecting coins from folks playing an array of three-digit combinations for small amounts. She figured that modest money would add up over the weeks and months as long as no one hit. And if someone did hit, she'd have the hundred dollars in reserve for payouts. Uncle John thought it made sense.

"I can make it with one hundred dollars," she repeated. "Do you have it?"

"I said, 'Yeah Fannie, I got it.'" (That same year, 1958, Berry Gordy borrowed $800 from his family's "credit fund" to launch Motown Records.)

With the loan money, she got started right way. Week after week, Mama took in those pennies and dimes and nickels and quarters from customers playing an array of combinations, every day except Sunday. People could bet on "the Detroit race" or "the Pontiac race" or both. Each had two winning three-digit numbers, hence Mama asking all her customers: "You want this number played both races, Detroit and Pontiac?" as she recorded the letters D&P beside their bets. Cutoff time was late afternoon, early evening. By dusk, the "first race" digits hit the streets, and by dinnertime, word had spread and everyone knew both sets of winning numbers in both races.

The winning numbers came from two different sources. The Pontiac number came from actual racing forms based on results from preselected racetracks—from the Fair Grounds at

New Orleans to Aqueduct in New York to Washington Park outside Chicago—and bettors could compute it themselves: All the racetrack payoffs for win, place, and show in the first four races were added up. The first number at the left of the decimal point became the first of the three winning digits. This process was repeated to get a total of the pari-mutuel winning payoffs for the first five races, and the number to the left of the decimal point became the second winning number; the process was carried out a third time for the winning pay-off's total in the first six races, again using the number to the left of the decimal. Those three tabulated digits became the first Pontiac winning number. The second three-digit winner was compiled similarly: the winning digit for the sixth race was always used as the first digit; the race payoffs for the seventh race were totaled, and the digit to the left of the decimal point became the second winning digit. This formula was repeated for the eighth race, and Numbers operators had their second three-digit winning number. On a given day, for example, 692 and 281 or 784 and 431 could be the winning numbers for Pontiac.

Aunt Florence says Fannie could do those calculations herself, using the requisite *Daily Racing Form*. And she had some access to those forms, thanks to my uncle John, given that he was a horseman at the local racetrack (when he was working the New Orleans racetrack, he'd call long-distance to give her the winning races), so she often knew the winning number before most. But like a lot of people, Florence didn't understand the formula. "I never did figure out how they chose the numbers," she admits. "I never did know how you did that shit."

Meanwhile, the Detroit number was more mysteriously

derived, so that no one knew exactly where it came from. Over the years the widely held belief was that it was fixed, completely made up by the Number-service bosses. The Detroit number, they say, was based on the least heavily played combinations for a given day. They called it "hit protection" as a way to prevent huge payouts. It's unclear when this became widely known, as folks did still play the Detroit number, which at least looked legit, its winning combinations mimicking the Pontiac number by using the last digit of one three-digit combination as the first digit for the second (e.g., 809 and 973). And some people did hit.

Following all these convoluted calculations, someone high up in Detroit's racket received all four winning three-digit numbers via a long-distance phone call from a Number-service boss in, they say, Chicago. And thus the day's numbers hit the streets.

Anyone who has bought a daily lottery ticket in recent years will recognize the game's potential reward: If a customer played one of the winning combinations, with its 500-to-1 payout, a 25-cent bet on 973, for example, garnered $125. If that customer played the same number "boxed"—a way to bet on all possible combinations—she'd win a payout of 80-to-1, or $20. That payout is based on the fact that there are six different ways the number 973 can fall, so it's a six-way box. A number with two of the same digits, like 977, garners more money when boxed for the same twenty-five cents—$40—because there are only three ways the combinations can fall. Higher odds equal a handsomer payout.

Because Mama's initial reserve, or "bank," was $100, she had to make the daily calculation to determine how much to allow each customer to play, or to "cap" their bets, to ensure that she could pay out all potential hits. My aunt and uncle both say that from the beginning, Fannie could do that math in her head; I'm guessing she didn't accept any bets on a single number that totaled more than a $90 payout. Luckily the combination of three digits is seemingly infinite but actually has *600 different possibilities;* folks played a variety of them, and as long as no one hit for too much, the coins added up to a small profit. Numbers is a gamble for both the player and the banker. But it favors the house. The odds of winning with a three-digit number are 1,000 to 1.

As Aunt Florence notes, "It's hard to hit them numbers."

Even in her conservatism, my mother would've made profits of roughly $25 a week, which certainly was much-needed household income. And once the Numbers provided her with a little extra money, her giving to others stepped up.

"I remember she would often share whatever food she had from the grocery store," recalls Elaine, whose family moved into the same four-flat house on Clarendon back in 1958. "She would say, 'I bought a couple extra chickens, I bought some extra greens, I bought' whatever it was; but you could tell it was a little bit beyond what she would normally buy; it would be a variety of food and it would be in several bags; and so she would just freely give it to you; and if you tried to offer her money, she would *not* take it; she would refuse and throw her hand up and say, 'Oh no, that's not necessary. That's not what I did that for and don't worry about it.' And that was the way that she was with not only our family, but other people on the street."

It was then too that a pattern in my mother's life first

emerged in Detroit: helping to shape the life of a teenage girl. "God sent her to me at the right time in my life," admits Elaine. "When I got about thirteen or fourteen, talking back and getting a beating, getting in trouble often, I'd run away from home, straight to Fannie's. And she'd hear my side of the story and then she'd give me food for thought. 'Maybe you could have done it this way' or 'You could have done it that way.' And she was very confidential. If I did something I had no business doing, I could tell her and she wouldn't tell on me. I'd never hear it again unless I told it."

Throughout that time, Elaine says she and her family, who became so close to us the children called each other cousins, weren't aware that Fannie ran the Numbers. "I don't remember seeing her do that at all," she insists.

This is a recurring theme, my mother's secrecy about her line of work. Apart from her customers, people in her life had no idea she was "in Numbers." I marvel at this because Cousin Elaine, for instance, was an integral part of our lives, in and out of our home daily. In fact, she and others only learned the full story when I told them a few years ago. My mother was the embodiment of discretion.

Florence and her husband, Uncle Gene, soon came to visit. "They wasn't doing they best then, but they was doing a little better," recalls Aunt Florence. "We went to Belle Isle and Fannie say, 'Y'all ought to move here.' We went back and I worked and I was saving my little change every week, 'cause I knew I was on my way."

That fall, my parents' landlord, a black man named Mr. Saddlewhite, saw my mother planting bulbs in the front yard of the four-family house and confessed to her that he also owned the two-family house across the street. He told her he liked how she took care of his property and that if she could swing the $75-a-month rent, the better place was hers. The address was 8878. They couldn't afford it per se, even though my father had begun moonlighting as a house painter to supplement his unsteady factory work and she was making some money from her penny Numbers business. She took the place anyway. It was bigger, and the family of six could use the space. Also, Mama was pregnant again.

For the next couple months, they barely got by. They needed more steady money, and that was when my mother turned to Wingate and began working for him as a bookie—handing over her customers and using Wingate's hefty bank to accept larger bets from more people. The percentage he gave her helped create a striking contrast to how the Davis family had lived just a year before.

Meanwhile, Florence did migrate to Detroit, along with her young son (her husband joined them later), moving into the available flat above Fannie and John T.'s place. "When I came here, I had twenty-five hundred dollars in my brassiere I had saved up," recalls my aunt. Her dream always had been to come to the North and be with her big sister Fannie. And she did it. "I came here, Honey, and hell, I was happy."

That May, I was born two months premature at Henry Ford Hospital, where my mother paid for the dignity of a private room. At birth, I weighed 4 pounds and 11 ounces; it turns out that 411 was a popular number to play, and seen as a good-luck combination. Maybe that's why Mama once told me: "You were born lucky." Or maybe it's because I was the first of her children born in comfort.

While she waited for me to come home from the hospital, where I remained in an incubator for weeks, Mama bought an entire suite of French Provincial baby furniture. The cream-colored crib with ruffled canopy, matching dresser, and child's armoire paired with a white layette trimmed in lace were so exquisite that people streamed into the house to ooh and aah over "the baby's room" before I came home. (I can still conjure that suite with its little-girl armoire, as it remained in my bedroom for several years.) For my mother, the purchase was a way to celebrate my healthy arrival in the world. It was still risky for a baby to be born at thirty-two weeks back then. In fact, just before my birth, doctors discovered why premature babies were developing a disorder known as gray baby syndrome and dying. The usual doses of an antibiotic known as chloramphenicol, routinely given to preemies as a prophylactic, turned out to be at toxic levels. By the time I came along in 1960, some babies were still receiving the drug, but doctors at renowned hospitals like Henry Ford knew better than to administer it, luckily for me. The high-end baby furniture also symbolized my mother's achievement: five years after arriving as a migrant, Fannie had climbed her family out of the poorhouse, and that indulgent splurge punctuated the fact.

Now, in 1962, she'd decided to stop working for Wingate, taking a chance on herself as her own boss. The risk, she knew, could plunge us backward. But risk is the linchpin of success in the Numbers: The only ways to make any real money are either to go long enough without anyone hitting, which eventually is bad for business since folks want to feel they have good luck with you, or to gamble with the odds while your customers are gambling against them. The hope is to go long enough "holding tickets" without getting hit hard, while you build up your cash reserve. If someone *does* hit big too soon, you lose. And my mother had a lot to lose: our beloved Broadstreet.

Mama was a nervous wreck each day as she waited for the winning number to come out. To alleviate stress, she created a daily ritual. With her older children at school, she'd carry me in her arms to the movies at the Mercury Theater on Schaefer Highway. "She'd just set up there in the dark, and wait it out," says Uncle John. The moving pictures calmed Mama, and each week that went by without a big payout allowed her to build up her reserve.

As she sat in that darkened theater watching Natalie Wood in *Splendor in the Grass* and Audrey Hepburn in *Breakfast at Tiffany's* and Diahann Carroll in *Paris Blues* with me cuddled in her arms, a quiet baby, she held fast to her belief that *God helps those who help themselves.*

Three

Fannie at the Fountainebleau, Miami Beach, December 1968

My first cogent memory is sitting beside my parents in the den on Broadstreet. We're watching TV coverage of John F. Kennedy's funeral. I remember snatches of images: little John-John saluting, Mama crying, horses drawing the hearse, Daddy comforting his wife.

I was both parents' child then, sleeping between them each night in their big bed, my small leg thrown across one of their bodies "making sure she stays the baby," my father would jokingly say to his friends. And they were a unit. Mama took folks' numbers, and Daddy collected their bets and their money from "out in the streets." He once served brief time after he and Mama got stopped for a traffic violation and were caught with Numbers tickets on them. Daddy later told me he gladly took that rap, because "jail was no place for a woman." He was charged, likely served mere hours, and was out after paying a fine, the custom back then. Law enforcement had its eyes instead on the big operations; Detroit's Numbers racket was now an estimated $15-million-a-year enterprise. In fact the year before, 1962, just months into Mama's efforts to work for herself, as she waited it out in that movie theater, authorities executed what became known as the infamous Gotham raid.

Detroit's Hotel Gotham had been internationally famous, and throughout most of its existence, blacks weren't allowed there as guests. While Jim Crow is equated with the South, the North was no stranger to the same de facto racist policies, and the Hotel Gotham was one clear example. That is, until a man named John White bought it in 1943; the hotel suddenly became *the* place for African-American travelers denied accommodations in the downtown hotels, many of them entertainers. The ironically named White was a black man who could pass for white, which apparently helped him purchase the nine-story twin-towered hotel for a quarter million dollars; sellers thought they were selling to a Caucasian man. Also, John White and his partner had Numbers money.

Located on the corner of John R Street and Orchestra Place—near Paradise Valley, the city's black cultural hub—the top-notch 200-room hotel was known for its elegance and the comfort it provided. A key feature was the Ebony Room, the hotel's restaurant, known for African carvings and a famous "high-class" chef. Its guests were a who's who of black America, including civil rights lawyer Thurgood Marshall, Billie Holiday, Jackie Robinson, Ella Fitzgerald and Duke Ellington. Langston Hughes once called the hotel "a kind of minor miracle" for being owned, managed, and staffed by blacks.

The Gotham was also headquarters for White's Numbers

racket and that of Detroit's other black Numbers operators. White had once worked for Roxborough, the city's founding Numbers man, who set the bar high in smudging the lines between an informal and a formal economy: Roxborough was the first to use the wealth he amassed in Numbers to invest in legal businesses, everything from an insurance company to a country club to a weekly newspaper to a bowling alley—providing services to African-Americans that racism had denied them. White learned well from his mentor, not only taking over where Roxborough left off; he also bought the Hotel Gotham to give black folks a luxury service they sorely needed and deserved. And like Roxborough and other Numbers men before him, White was a staunch race man who supported black pride, requiring all his employees to be both registered voters and members of the NAACP. In fact, he single-handedly kept the city's fledgling NAACP branch afloat and also gave generously to the Detroit Urban League. Both civil rights organizations would of course become critical to the fight for equality waged by blacks in the 1960s.

It's worth noting that by the time Roxborough and others began serving prison sentences for "conspiracy to protect the numbers racket" in 1944 (convicted by an all-white jury), blacks in Detroit controlled *less than 50 percent* of Numbers operations. That's also the point at which Roxborough gave up control of the wire service to Detroit's Mafia. Controlling the wire service essentially meant controlling the entire Numbers operation, because back then the wire service provided the daily numbers, and whoever controlled it decided from which racetracks winning numbers would be drawn.

In 1951, the black-themed magazine *Color* reported a

"War On Number Racket Kings" on its cover, claiming: "Huge profits lure organized crime bosses into the numbers game." Peter Licavoli, a notorious Italian boss, was head of Detroit's Mafia for many years and reportedly owned at least two Numbers businesses throughout the 1950s; he's credited with helping to expand the Numbers game in the city and ensuring that more whites owned and controlled those operations. John White was one of a very few black men in the 1940s and 1950s who managed to hang on and compete as Numbers kings.

By the time of the Gotham raid, the hotel was already targeted under eminent domain laws, to make room for a medical center as part of the city's "urban renewal" plan, which cut right through traditional black neighborhoods. But some of the hotel's full-time residents remained, many of them White's friends and associates whom he claimed he kept on the premises to maintain insurance coverage, and protect against vandals. The hotel was clearly still operating as a Numbers factory; authorities knew this, claiming that the Gotham was the headquarters for a "gigantic numbers operation," and they were determined to crack down.

Dubbed "an unprecedented raid" in the history of the Detroit police department, the over-the-top ambush involved two busloads of Treasury agents, some brought from Chicago, busting into the hotel at 5 p.m. on a Friday, when numbers operators would allegedly be in their rooms counting their receipts. Men came in blazing, with hammers and axes, and ultimately hacked their way through every one of the hotel's 174 rooms; White was irate and called the raid "a needless and uncalled for binge."

White accused the Feds and the local vice squad of breaking in "like members of the Notre Dame football team." He further accused them of being there over an hour "smashing everything in sight" before they showed him a warrant. He was quoted in the *Michigan Chronicle*, the city's black newspaper, pointing out the fact that "no one was caught in the actual operation of numbers." Apparently, officials took possession of his hotel for twenty-four hours, and, according to White, drank up all his personal whisky, soda pop, and even some milk. He said they also drank "untold amounts of whisky" belonging to his permanent guests, and even took ten new, unused packs of pinochle cards. White was convinced that the raid, led by a member of the IRS Intelligence Division, was a ploy by Treasury agents "bucking for promotion."

Meanwhile, police found at least one Numbers office on every floor, each with its own adding machines and blacked-out windows. Linen closets contained boxes of coin wrappers. Raiding officers confiscated eleven safes, which contained $49,000 in cash, records, and other gambling paraphernalia. Even though no one was in fact caught in the act, forty-one people were arrested, including White himself and another well-known Numbers operator; some were charged with violation of the US gambling code, and others with violation of the state gambling law. Interestingly, Eddie Wingate, whom my mother had just disassociated herself from and whose Numbers headquarters was also located in the Gotham, wasn't there that day, so he avoided arrest. By then, Wingate was considered one of the city's top Numbers operators.

Detroit's police commissioner, George Edwards, who claimed to have confiscated 160,000 bet slips, proclaimed, "I am certain that quite a crimp was put into the business by this raid."

I imagine my mother spreading out the *Detroit Free Press*, which she read religiously every day from her bedroom perch, and seeing the coverage of the raid. Did it frighten her? Make her even more cautious? Or was she clear that the way to stay in the business was to do so under the radar on a small, mom-and-pop level? I suspect that the Gotham bust reinforced her determination to stay low-key; she had no desire to become "big-time," à la the biggest woman Number runner in history: the notorious 1930s legend Stephanie St. Clair, known as Madame Queen, who dominated New York's Numbers racket in her heyday. Greed and power were *not* my mother's thing. Still, the raid had to be unnerving. She could not afford to get busted. Nor could she afford to leave the Numbers alone.

"Fannie always was a hustler," explains Aunt Florence. "I guess she got that honest from my daddy. She didn't give up. And she kept going, kept pushing, pushing, pushing until she got what she wanted."

The raid apparently did put a chill on the entire Numbers community, but it never slowed down the Numbers business itself; hardly. In fact, many Numbers bankers began using their proceeds to aggressively fund Detroit's growing civil rights movement, as they saw the bust as an attack on the Hotel Gotham specifically because it was black-owned, and because blacks were generating so much wealth within its walls. Eight months after the raid, the Gotham was demolished, a sight that brought White to tears—two of the city's most successful black businesses, one legit, one illicit, both filling the needs of the black community in ways its government had neglected, were gone.

A year later, while awaiting trial, John White died at age fifty-five from a heart ailment. It was the end of an era.

With White and his Gotham Numbers factory no more, the structure of the city's Numbers games changed. Displacement of concentrated black communities, thanks to the so-called urban renewal that sacrificed thousands of buildings, helped to decentralize the Numbers, which were no longer run out of large headquarters. This allowed for the creation and proliferation of small operations, modest enterprises like my mother's. Whereas a major "house" employed numerous people to perform the jobs of door-to-door ticket writers, those taking numbers via phone, pickup men collecting bets and money, and a bevy of bookkeepers and tabulators, Fannie's business was a one-woman microcosm of all that: she did every job.

In addition to this new business model for the Numbers, by then black Detroiters were facing the hardship of high unemployment, with one in five adults without jobs, or working within the so-called informal economy. With the auto companies already outsourcing jobs, that number grew as the decade went on.

These twin conditions at play, Mama's fledgling business took hold. Along with millions of other blacks, my mother watched on TV as Dr. King delivered his speech at the March on Washington. She heard him clearly say, "We have come to our nation's capital to cash a check. When the architects of our republic wrote the magnificent words of the Constitution and the Declaration of Independence, they were signing a promissory note to which every American was to fall heir.

This note was a promise that all men, yes, black men as well as white men, would be guaranteed the unalienable rights of life, liberty, and the pursuit of happiness...America has given the Negro people a bad check."

More and more folks looked to the Numbers as a major source of hope, yes, but mostly as a right of survival, and Mama's customer base began to grow. Here another memory asserts itself: being with my parents, together, for the last time. We are once again in the den as Mama and Daddy sit on its white leather love seat, watching me play. I am four, and holding a Squirt bottle, its green glass a rivulet of swirls that fascinates me; I run my small hands over its smooth curves. Suddenly I drop the bottle on the hardwood floor and it shatters. What I remember next is Daddy carrying me from his long silver car, up the walkway of our home, through the front door. My right foot is bandaged, as I've just received stitches across its instep. I can still detect the faintest, faintest trace of a scar there, reassuring me that the memory is real.

Once we reenter the house, I am a daddy's girl. Held safely in his arms, feeling the stubble from his beard tickle my face, crossing the threshold, I'm his child. Mama is there, for sure, running her business at the dining room table, taking customers' numbers from bed, coming into the house from the outside world, going back out, cooking, talking on the phone—an ever-present life-force. She takes me shopping, combs my wild hair, lets me hang out beside her in the basement as she does laundry. But the day-to-day of my life is spent with Daddy, in the den. He now sleeps downstairs while she, Mama, sleeps upstairs. They are not together, in the same house. I never hear one argument between them, but barely any conversation either. And it's Daddy I sleep with every night, literally curled atop his broad back. (I once awake to Mama and her good friend Miss Betty peering at us through the glass of the den's French doors; Mama is pointing and smiling.)

It's Daddy who teaches me to tie my shoes, tell time, read. I start kindergarten and Daddy alone escorts me to my first day of school. When Malcolm X, whom my oldest sister, Deborah, would go to hear speak at Temple Number One on Linwood Avenue, is gunned down, only Daddy and I watch the coverage together on the den's Magnavox TV.

Age and distance now allow me to see what was happening. Daddy's life, due largely to his poor health, was shrinking. His high blood pressure was consistently stroke-level, causing daily migraines, which he tried to mitigate with Stanback "headache powder" (crushed aspirin) poured onto his tongue and washed back with Pepsi-Colas. While still a little girl, I placed cool washcloths across his forehead to help alleviate the pain. His last day working at General Motors' Pontiac Division was October 2, 1963, when he was injured at work; that coupled with his hypertension led to his being one of the youngest men at GM to receive disability. He was thirty-seven. It would take more than eight years for the auto company to settle his case. When I was a teenager, Daddy unfolded the settlement letter—worn and nearly tattered—and spread it out before me. "This is how they did me," he said. It showed that GM's entire liability had been "redeemed" by a single payment "in lieu of weekly payments and past, present, and future medical benefits" of $1,000. From that payment, $200 was deducted for attorneys' fees, and another $90 for medical expenses. He received a total of $710 in disability payment. Interestingly, months before my father was injured and let go from the Pontiac plant, Dr. King led over 125,000 people through Detroit's streets to protest just such discrimination in workplaces. There, he told the crowd, "I have a dream this afternoon that my four little children will not come up in the same young days that I came up within, but they will be judged on the basis of the content of their character, not the color of their skin," a precursor to his famous March on Washington speech.

Daddy, who was never to work again, had time on his hands, and he chose to largely spend that time with me. My parents had been childhood sweethearts, married as teens, had five children together, migrated north, launched a Numbers business, moved into a spacious family home. But the marriage was not holding up; who can say exactly why? "They just grew apart," says Aunt Florence. "They just grew apart."

I do know this: I was the last vestige of what they'd once shared. I was their baby, and Daddy knew there'd be no more babies between him and Fannie. He clung to me and I happily clung back.

Mama, now the sole breadwinner, didn't have that kind of time on her hands. Everything was on her. It was on her to pay the house note and handle every leaky faucet and roof and furnace repair that came with home ownership; it was on her to pay the light and heat bills, keep the refrigerator full, buy her own car, and keep both hers and Daddy's running; it was on her to furnish the house and pay medical expenses, insurance premiums, and credit card bills—never mind the meals in restaurants and excursions and well-made clothes and shelves full of books she was hell-bent on giving us. So inspired, Mama built her business. She did it by amassing steady, loyal customers who turned in their numbers only to her. Mama's distinction was her reputation. She was known for being honest, reliable, fair, and tough—all very important qualities in an underground business with few checks and balances. People could lie, cheat, steal, and who would stop them? Folks knew that when it was time to turn in their numbers, Fannie would be there to take them; they knew that when they hit with her they'd get paid the next day. ("It's not my money. What the hell does it need to hang around my house for?") They knew that she wouldn't discuss their business with other customers. They knew that she'd have clear records for every transaction. And they knew that if they didn't pay their bills, she'd politely drop them.

"You expect your money when you hit, don't you?" she'd say to a customer. "Well, I expect mine when you don't." She didn't understand people's "get-over" mentality. "What makes somebody think they can sit on their ass and play numbers all week, and then not pay for them?" she'd say, incredulous. "That don't make no damn sense."

In fact, while most bookies accepted tips when their customers hit, Mama did not. "I get my tip when you pay me on time," she'd say. Another cardinal rule that helped Mama's business thrive: she didn't believe in "playing up your profits." To be sure, she still played her pet number, 788, regularly, and other numbers that she'd get hunches on too. But she ironically lacked a gambler's mentality. To her, playing numbers was an investment in her business. So she placed a cap on what she herself played. And throughout the years, when she *did* hit—reaffirming her reputation as a lucky woman—she always put away a big portion of it. Having a stockpile of cash is vital to someone who banks the Numbers.

What also aided the growth of my mother's business was that her customers played heavy. Despite the fact that the city's auto industry was on an overall downward spiral that had begun a decade before, thanks to a "cyclical boom"—a brief boom inside a broader downward trend—in the mid- and late-1960s, many had steady work; in fact, for those blacks who had been at the plants long enough to secure good jobs with benefits protected by the union, salaries were pretty good. That meant folks had more disposable income to play more numbers, more often, for higher amounts. That also meant Mama stayed busy.

During that time, Mama expanded her operation by taking the numbers of those who themselves were taking others' numbers. Each "book," as it was known, was a customer who herself had a few customers. As Mama's reputation for fairness and honesty grew, more people, bookies themselves, wanted to turn in their own business to her, and she eventually had several books, as many as ten at her height. This was small compared to a major numbers man like Wingate, who had numerous bookies working for him, turning in dozens of books; Wingate reportedly made millions a year in his heyday, with a business widely believed to be connected to Detroit's Italian Mafia. Still, Mama had by any measure a robust roster of customers.

"You can't make it off of no two or three books," explains Aunt Florence. "You got to have a volume of business to really make it." And by the mid-1960s Mama had volume.

As my cousin Bill puts it: "Fannie came up in the world, she did."

Toni Morrison once said of Muhammad Ali's upbringing, "It was middle class, but *black* middle class, black *Southern* middle class, which is not white middle class at all." Our lives were the Northern equivalent of that, with a twist. Numbers provided the twist, allowing Mama to become a lucrative small business owner in the city's hierarchical Numbers racket.

To punctuate her early success, and for me a reminder of its fragility, Mama finally had her own name placed on the land contract for our home—three and a half years after Mr. Colvin "purchased" it for her. That's how long it took Mr. Prince, the seller, to trust my mother enough—was he waiting to see if she'd miss a payment?—and officially enter into a legal arrangement with her as the actual buyer. Now at least Mr. Colvin couldn't take Broadstreet from us. The transaction was recorded with the Register of Deeds on October 6, 1964:

> For a valuable consideration, receipt of which is acknowledged, the undersigned assignor hereby assign to Fannie Drumright (sic) Davis the assignee a certain land contract dated April 15, 1961, executed between Torkom Prince and Beatrice Prince, his wife as Seller, and *Wallace Colvin as Purchaser,* for the sale of land situated in the city of Detroit, Wayne County, Michigan described as Lot 427 Russell Woods Subdivision of part of ¼ section 11 and 12, 10,000 acre Tract, Liber 34, Plats, Page 3, Wayne County Records, Commonly known as 12836 Broadstreet.

* * *

Throughout her first decade in the business, Mama took bets from customers on numbers for higher and higher amounts, which provided more revenue, which came with more risk. If a customer hit big, it could potentially wipe her out. A number played for $5, after all, could bring its winner $2,500, and if several customers bet on the same number and hit, Mama would have to come up with several thousand dollars on one day. Cash flow was the key. That's where Len Taylor came in. He too was one of the biggest Numbers men in the city, but a low-key contrast to the notorious Wingate, whom Mama had scarily owed all that money to. Mr. Taylor was benevolent and kind, and when he befriended my mother, she knew she could trust him.

"Taylor was nice," says Aunt Florence. "When Fannie was getting hit heavy, he would take the business from her and he would give her so much money, a percentage each week, off of what she turned in to him until she could get her nest egg built back up."

Once Mama got that nest egg rebuilt, Mr. Taylor would return her business—all her books—to her. In this way, Mama went back and forth between being a bookie and a banker. And she never had to worry about him taking her customers away from her. She turned over and reclaimed her business from Taylor a few times over the course of the three decades she was in the Numbers. Another way Mr. Taylor was helpful was to act as an insurance policy. If she noticed on a given day that a number was being "played heavy" by several customers, she'd "relay" that same number to Mr. Taylor for enough money to cover the cost if it came out. Only the handful of big Number men like

Taylor could afford to take a bet on a number played for several dollars, and depending on who it was and whether they liked the person, those big bankers might choose not to do it. So Mama benefited greatly from her relationship with Mr. Taylor, able to grow her business and make a good living thanks to an occasional safety net.

What this meant for my family was that we stayed intact. Unlike so many African-Americans in precarious living situations, Mama wasn't forced to leave her children at home with just each other, while she went to work for low pay. Every day when we came home from school, my mother was there. In fact, my siblings and I never had babysitters. My mother didn't believe in them. My father, facing debilitating health problems, didn't have to face an impoverished life alongside them. And we, their children, could reasonably expect to someday do better than our parents.

Looking back, the 1960s were Mama's best decade as a number runner, an enterprise she'd only begun in 1958. Certainly from my perspective, it was a heyday. My childhood memories are awash in the sights and sounds of Mama running her business, the rhythm of her days: early hours on the phone, taking customers' numbers, a lull in late afternoon, when she'd hide the business in places she felt enhanced her own luck—under her mattress, in the freezer so as to take the "heat" off, or in her bedroom closet. At dusk a phone call announcing the day's numbers, and the flurry of activity that ensued. Hers was a photographic memory when it came to numbers, so she often knew before confirming whether any customers had hit, and if so, who'd hit for what. I still see Mama checking her business: First, she'd go over the numbers taken via phone and recorded in her notebook, red pen in hand. If she found a hit, she'd circle it. Next, she went to the "stuff" as she called it that had been collected "out in the streets," i.e., picked up from customers by a runner—usually a friend's son or family friend she'd employed. Those bets were written on small slips of paper known as tickets. For those, she'd wet her finger and go through each ticket one by one. All my siblings helped at different times with this task. Going through the business to spot hits was a serious undertaking, because to miss a hit was called an overlook, a major faux pas. (Of course, customers who'd hit often started the phone ringing minutes after the number came out.) If a ticket had a hit on it, she'd pull it out and circle the three-digit number. Eventually that ticket would get stapled to the customer's end-of-the-week tally, or "tape."

Mama ran customers' tapes once a week. I still conjure the *rat-a-tat, rat-a-tat, rat-a-tat* of the adding machine, and the trill every time she hit the Total button. She provided a breakdown for each customer of what was played for the week, minus both the customer's percentage and what numbers were hit, totaling the final bill—money owed to her (the payout), or a break-even amount if the customer "hit out," or money owed the customer if the hits totaled more than the customer's ticket (week's worth of numbers played). Customers who had hits from business taken over the phone got a "fly sheet," a piece of scratch-pad paper listing the winning numbers, how much they were played for, and how much money was won. This fly sheet got stapled to the tape. I can see her now, holding those white sheets in her hand, hear her say, "I got your tape right here, Cecil. I can tell you exactly what you owe."

One of my most cogent memories is watching Mama count money. Whether she was double-checking what she'd collected from a customer while he or she was standing there, or gathering money for a payout, she always counted the same way: She'd spread out the bills in her hands like they were cards, or place them before her on the table, and rearrange them in order of descending denominations. Then she'd gather them up and count the money, hands a blur as she did so with speed; best of all, she'd pause to turn bills around, so that every president's face looked in the same direction. She was like a bank teller, but more so. I always marveled at her skill, and watching her count cash is an image that freeze-frames in my mind.

Nothing captures my wondrous childhood of abundance more than memories of Christmas morning. I'd wake to find a plethora of toys and presents tumbled out from under the all-white tree with gold ornaments (because Mama loved monochromatic Christmas decorations), so much so that there was nowhere to walk. "Christmas is for children," Mama declared. "The rest of us just need to understand that."

We all had the latest fashions. I can often remember a specific time by what my siblings wore: Deborah in stylish shifts and vests from Lane Bryant; Dianne in her myriad colorful mohair sweaters with matching pumps; Anthony in his head-to-toe red or purple or blue or green outfits, down to the matching shoes; Rita and her array of knee-high boots showing off her big, pretty legs. I think of my own favorite outfits: the sky-blue brocade ensemble worn for Easter; the red-and-white polka-dot dress with the white smock that held the matching polka-dot handkerchief, worn with my black-and-white polka-dot patent leather shoes; the orange plaid skirt and navy Nehru jacket worn with orange fishnet stockings, the white go-go boots. And my all-time favorite: a reversible leopard-print velour coat Mama purchased for me while in New York for its 1964–1965 World's Fair.

Mama was hands down the best dressed in our family. She had a thing for lush baby-leather purses, furs, and stylish shoes. A soft white-and-gray mink cape, with thin gray vertical leather strips running through it, still hangs in my bedroom closet. She sometimes wore it with a matching mink muffler. Her initials, FDR, are inscribed on the silk lining. She also loved jewelry and had a collection of gold chains and thin-banded, elegant watches and bracelets, many of them diamond-encrusted. My favorite was a necklace with a pot of shaved gold dangling from it. And for as long as I can remember, she wore a 1.75-carat diamond solitaire on her ring finger. That diamond now hangs from a necklace I often wear.

Also, Mama always drove a new car, in custom colors like powder blue and pearl white. She made it clear she didn't believe in sacrificing and doing without as a martyr for her children. She was not what writer Hilton Als has dubbed a "Negress," a black woman who has no life beyond others' needs. She believed in self-care—long baths, naps, vacations, spending money on herself. "If I don't have shoes on my feet, that's a problem for *you*," she'd tell us. Those shoes might as well be high-quality and fashionable.

When I close my eyes and envision my mother, I see her wearing her signature style accessory—an Hermès scarf, one of those colorful and intricately designed squares of silk made exclusively in France. She had a collection of them, used to protect her hair from rain, to cover fresh curls as she left the beauty shop, and as an option for days when she didn't feel like styling her hair. She was never precious with these scarves, which sometimes had pomade on them, or got slightly tattered, and were often strewn across a chair or on the bathroom vanity. I didn't even know the distinction of Hermès scarves until I was an adult. I just knew they were pretty, and my mother had a lot of them.

"Fannie bought whatever she wanted," proclaims Aunt Florence. "Wasn't nothing she did want that she didn't get; if she could see it, she went and got it; she wasn't like a lot of people, have that money and too stingy to buy the things that you want. She lived."

Doing well also put Mama's giving on steroids. She had a soft spot for motherless children in particular. "Nobody replaces a mother's love," she'd often say. I will always remember Spook, a quiet, gentle teenage boy in our neighborhood. Kids called him Spook because he was very dark-skinned. Once, in the basement, I sat beside him as he sewed up a busted seam in his winter coat. I watched him, fascinated, as he pulled the heavy black thread through the thick fabric. "My mother taught me to sew," he told me. His mother had recently died, and he was headed somewhere far away to live with a relative, because his own father made a difference between him and his lighter-skinned brother. Spook had little to take with him. Mama went shopping and bought him new underwear and shirts and pants and socks to send him on his way. "A fresh start requires fresh clothes," she said.

Some comments I never heard from my mother: *Do you*

think money grows on trees? That's too expensive. We can't afford that. It's not worth it, you'll just outgrow it. That's a waste of money.

What she did say: "Each child has his or her day. When I'm shopping for one, I'm just shopping for one. So when you see me come in the house with a big bag, if it's not your day, don't ask, 'What'd you get me?'"

One of her pet peeves was seeing parents buy too-big clothes for their children so they could grow into them. "Just buy the child clothes in her size," she'd say. "Who wants to wear something that doesn't fit?"

Our family might've fully entered the world of the city's *black bourgeoisie*—or even its progressive black activist intelligentsia counterpart—if Mama's had been a legal enterprise like a funeral parlor or dry cleaner's or restaurant, if she'd been a self-made woman in a more legitimate way. We might've elevated ourselves to the status of the Talented Tenth, as W. E. B. Dubois famously dubbed educated and privileged blacks, as so many African-Americans before and after have done. But the Numbers were illegal, so that was not an option. (One striking exception to this status-conscious rule was Roxborough, who as the founding father of Detroit's Numbers racket was from one of the city's privileged African-American families. Already part of the black upper class, he remained within that elite milieu even though people knew exactly how he made his money.)

Basically, because my parents weren't college-educated professionals with fair skin and an air of entitlement, we were exempt from what critic Margo Jefferson calls *Negroland*, "a small region of Negro America where residents were sheltered by a certain amount of privilege and plenty." We were not that group of black folks, which ironically meant we didn't have the same constraints on us to uplift the race through respectability. Funny thing, without those strictures, my mother was able to create generational wealth in ways that more so-called respectable blacks were not. To be sure, Mama did demand we follow certain dictates to avoid what she called "low-class" behavior, like being loud in public or going barefoot outside or having discarded objects on the front lawn. As a migrant from the South, she didn't want to be seen as "country."

We didn't "summer" at Idlewild resort (the "Black Eden") in Michigan's rural Lake County alongside Detroit's black upper class, but we *did* go places. We drove across the Ambassador Bridge to Windsor, Ontario, to have Chinese food dinners. In the winter we took day trips north to Frankenmuth, Michigan, home of "the world's largest Christmas store," where Mama bought pretty ornaments for the tree. And I found myself alone on a plane for the first time, age eight, headed to a tiny town in Ohio to visit my mother's childhood friend, Aunt Maria, for a summer week because Mama overheard me saying I wondered what it felt like to fly.

We may not have attended performances at the Detroit Opera House or by the city's symphony orchestra, nor visited the Detroit Institute of Arts regularly, but we had our own cultural outings. "It's good to expose kids to things," Mama would say, and expose us she did. Memories tumble forward: me, my cousins, and neighborhood friends at the Barnum & Bailey Circus at Cobo Hall, our little hands filled with caramel popcorn; at the Ice Capades, transfixed by the skaters' amazing pirouettes; wrapped warm in a blanket during languid nights at the drive-in theater, Daddy's silver Buick deuce-and-a-quarter filled with hot dogs and other goodies from the concession stand; riding in Mama's Riviera, headed to dinner at upscale places like Sindbad's Restaurant and Marina with its view of the Detroit River, and Joe Muer Seafood Restaurant, where I learned both to place a cloth napkin in my lap and to eat fresh oyster soup with little circles of oyster crackers. And we rode to Belle Isle just "to be by some water" as Mama put it, and throw coins into its changing-colors fountain, a good-luck ritual my mother believed in.

Another highlight was trips to the Hazel Park Raceway to see my uncle John's racehorses run. Because John was that rarity, an African-American horse trainer, watching his Thoroughbreds—with names like Bitter Blue, Copper Quest, Nice & Playful, and his prized Michigan Mile winner, Thumbsucker—perform was our version of the Royal Ascot. I loved all of it, from the starting shot, to the crowds' yells during the adrenaline-fueled races, to the photographers' blinding flash inside the winner's circle, where discarded tickets scattered across the ground like oversized confetti.

My brother and sisters and I didn't attend private school on the campus of Cranbrook, the sprawling center designed in part by architect Eliel Saarinen, nor at University Liggett School in Grosse Pointe Woods; but Mama did believe in supporting our intellectual and creative interests. There were French lessons for Deborah; a personal hi-fi for Anthony, along with a stack of Motown albums and a microphone, so he could work out his dance routines ("I brushed my teeth every morning to the Temptations' 'My Girl' for a whole year," Mama later reflected); a subscription to *World Book*

Encyclopedia for Rita's book reports; and for me stacks of Dr. Seuss books piled onto the wide built-in shelf in my room, alongside my own portable record player with LPs of recorded fairy tales; I spent whole afternoons listening to *Peter and the Wolf* and dramatic readings of "Pinocchio" and "Little Red Riding Hood." As I grew older, my mother, knowing how much I loved to read, subscribed to Readers' Digest Condensed Books, tossing a brown package on my bed every couple of weeks; I began devouring abridged versions of classic novels, from *Wuthering Heights* to *The Call of the Wild* to *The Adventures of Huckleberry Finn.*

There were no debutante "coming out" balls, no membership in Jack and Jill, the invitation-only group for upper-middle-class African-American youth, no sorority-based affairs. I knew nothing about these things, didn't have friends who were part of that world. Society validation didn't interest Mama. I suspect she understood that she wouldn't have fit in, wouldn't have been welcomed anyway. That didn't stop her from celebrating our big moments with grand gestures. When my sister Dianne married, my mother planned an elaborate engagement party for her at the Hotel St. Regis. And years later, I'd have my own Sweet Sixteen party at a downtown hotel.

We were our own social class, what I've dubbed *blue-collar black bourgeoisie,* part of that subset of black culture, so invisible to the mainstream, folks whose livelihood came from jobs at the post office and as city workers and sales clerks on commission in department stores, or as number runners. Folks who didn't go to college yet were smart, industrious, and, yes, educated about and by the world around us. Detroit itself gave us the bourgeois part: We lived in a very nice house—one of many left behind by all those fleeing whites—on the west side of town, dubbed the "best side"; like my friends' families, we defined our middle-class status largely by the upscale homes we inhabited. Thanks again to Detroit's uniqueness, we had family members and friends, and in Mama's case customers, who were making decent money in the plants, wages that could bring you a good living even before you added overtime. Mama's customers played heavy, keeping her cash flowing, and so our family benefited. As my high school friend Elliott said about us, we were "living your west-side *bougie* lives."

No other American city had quite that complement of twin conditions: good-paying jobs and affordable, available housing stock for the city's black population; meanwhile, black businesses provided many of the services we needed and craved. For some, that included a thriving industry of "boosters," who shoplifted clothing and accessories from department stores and sold them to customers in makeshift stores set up in their basements on weekends. In a city of hustlers, where the lines of legality and illegality stayed smudged, these boosters—all women—made good livings, with Numbers folks as their key clients. (One booster named her store Jackie's Finer Designs, and she had guards watching customers, to make sure no one stole the merchandise that she had stolen.) I visited a booster's shop with Mama at least once, but she preferred store-bought clothes.

Indeed, by then Detroit City *was* the place to be for blacks, had hit its sweet spot. It would be years before the encroaching effects of white flight and a downsized auto industry unleashed their massive destabilizing forces upon the city. The US economy was still in its so-called golden age of high economic growth coupled with low unemployment and inflation. Unions were strong.

Still, maintaining our blue-collar bourgeois status took its toll on my mother. I remember across those same years that Mama sometimes slept for hours after taking customers' numbers, and before she closed the door on her bedroom, she gave strict orders not to disturb her. My sister Dianne would say to us younger children: "Whatever you do, try not to get on Fannie's nerves." And on Saturdays—the day we all had to clean the house—she'd go collecting, leaving in a bad mood, coming home exhausted. Only later did I learn why: Dealing with folks when you needed to collect their money wasn't easy. Some didn't answer their door or asked you to come back later, or didn't have it all, or wanted you to come in and visit…it was stressful. No numbers ran on Sunday, which was Mama's day off, but portions of that day were often spent tallying customers' weekly bills and collecting payments she hadn't gotten before.

We all collectively and viscerally understood the need to protect Mama from any undue stress. This led to my siblings and me keeping certain upsetting news from her, because we all knew she "had enough on her." We kept secrets from Mama to protect her.

I didn't explicitly know the pressure my mother was under back then, but she was ever on my mind, just as she was on every family member's mind. *What will Fannie think?* was an unspoken question for all situations, because it would affect what she did, and what she did affected all of us. It was as though we moved in a planetary orbit around her, the sun. As the baby, this meant I was both in thrall to and slightly intimidated by my mother. I thought of her as a queen with the bed as her throne, Mama ever on the phone or giving orders or disciplining us or saying, "Here, I bought this for you." She was also the engine that kept our world humming. And no one, myself included, wanted to get on Mama's bad side. Nothing angered her more than the perception that she wasn't being respected, particularly by any of her children. "Respect is earned," she'd say, and we wanted to earn hers. None of us ever talked back or "sassed" her, as she called it; that was not even an option. My mother did not play; she took a hard line on respecting your parents, with no ifs, ands, or buts. You just did, end of story. And if you didn't, well, she had a belt waiting for you.

I was spending a lot of my time in the den with Daddy, but I could see that he wasn't the one in charge. I got emotional nourishment from one parent, and a sense of security from the other. Daddy gave me lots of hugs, but I was clear that Mama was the one who knew how to defend me against outside forces, like my first-grade teacher. Mama once said to me, when I was a young woman: "I wish I'd had the time to hug my kids more, but I was busy trying to make a better life for you."

Throughout the mid-to-late 1960s, all around us, Detroit was changing, becoming more radical, more aware of its role as a central locale of the civil rights movement. As a child, I didn't know that the city had one of the country's largest chapters of both the NAACP and the Urban League, thanks in large part to heavy contributions from local Numbers men and women, including my own mother. I didn't know that

Stokely Carmichael chose Detroit's Cobo Hall to give a seminal speech, during which he shouted out to the crowd, which included my nineteen-year-old sister, Deborah: "It's time to get some black power!" Nor did I know that Coleman Young, a firebrand spokesman for racial justice, was helping make Detroit a hotbed of labor activism, nor that black autoworkers were becoming more militant on shop floors to push back against factories' discrimination.

But I did witness Detroit lifting black consciousness and becoming a symbol for the nation, when my mother took me to a church service at the Shrine of the Black Madonna, founded by Reverend Albert Cleage, Jr. I was seven years old, and will never forget the shock and thrill I felt inside that sacred place on Linwood Avenue, staring up at a painting of a blue-black Madonna holding a black baby Jesus, this eighteen-foot mural towering over us from the church's sanctuary. That arresting image was unlike anything I'd witnessed in my young life, and the message it sent was clear: black people come from God. That meant everything to me.

Meanwhile, the country was deep in the Vietnam War, which Muhammad Ali had refused to fight, famously saying, "My conscience won't let me go shoot my brother, or some darker people, or some poor hungry people in the mud for big powerful America. And shoot them for what? They never called me nigger, they never lynched me, they didn't put no dogs on me, they didn't rob me of my nationality, rape and kill my mother and father. . . . Just take me to jail."

Because I was so young, when I think of the fraught sixties, I think of Motown music and their artists, our local royalty. I remember the up-tempo, happy songs blasting from our living room hi-fi, songs my siblings and I loved to dance to—Martha and the Vandellas' "Heat Wave," and the Miracles' "Mickey's Monkey" and "Come On Do the Jerk," and Mary Wells's "My Guy." Mama never joined in, but she never said, "Turn that music down," either. I used to try to sneak a glance at Diana Ross, sometimes standing outside her corner house just a couple of blocks from Broadstreet, waiting for her to leave. One day, I saw her and waved shyly. She waved back. Certainly, Detroit was having its heyday as Hitsville, USA, *and* the Motor City. The city's population, while no longer at its height, was still 1.6 million, with black folks nearly half a million of its residents. I could feel that proud energy even as a child. It was as though Marvin Gaye was singing an ode to *us* when he sang, "You are my pride and joy."

And a sense of possibility was in the air. My cousin Jewell and I got to be flower girls in a wedding, wearing pretty white lace dresses with pink ribbons around our waists and mini lace veils atop our heads. In our innocence, she and I rode through the streets atop the back seat of a convertible, our veils fluttering in the breeze as the bride and groom sat up front. And that same year, 1966, our family was excited about another wedding, that of Pete Moore from the Miracles. What made this an extraordinary affair was that my sister Dianne knew his bride, Tina. That meant she got to go to the wedding, and that meant she'd get to meet Smokey Robinson. Dianne had a teenage girl's crush on Smokey, sang all his songs in a sweet voice mimicking his own falsetto. In a photograph from the reception, there she is, Dianne, wearing a red skirt suit with a ruffled blouse, standing beside Smokey. He has his arm around her, and she's beaming.

Cousin Bill also had a nice wedding, and in spring of 1967, he and his new wife, Susie, came to Detroit for their honeymoon. "I never will forget," recalls Bill. "Fannie bought me a blue suit that had one button; seemed like the suit changed colors. And she bought me some knit shirts; then she sent my wife with Dianne and bought her a wardrobe. That's just how she was, always thinking about others, giving things, helping people."

Bill also remembers my father's gratitude. "Your daddy said, 'Thank you, Bill, for going back and telling folks in Nashville that we were doing all right back in fifty-eight.'" My cousin points out that "By then, y'all were doing real good."

In many ways, we were: Deborah was in her senior year at Wayne State University, majoring in English (deterred by her advisor from majoring in psychology, a "useless choice" for a Negro girl); Dianne was attending Oakland Community College and had met the man she'd eventually marry. Anthony was finishing junior high and making good grades. Rita was gathering a reputation as a best friend, becoming one of the popular girls at school. And I was enjoying second grade at Winterhalter Elementary, with a teacher who never asked questions about my parents, let alone my shoes.

But another world was brewing outside our doors. Older blacks who'd managed to secure jobs in the plants still had theirs, but unemployment for young black men, for those older blacks' own sons, was between 25 and 30 percent, with few prospects of improvement. As James Baldwin once wrote, "The most dangerous creation of any society is that man who has nothing to lose." The city's black poor were in the same situation their migrating predecessors had been in thirty years before, relegated to overcrowded, depressed inner-city ghettos. Whole sections of the city were off-limits to blacks, thanks to white residents' violent tactics, with twenty-five crosses burned on city lawns in 1965 alone. The only two groups of whites ever-present in black neighborhoods were opportunistic shopkeepers and police. I still remember my father talking about how Mr. Stein, who owned the corner store near our home, overcharged for his cold cuts, which were more often than not near rancid.

Tempers flared across the city. On July 23, 1967, my cousins Ava and Buddy arrived from Nashville. Ava, who was twelve, remembers that it was *such* a big deal for them. They took the train up; neither had ever traveled that far before. She'd been looking forward to their big trip to Detroit all summer. Her father, my uncle Napoleon, had just died and my mother had invited her niece and nephew to come visit as a little getaway, a treat. They got to the city, which was in the midst of a heat wave, and made their way to Broadstreet. As fate would have it, that was the day that police had busted a "blind pig," an illegal after-hours joint on Twelfth Street, a stone's throw from Delaware Street, where my family had begun its life in Detroit. These blind pigs, which got their start as Prohibition saloons, remained the go-to nightlife spots for black folks well into the sixties. Even after desegregation, working-class folks preferred the blind pigs; most of these men and women toiled long hours on assembly lines in the city's plants, and here were places where they could recuperate and seek some pleasure, where "the night time becomes the right time." Police raids on these spots were commonplace, "an unwise attempt by a white middle class to foist its morals on the lower class," said Errol Miller, a representative of the US Justice Department at the time. Police had attempted to raid this particular blind pig nine times the previous year.

At three in the morning, an undercover officer gained entrance to the pig, and soon after, his commanding officer and crew broke down the door with a sledgehammer and charged in, finding a crowd of nearly one hundred people; owners of the pig were hosting a party for two men who'd recently returned from Vietnam and one who was about to leave for the war. The sergeant decided to arrest everyone present—on the claim that the after-hours club was operating illegally—and transported the partygoers to jail in four paddy wagons.

While this was happening, a crowd that grew to two hundred people gathered in the streets outside; the crowd got hostile when it witnessed police officers' rough treatment of the men and women, from pushing to kicking to arm-twisting. Someone yelled, "Black Power! Don't let them take our people away!" and quickly folks started throwing bricks, rocks, and beer cans at the police; one bottle smashed through the last police cruiser to leave the scene, and what forever came to be known in the media as the "Detroit riot," what government officials dubbed Detroit's "civil disturbance," and what blacks called the "Great Rebellion," erupted. The crowd grew to three thousand by 8 a.m. Chaos ensued, and the uprising raged on.

"By the time we got to the house, we saw it on the television, all the looting and burning," recalls Ava. "I remember being real scared. I'd never seen anything like it in my life.... It was a long time before I wanted to come back."

I spent the days of Detroit's uprising lying prone on the floor of our home, below the windows that faced Broadstreet Avenue, hoping to avoid stray bullets. Instead of gunfire, however, there was eerie quiet on our block, interrupted only by National Guardsmen who rolled down our street in armored tanks, their megaphones ordering residents to "Stay inside. This is an order. Stay inside."

No numbers ran during that entire week, as looting, burning, and violence wore on for five days. A combined force of nearly seventeen thousand officers, National Guardsmen, and federal troops was sent in, and by the time the uprising was suppressed, as many as 155,000 rounds of ammunition had been fired by law enforcement; forty-three people were dead—thirty of them African-Americans, including a four-year-old girl named Tonya, victim to a .50-caliber bullet fired by the National Guard; more than seven thousand people were arrested on riot-related charges. During those few days, Detroit cops also tortured and brutally killed three black teenagers in what became known as the Algiers Motel incident. And the entire area around Twelfth Street was in ruins. The remnants of that damage remained for decades, much of it incredibly never rebuilt, even as the street was renamed Rosa Parks Boulevard.

During most of those five days, the city was all but shut down, with businesses, factories, and schools closed. Rumors flew that Russell Woods Park, just a couple of blocks from our home, would be set on fire, the entire area supposedly a target. My parents were nervous wrecks, and so with my visiting cousins tucked in for the night beside us, my father stayed awake each of those five nights, keeping watch from the front window, guarding the house from angry rioters who had nothing to lose. My family had Broadstreet to lose, and that was everything.

When it was all over, we were lucky. More than twenty-five hundred buildings had been looted and burned, but our beloved house remained intact. But I suddenly developed a paralyzing fear of the outside world, of losing Daddy to it, and began a habit of grabbing on to his leg every time he tried to leave the house. I was seven and had seen armored tanks roll down our street. I could sense a looming catastrophe coming to get us.

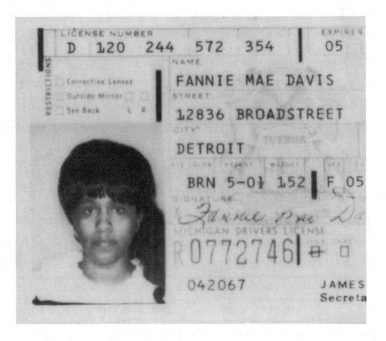

Four

Fannie and Burt on their wedding day, April 10, 1969

Mama celebrated her fortieth birthday with a "surprise" birthday party, which I doubt was really a surprise because my mother didn't like to be surprised, and everyone who knew her knew that about her. Still, I remember the excitement surrounding the whole evening. The party was a big one with lots of guests, hosted by Mama's best friend, Lula, at her home just a couple of blocks from Broadstreet. I can imagine how good it felt for Mama to be at that point in her life, with five children ranging in age from eight to twenty-one, and having come so far in the decade since she'd arrived in Detroit. That cold-water flat on Delaware was a distant memory, as Mama's thriving business was celebrating its tenth year. I'd never seen my mother so beautiful. I don't recall what she wore that day or how her hair was styled, just the light in her eyes and my own adoration. Mama often said that forty was the perfect age: not too young, not too old. That day, it showed.

My father was at the party, which is where my most treasured picture of him was taken. In that photo, my cousin Jewell and I are sitting on Daddy's lap. He wears a crisp white shirt unbuttoned at the neck, and looks lovingly at me; my head is down as I fiddle with a bow on my silvery new organza dress. It's one of the only pictures that remain of Daddy taken during my lifetime, and it's the last time he appears anywhere as my mother's husband. They've been married twenty-two years by then. I recall his nervous excitement about the party, as if he knows things could still go either way.

I now see what a precarious time it was for our family. Both my oldest sister, Deborah, and my brother, Anthony, had begun experimenting with "smack," i.e., heroin. Dianne was dating a man Daddy didn't approve of, which caused friction between her and our father, and my parents were living separately in the same house. Rita was still writing letters to God, asking him to keep her from worrying. One month before the party, Dr. King had been assassinated. As we all watched the funeral procession on TV, it was the first time I saw my mother cry—so rare an occurrence I only recall one other time. The day before, on April third, I'd made a giant card with too many candles to celebrate my father's birthday. Daddy kept saying, "He was three years younger than me. The man was three years younger than *me*." I thought King looked a lot like Daddy; and his wife, Coretta, reminded me of my mother—same complexion and hair and beauty and what I now recognize as quiet dignity. Because Coretta's sadness and tragedy leapt out from the TV screen, their resemblance scared me. Turns out, Coretta was just one year older than Mama. My parents, as contemporaries of the Kings, felt the loss intimately, as we do when our same-age friends die. And I felt the worrisome way you do when your friend's parent dies.

In response to King's death, Congress would finally pass the Fair Housing Act, which he and others had fought so very hard for—a triumph my mother understood firsthand, having been denied a mortgage for our home because of federal law. Barely a month after Mama's birthday party, Robert F. Kennedy was assassinated, and the toll of the dead, missing, and wounded in Vietnam reached over 100,000. By that summer, Olympic medalists Tommie Smith and John Carlos would each raise a black-gloved fist during "The Star-Spangled Banner" as a sign of black power. In Detroit, the black labor movement was gaining steam as four thousand racially integrated autoworkers staged a wildcat strike at Chrysler's Dodge plant over assembly-line speedups and other grievances; meanwhile, Motown Records was mired in legal battles with its premier songwriting team, Holland-Dozier-Holland, over unfair royalty contracts. Richard Nixon was elected president.

And it turns out, I hadn't been holding on to Daddy's leg for naught. That November, while I made my way through third grade, my father moved out. I'd slept atop his back or beside him every night, in the den where he stayed, for as long as I could remember, and I deeply felt his absence. Mama had just given me a fuzzy stuffed tiger she'd bought at Tiger Stadium, where she'd treated friends to see the Detroit Tigers play and actually win the World Series. I wasn't a child who cared for stuffed animals, but I clung to my soft gold-and-black-striped tiger every night, cradling it in lieu of Daddy. When I went to visit my father in his new flat, he sat me on his lap and explained the meaning of the word *divorce*, a word so scary that I cried into my Wonder Bread bologna sandwich. When I asked if I could live with him, he said quietly, "No. I can't take care of you the way your mama can."

Because my mother was in charge, because she made her own money, I suspect she could more easily make a tough decision that most women couldn't. The family Numbers operation had been built by Mama—*she* controlled it. Or, as Aunt Florence puts it to me: "It wasn't so much your daddy that was doing it. It was *her* that carried the load. She carried that load."

While visiting Daddy, the scary word still in my head, I sat at his table and wrote him a letter on notebook paper, in block letters colored with Crayola crayons. Atop the letter I wrote: *I love my Daddy.* Then I wrote:

Dear Daddy, I don't want to leave you. But I won't worry. Can I call you when I get home? Are you going to come over for Thanksgiving? If you can't come, I'll send you a plate of food. Good-by. Love always, Bridgit.

In December, Mama gave herself an early Christmas present: she took a much-anticipated trip to Miami Beach, Florida, for a winter holiday at the popular beachfront resort, the Fontainebleau.

When Mama went on vacation at the end of 1968, she had a lot to celebrate, and a lot to escape: Across a decade, she'd established and maintained her reputation as a woman who banked the Numbers, a rarity in a man's world. And she was newly separated. So what a big trip! Three girlfriends each without their men, all fortyish, traveled together to stay at the iconic, world-renowned, oceanfront hotel. My mother got the idea for herself and Lula and Mildred to stay at America's Riviera, its French name pronounced the Anglicized way, as the "Fountain Blue." She must've gotten more and more excited when she read the hotel's brochure, which gushed: *All our resources and efforts have been channeled to creating a resort designed to fulfill your every desire.... We have tried to anticipate your needs, and as proof of our sincerity, we will continue to improve and add features to enhance your stay and to stimulate your vacation.* Mama loved to travel, and not in long car trips down South to visit family like so many migrated blacks. She preferred to fly.

Who knows where Mama got the idea to vacation at the Fontainebleau? Maybe she'd dreamed of staying there ever since seeing Frank Sinatra welcome Elvis back home from the army, on the TV special broadcast from the hotel's famed La Ronde Supper Club just ten days before I was born. Maybe she'd read that Sammy Davis Jr. and the Will Mastin Trio had performed there in 1961. Perhaps she'd seen it featured in James Bond's 1964 classic *Goldfinger,* in a sweeping aerial shot that follows the opening credits. In fact, the month before Mama's visit, *Lady in Cement,* filmed at the hotel and starring Frank Sinatra and Raquel Welch, opened in movie theaters.

The Fountainebleau also had its notoriety. Rumors abounded of the hotel's ties to and possible ownership by the Mafia. That link was never proven, though, and in an April 1968 article the *Miami Herald* retracted its claim, stating in part that after an intensive investigation, "We are of the opinion that the Fontainebleau Hotel is not owned or controlled by any gangsters or underworld characters." As a result of that statement, the hotel's owner, Ben Novack, withdrew his defamation suit against the newspaper. Mama was certainly no stranger to the Mafia. While she never had direct contact with organized crime, I often heard her refer with disdain to "the Dagos"—the Italian Mafia—as the ones who actually controlled the Numbers in the black community.

My mother could afford the trip, and maybe that's the simple reason she decided to vacation in Miami. And if you were with Fannie, your own experience got elevated alongside hers. She liked sharing the good life. Both Mildred and Lula were thrilled to be joining their best friend for a holiday during the high season. That trip was the biggest one Mama had taken to date, and it has stood tall in family lore, giving my mother's life another layer of distinction: on a vacation. To a resort. For the wealthy. Where it's warm in winter.

A few photos from that trip remain, taken with my mother's brand-new Polaroid camera. My favorite was snapped in front of the hotel. My mother stands in the middle, flanked by her girlfriends: three black women, none of them entertainers nor entertainers' wives nor employees of the hotel. All of them heavyset and working-class. Wearing dark sunglasses. Looking good. Divas. When I look closely at the photograph, I see shimmering details: While Lula wears a practical, inexpensive top and skirt, and Mildred wears a simple shift, Mama wears a crisp cotton wrap dress in soft pink, with a ruffled collar. The dress's cinched waist flatters her figure, as does the flowing, loose skirt. Her sunglasses stand out, as the others wear oval ones in white and hot pink, respectively, chosen from a rack in a drugstore. Mama's are a soft shade of pink, rectangular, mother-of-pearl. They complement her face. She has on the faintest hint of lipstick, and stands more sexily than the other women, chest out, shoulders back. She's definitely wearing a better bra.

In another iconic photo, my mother and her girlfriend are still in their pajamas, having breakfast in their room. Knowing that the scene evoked the epitome of luxury and indulgence, they happily captured it for posterity. The room's décor is cream-colored French Provincial, one of my mother's favorite styles. The linen-clothed table has atop it a breakfast served on china, actual silverware, water in crystal wineglasses, flowers in a bud vase, and a basket of fresh bread at its center. Mama always loved room service, and maybe this trip was the genesis of that love affair. Mildred is dressed in functional man-style pajamas, but Mama is wearing one of her pretty signature robes, this one short and white, its cuffs and collar trimmed in satin. Beneath, she wears a turquoise nightgown. The diamond ring on her finger sparkles.

Later, dressed in a stylish black bathing suit, she lounged by the elevated outdoor pool at the Cabana Club, overlooking the Atlantic. Another vacationing woman came up to her and asked, "How in the world did you get such a beautiful tan?" My mother lifted her mother-of-pearl sunglasses to look at the white woman and said, "I was born with mine." Then she lowered her sunglasses.

This was classic Fannie. Of course my mother was acutely aware that she was in Florida, and that the South was still the South. But she also knew that being in that particular place was an equalizing force, and as such she could speak her mind.

She could declare her pride in being black by noting its built-in advantages. Besides, she welcomed the chance to make fun of the ironic quest by whites to darken their skins even as they shunned the actual Negroes whom they were desperately lying in the sun to resemble. Mama was the first person I ever heard say, "They want everything we got but the burden."

On a spring morning weeks before my ninth birthday, Mama summoned me to her room, where she was sitting up in bed, propped against big fluffy pillows. As I stood before her, she announced that she was getting married. She explained that I would have a stepfather, and I asked if he'd be mean like the stepmother in "Cinderella." She assured me he would not. I think she asked me if I was okay with this. I think I said yes.

I'd never met this man who was to become my stepfather until moments before he and Mama said "I do." I was too young to fully process what was happening, but I remember how I felt: deeply conflicted. I was a daddy's girl, and I wanted to remain loyal to my father. But I also wanted to please my mother. That very same evening, surrounded by her friends and family, Mama married this new man in a ceremony held in the living room of his modest home. She was nearly the same age as Jackie O, and he was fifty-three, the same age as Sinatra. To me, they couldn't have been more glamorous: She wore an off-white two-piece suit, its jacket collar in soft white mink, and a chic short wig that made her resemble Diahann Carroll in *Julia,* the popular TV show. On her delicate wrist Mama wore a thin-band, diamond-encrusted watch that I would later wear on my own wedding day. The new man wore a sharp, shimmery gray suit with a colorful tie and coordinated aqua shirt. No one would ever guess that he was color-blind. The date was April 10, 1969 (as it turns out, my future husband's second birthday), and the new man was Burtran A. Robinson. Burt, as he was known, later told me when I most needed to hear it that he'd waited a decade to marry my mother, the love of his life.

I don't doubt that. In one of my all-time favorite photographs, she sits beside Burt wearing a dark mink-collared jacket, and with it a white mink hat, her long black hair flowing beneath. She has on lightly frosted lipstick and a slight smile as she stares into the camera, her fingers around a champagne glass. Two bottles of bubbly are on the table. "Who goes on a date wearing a mink hat?" my sister Rita once quipped as we scrutinized the photo, by then adults ourselves. "Mama was so straitlaced! She looks like she's on her way to church." I thought she looked like a woman who knew happiness.

For the rest of his life with her, that photo stayed atop my stepfather's giant floor-model TV, prominently on display in his basement office. He outlived my mother, and after Burt became ill with Alzheimer's, Rita surprised me on my birthday with the photo, which she'd had to go through some effort to retrieve from his current wife. Only then did I bother to take the photo out of its frame and flip it over. There, written in Burt's handwriting: *Phelps Cocktail Lounge, April 1965.* Three years before Mama's divorce from Daddy, and four years before she and Burt married.

My father once saw that photograph during a visit to our new home, grabbed it, and slammed it facedown with fury. "Your mama and I were still married when they took that picture," he told me. Why didn't I take him seriously? Maybe because I was still so young? Maybe because I didn't want to do the math, believe its implications? Now I can't help but wonder if that math better explains why my mother slept a lot during my early childhood? Was she not only tired from running the Numbers, but depressed? Did she take a Valium before crawling into bed some nights? Because she was in love with one man but stuck in a dead-end marriage to another?

Mama should've felt she was starting over after her wedding, but she and Burt didn't live together as husband and wife for another six months. I don't know exactly why. She hadn't told her ex-husband, John T., that she'd remarried, and she apparently insisted that no one else tell him. I've turned this fact over myriad times across the distance of many years, and I still don't know exactly why she didn't tell Daddy. I wish I could ask her, but it never occurred to me to do so while she was alive. I doubt I would've had the courage to, anyway. The question itself suggests judgment, and who was I to judge? Last thing I ever wanted was to hurt Mama's feelings, in any way.

I do know that she was terrible at giving anyone bad news. Some people have a knack for it, a relish even. Not her. She hated it, actually seemed incapable of it; and so I can imagine that even though she didn't want to be married to Daddy anymore, even though he couldn't be the husband she needed, she didn't want to hurt him. But after more than two decades of marriage, she knew it would. And this was not the kind of news you pass off for someone else to tell. Sometimes my mother kept secrets not out of necessity but rather out of protectiveness, and I believe this was one of those times. She also didn't know how my father would react. Would he try to stop the wedding? Threaten to hurt himself? Make her feel wracked with guilt? Who could know? So she avoided telling him. Of course, that ended up hurting Daddy more when he eventually found out.

Looking back, I realize Mama had to first extricate herself and her younger children from Broadstreet, because there was no way in hell that she'd move her new husband into our beloved family home. She needed time to find a new place for us. As the weeks passed and we remained on Broadstreet, I saw Daddy every weekend; yet I didn't tell him that Mama had remarried. I later learned that Mama and my siblings were all terrified that I *would* tell him, because they knew my allegiance was to him. This is why my mother told me of her remarriage at the last possible moment, on the morning of her wedding. Funny thing, I don't remember Mama telling me *not* to tell Daddy. Did she suspect I would, and figured Daddy would then confront her about it, and she'd be forced to get the painful mess out of the way? I don't know. But I never did tell him. I could be relied upon not to reveal the biggest secret of all, our number-running lives. I understood secrets and I valued them all equally. But I didn't tell Daddy mostly because I was fiercely protective of him, and I knew he still loved Mama. Besides, for months after the wedding ceremony, I never saw my new stepfather anyway. Out of sight, out of mind.

With a big secret in my belly, I spent much of that summer at my cousin Jewell's house at endless sleepovers, riding my bike, hanging with the neighborhood kids, away from my family's holding pattern. Together, Jewell and I played jacks and hula-hooped and jumped rope and even watched men land on the moon. One day I noticed a lump on the back of my knee.

Aunt Florence thought it was a giant mosquito bite, and I recall her spraying antihistamine on it, to relieve the swelling. But the lump grew and grew until it was hard to bend my leg. A doctor's visit followed, and I was soon admitted to Henry Ford Hospital for surgery. My father later told me that the surgeon wouldn't know until he "went in" whether the cyst was malignant or not, and that he and Mama had given the hospital permission to amputate my leg if need be. "Those were the longest damn hours of my life," he said. "I aged something mighty that day."

When I woke up, my left leg was bandaged but still there. The cyst had been benign, and doctors had easily removed it. Lucky me, again. I recall Daddy sitting with me in the hospital room, and I recall Mama sitting with me too; was Burt beside her? I don't recall, just that my parents were both there, but never at the same time. I remember taking note of that fact, finding it odd. Maybe it made me sad.

That was also the summer Mama purchased a gun, a Smith & Wesson .38 special revolver. I only know this because I recently found the receipt. She bought it on July 3, 1969, and it cost $71.50 plus some kind of tax called OTGS for $4.85. I don't know why she bought a gun that particular day but I do know she wasn't afraid to use it. Maybe this was the one she kept in her purse, as the other pistol would soon be kept in the new home's linen closet, underneath the eyelet-trimmed sheets, lace tablecloth, and linen napkins. This fact gave me a bit of comfort, made me feel she'd be safer out there in the streets, and that we'd be safer at home. "Let somebody break into my house," Mama used to say. "I'll blow their ass away, then call the police and tell them to come clean my damn carpet." I loved hearing her say that, loved believing she was that fearless, and that clear about her rights.

Our family's second secret, which was in place for six months, affected Rita the most, as a young teen all too aware that her mother had remarried, her father couldn't know, and the secret had to be maintained until we moved. Rita desperately wanted us to start our new, less stealthily lived lives. In one letter she stuffed into the family Bible dated September 26, 1969, my thirteen-year-old sister wrote:

> *Dear God, I know you are saying that I am changing. I curse and smoke. But I have stopped because I know it isn't right. Bless all my friends and enemies and forgive me for my wrong. Please let us hurry up and move in the new house.*
>
> *Thank you, Rita*

As the moving date loomed, I wasn't like Rita, aware of what I'd be leaving behind and going toward. I didn't know enough to worry about leaving my bedroom's beloved window seat, my basement playroom, my hiding spot in the attic, and the unfinished tree house Daddy was building for me in the backyard.

Weeks after the school year began, we finally did move, to a house farther west in the city with the improbable address 3456 West Seven Mile Road. It was one mile from the road that divided Detroit from its neighboring suburb, Southfield, the street made famous by the film about rapper Eminen's life, *8 Mile*. The house sat on the edge of Sherwood Forest, a privately patrolled district known for its architecturally distinct houses and quiet, winding streets. A few blocks away stood a Frank Lloyd Wright–designed house in the city's tony Palmer Woods section. On moving day, Mama sat cross-legged on the gold-colored carpet of our new, spacious living room, unpacking yellow china, looked over at me, and said: "We're gonna be happy now." I wanted nothing more than for my mother to be happy. I knew enough to know that she hadn't been. As for the rest of us, we all knew that a life in which one parent lived upstairs and one lived downstairs, barely speaking, wasn't normal. I hadn't been unhappy on Broadstreet, but I understood why things needed to change.

Only Rita and I moved to the new house with Mama and my new stepfather, Burt. Each of my older siblings chose a new path for himself or herself, marking the moment when we ceased forever to all live together as a family, under the same roof. Twenty-two-year-old Deborah, who'd recently seen Jimi Hendrix perform at Cobo Hall and was fully absorbed in the psychedelic, free-love moment, went to live with her boyfriend (Mama called it "shacking up"); twenty-year-old Dianne, newly married, moved into my stepfather's former home. And seventeen-year-old Anthony stayed on Broadstreet, where Daddy moved back in to live with him. Daddy later told me about their winter together that year, how the heat was turned off, and how cold the house was, how they stayed warm by burning a fire in the fireplace. It touched my father's heart that his son didn't abandon him. "He coulda gone on over to the new house with y'all," said Daddy. "But he chose to tough it out with me."

Why didn't Mama, who was living well in a new house with a new husband, give her son and ex-husband money to pay the heating bill? This from the same woman who used to joke that she was the only ex-wife she knew ordered by a judge to pay her husband alimony. I don't know if that decree really came down, only that in the years that followed, Daddy knew he could turn to Fannie repeatedly for help. And over the years, he did.

"Honey, she was good to John T.," says Aunt Florence, setting the record straight. "John T. himself would tell you if he could; Fannie was nice to him, all through his life, she was nice to him."

I think it was pride that forced my father and brother to suffer through that cold winter. My father was so upset that we'd moved out and on, away from him, and that hurt didn't allow him to ask for help. And my brother? He was a loyal son. And Mama? Maybe she didn't know. Maybe she was distracted by her new life.

Luckily, my stepfather, Burt, a handsome, jocular, gray-eyed man, was good to me from the start; he affectionately called me Chicken, taught me how to bowl, chauffeured me around to my childhood activities. And he never tried to usurp my father, which made living with Burt stress-free. He reminded me of the affable, kind Uncle Bill on the popular sixties sitcom *Family Affair*. Having been a crane operator for Ford Motor Company, Burt was working in the decidedly unglamorous job of garbage collector by the time he entered our lives. Soon after, he retired. I recall no sense of frustrated ambition in Burt, although he did like to read get-rich-quick books. He happily helped out Mama with her business, mainly as a pickup man. Financially, he brought not only his regular paycheck and then his pension to the marriage, but also health insurance. No question, though, that marrying my mother raised his standard of living.

Our new house was vastly different from the old, a stylish gray brick modern two-family built in 1956, thirty years after Broadstreet, a classic Colonial built in 1926. The house we quickly dubbed Seven Mile appeared roomy, with its wide open living/dining area, its den with wraparound built-ins, and a picture window that nearly covered an entire front wall; but it was a two-story duplex with a replica apartment above, for renting out, and it was actually much smaller than Broadstreet. In this new house, with its two-bedroom, ranch-style layout, we'd all live as a family on one level. It was a challenging place for Mama to run her business. She had to do so either in the kitchen, which was itself small and the first place people entered from the side door, or in her bedroom, which was a short distance down the hall. Voices carried. On Broadstreet, we'd had three different floors, which meant what took place upstairs couldn't be heard downstairs. On Seven Mile, the sound of ringing phones was ubiquitous. I worried that my friends could easily detect that something was going on, and so began an anxious ritual of closing doors and drawers, hiding Numbers paraphernalia, quickly answering the phone to hush its mouth. For me, keeping our secret was tough on Seven Mile, especially when I learned that the police department's Twelfth Precinct station was less than a mile from our home.

Meanwhile, I was the new girl in fourth grade at Hampton Elementary. For my first day, Burt had presented me with a set of multicolored pencils that he'd special-ordered, each with my name printed on it. On that day, the table captain in science class, a girl named Diane, sharpened all my pencils so short that my name disappeared on every one. Diane and I went on to become best friends—still are—but that moment of seeing my name gone stays with me, as I didn't know who I was in this new place, with a new configuration of parents, so far away from Broadstreet, yet with the same family secret. That fall is forever captured for me by the Jackson 5's "I Want You Back." I played the 45 of the hit single on my portable Tele-Tone record player over and over. I wanted my old life, where men didn't bowl, and we didn't eat strange new food like chocolate Cream of Wheat on yellow china dishes, and I didn't sleep in a new twin bed beside my sister's twin bed, instead of beside my father. *Spare me of this cause,* sang Michael. *Give me back what I lost.*

Shortly after we moved, Daddy came to visit us. Mama wasn't home. He discovered she'd remarried only when he spotted Burt's clothes in the bedroom closet. I will never forget the shocked and hurt look on his face. "Somebody could've told me," he said. "Somebody could've at least done that."

After he left, my sisters tried to comfort me as I bawled, surrounding me as I sat in my and Rita's new bedroom, crying nonstop, inconsolable. I knew in my heart that I was the one who should've told him. "What if he tries to hurt himself?" I asked.

"He won't," said Dianne, the sister who mothered me most. "He loves you too much. He won't."

But I was rattled, wasn't sure where my loyalties should lie. Yes, Mama helped me pack my bags every weekend to spend with Daddy, but did she feel I betrayed her? And was I betraying Daddy by living with her?

Mama calmed my fears the next day when she gathered all

five children, aged nine to twenty-two, and sat us down in the big new living room. She stood before us and announced: "I am not related to John T., so I don't have to love and respect him forever. But he's your father, and you do." She paused. "Don't let me catch you forgetting that."

Then she turned and walked away, leaving my siblings and me sitting on the sofa in silence.

Bridgett and Daddy, May 1968

PART II

Hey, You Never Know

Fannie taking numbers, 1980s

Five

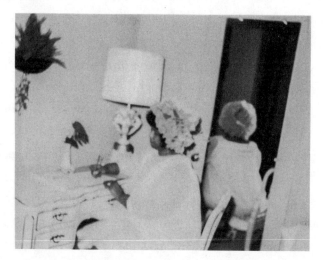

Fountainebleau Hotel Room, December 1968

The permeating smell of sage, frankincense, or sandalwood often wafted through our home, emanating from Mama's bedroom. There burned special incense molded into small charcoal-briquette cones, which she'd placed in a brass burner shaped like Aladdin's lamp. Mama would then brush away the ash to find, magically revealed at the bottom of the burner, a "lucky" three-digit number. Candles also burned seductively in our bathrooms. They were tall, thick and encased in glass, the kind found in *botánicas*, flames' shadows dancing across ceilings. Mama burned these long-lasting candles, always green, the color of money, for two days straight; when they'd finally burned down, a number to play awaited her at the bottom of the glass.

I liked both the incense and the candles, liked the act of conjuring up good via ritual. Also, I found comfort in the idea that our mystical household provided an extra layer of protection from the forces outside our door. The fact that Mama was the one performing the rituals added to her allure. To me, *she* was magic.

Of course, Mama also had more straightforward means of finding a number to "back," or play. She could, for example, buy a "tip sheet" sold at the city's party stores and novelty shops. These one-page printed circulars listed various three-digits posing as zodiac-sign or monthly or birthday "specials"; or as "long-overdue" or "gold pot" numbers—numbers anyone could ascribe personal meaning to, the way you might find meaning in your weekly horoscope in the Sunday paper. The outside world provided myriad numbers too. Every city, Detroit included, is a city of numbers. Mama could find a three-digit in a home address, as she'd done when she played ours and hit, buying our family home with the proceeds. But she also got numbers from the street addresses of businesses she patronized, dry cleaner's or shoe shop tickets, utility bills, traffic tickets, telephone numbers, and cars' license plates. Whenever we went to a Chinese restaurant, my mother read her fortune cookie not for the pithy advice, but for the so-called lucky numbers that always appeared on those little rectangles of paper. Travel itself brought several possible numbers for her to play: flight numbers, hotel room numbers, taxicab numbers, restaurant check amounts... Inspiration was everywhere.

Better yet were personal numbers, i.e., special numbers like family members' birthdays, anniversaries, death dates, birth times, and birth weights, all providing potential winning combinations. Added to that were people's pet numbers; Mama played her own personal pet number, 788, essentially every day. (She believed, along with most players, that the moment you "jump off a number," it comes out.) Other people's pet numbers were also possibilities. Mama might play a friend's pet number on her birthday, or if she ran into that person, or if she simply thought about him "out of the blue." And she often honored a deceased loved one's memory by playing that person's pet number on his or her birthday. Whatever numbers Mama herself played, she of course played with other bankers, otherwise she'd be betting against herself.

Aunt Florence too has had a few pet numbers over the years. "Two-eight-one helped put Jewell through college," she says about my cousin. "And three-three-nine? My kitchen was remodeled off of three-three-nine. Plus, that same number helped me buy two new cars."

Some numbers got played heavily once they appeared in the news or were associated with national events, such as the flight number of a crashed plane, or a famous historical date like November 22, 1963 (112) or December 7, 1941 (127). (A more recent example is September 11, i.e., 911, which is now popular with lottery players.) People also got numbers from films, the best-known being agent James Bond's 007; songs like the Marvelettes' sixties Motown hit, "Beechwood 4-5789," with its two sets of three digits (457 and 789), were another source; and from sports, all kinds of numbers abounded, such as the final score of a championship basketball game. Back in the 1930s, Detroiters regularly played boxer Joe Louis's weight. Mama would sometimes join the fray and play one of these pop-culture numbers, but rarely.

Triple-digit numbers like 222 and 888 were equally attractive options, especially two in particular from the Bible: 666 ("the mark of the beast" in Revelation) and 333 (in Ezekiel 33:3, the prophet blows his trumpet to warn people of coming tribulation). Speaking of the Bible, another well-played number was 318 (in Genesis, Abraham took 318 men to attack those who had captured Lot, apparently the only other three-digit that appears in the Bible). Any numbers like these deemed perennially popular were called "fancies." Some fancies had long histories, like 411 (my birth weight), first cited in an 1890 book as "the negro's lucky numbers." Players often knew by heart which numbers were fancies, and Aunt Florence can still rattle off several to me, including 110, 100, 310, and 313 (Detroit's area code). Another is 697, known as "the death row." Some bookies refused to accept a fancy because if it came out, too many customers would hit on it, creating massive payouts.

"If they pull a fancy, and you ain't big, it'll knock you out," Aunt Florence explains. "I remember once they pulled several fancies for a solid week, and them bookies, if they didn't have the money, they had to go."

Still other numbers were favored if they were perceived to be good "follow-ups," or numbers likely to fall soon after certain other numbers. Jewell told me that whenever the number for her mother's name, Florence, came out, within a day or two the number for her favorite aunt's name, Fannie, came out behind it—a guaranteed follow-up.

Mama's best way to "conjure up a number," as she called it, was via hunches. Her hunches were everything. The candles and incense and tip sheets were a means of reinforcing what numbers she already had "a good feeling about"; ditto for numbers out in the world—seeing a certain combination reinforced a hunch, provided a sign that yes, she should play *that* particular number on that particular day. It was important to respect your hunches, not ignore them or get distracted and fail to act upon these gifts of intuition. Mama's hunches were linked to, proof positive of, her good luck. People who are lucky have strong hunches, and win.

Mama had myriad ways of cultivating and enhancing her luck. Candles and incense, for instance, didn't always provide specific lucky numbers; rather, she burned them to generally attract luck. And I also sometimes found, tossed into one of our cluttered bathroom drawers, a bottle of "lucky oil" or "Chinese wash." Horseshoes were prominently nailed to our entryways; Mama collected miniature elephant figurines; and she carried a rabbit's foot on her keychain—all magnets for good fortune.

The word *luck* apparently originated as a gambling term, according to scholar Felicia George, whose 2015 dissertation is on the world of Detroit's Numbers. "Luck can be described as a power that brings good fortune or favor," she writes, quoting others and further defining luck as "the force at the core of the cosmos that governs chance events, that can be sometimes conjured but never coerced...that operates to overcome the uncertainty of the gambling situation."

Growing up, attracting good luck was never far from my mind. As a girl, I'd crawl through the itchy grass on my hands and knees in Aunt Florence's backyard, Jewell beside me, sun on our backs as we searched for four-leaf clovers to present to our mothers (it's a nice coincidence that Jewell and her family lived on a street named Cloverlawn). I wanted to be the one who found a lucky clover in that lawn of dandelions and crabgrass, but it was usually Jewell who found one, sometimes two. I couldn't stand that she was better at attracting a symbol of luck than me. I wanted to be seen as lucky by Mama, as I'd once been seen by Daddy, who'd sometimes take me to poker games, set me on his lap, and announce that "my baby right here is my good-luck charm." One day, I tore a three-leaf clover's petal in half and presented that to Mama. She made it clear she knew exactly what I'd done. "You can't fake being lucky," she said.

While Mama understood you couldn't coerce good luck, she did believe in rituals to thwart bad luck, which is why at the end of the business day she put customers' business in the freezer to "cool it off" or under her bed or in my closet to "hide" it from the day's winning numbers. Equally important to my mother was making sure people she perceived as unlucky kept their distance. She was suspicious of folks for whom *nothing* ever swung their way. Likewise, being around someone who was "always crying the blues" created unhealthy vibes and could make you miss a number, so had to be guarded against. "Too much hard luck rubs off," she'd say. (As an aside, Mama wasn't too particular about blues *music* either. The only blues song I ever heard her enjoy was a favorite by Dinah Washington, "This Bitter Earth," a sorrowful song that ends upliftingly with the line *I'm sure someone may answer my call and this bitter earth, ooh, may not be so bitter after all.*)

Cultivating good luck and avoiding bad was vital to Mama because luck was what sustained her livelihood. Just as comedy is serious business, Numbers playing is no game. She understood on a rational level that when she was a player, her odds of winning were long ("hard as it is to hit these damn numbers," she'd often say), and the numbers that fell were technically random. Still, logic didn't entirely rule, thus her efforts to enhance her odds by strengthening her luck—both in hitting a number herself and in *not* getting hit by customers. As someone who left little else in her life to "fate," Mama saw no contradiction in refusing to leave this game of chance to chance. She felt she must do *something* to mitigate the randomness of it all.

Even as she used luck enhancers, Mama didn't lean on any given ritual or charm to guarantee our security. My mother was too much of a pragmatist to believe wholeheartedly in magic. She took pride in being a Taurus, the sign of the zodiac known for a steadfast, earthbound feet-planted-on-the-ground approach to life. Common sense ruled. Likewise, she didn't give any credence to those who believed in hoodoo, voodoo, or black magic; she found those practices backward, the opposite of modernity. Just as she didn't believe putting a knife under your bed would "cut the pain" of an illness or that certain herbs could heal you ("Folks need to take their asses to a real doctor!"), neither did she believe someone could "work roots" on you to bring misfortune to your life. Only you controlled your own fate by your own actions because, as she saw it, God gave us free will. Luck to her was an offshoot of her disciplined and dynamic faith in herself, buttressed by her belief that if you do good, you attract good. Her rituals were backup efforts.

I find Mama represents a perfect blend of what Felicia George, the Numbers scholar, observes is the friction between two very different narratives that America tells about itself: The first is that this country was founded by "speculative men" who took chances to establish America, i.e., luck matters and "net worth" has nothing to do with "moral worth." In the second narrative, American heroes are self-made men and women who become successful through hard work and discipline, where "earthly rewards match ethical merits," leaving no place for luck. My mother was both speculative and self-made, combining her work ethic with her chance-taking; she embodied *both* values of a quintessential American.

Interestingly, I never heard my mother claim that winning numbers "come from God" (despite the fact that my sister used to write letters to Him, asking that certain numbers *not* come out). I think this is largely because my mother identified as a Christian, occasionally attending Unity Baptist Church, led by Reverend Stotts, a devout and truly devoted pastor whom she greatly admired. She respected the black church tradition—was in fact well versed in the Bible—and didn't like the implication that God was in the business of helping folks win numbers; Mama also disapproved of people who prayed for certain numbers to come out, or "fall," as they say, because she saw it as a reduction of God's role in our lives. Just as she pushed against the Christian tenets that suffering was holy, and that you must "stay on your knees praying to God" in hopes that he would answer your pleas, she felt you were a partner in your own good fortune.

"You take one step, God will take two," Mama loved to say.

Likewise, my mother didn't use church services as an opportunity to find numbers to play, as so many people she knew did. Many congregants would use a minister's selected

Bible verse to help them pick a "good three-digit," so that, for instance, Romans 12:2 would be 122 and Matthew 6:33 would be 633. Ditto for the chosen hymn numbers. A 1972 *Detroit Free Press* article quoted a Detroit Baptist minister who once famously said from the pulpit, "I know some of you are taking the numbers of our hymns and betting on them. I'm not saying whether I approve or not, but if you play them...be sure to box 'em." Certain preachers actually built their church followings on the claim that they had the ability to prophesy, and would give out numbers that had supposedly come to them in their dreams.

Given her belief that the poor and meek would *not* inherit the earth, my mother also enjoyed attending another very different Unity church, where followers practiced a "metaphysical Christianity" led by a legendary minister named Eric Butterworth. Butterworth, a leader of New Age thought and author of sixteen books, taught the Law of Attraction long before Deepak Chopra and Rhonda Byrne's *The Secret*. Some have called him "the twentieth-century Emerson." Butterworth was for many years minister of Unity's Detroit Temple, which he grew into Unity's largest church, attracting two thousand people every Sunday to the massive white-stoned structure located close to our future home beside Palmer Park; as minister, he led "worth-ship" services, espousing the belief that you attract good in your own life by being thankful in advance, by giving generously, and by believing that "Prosperity is one of God's greatest gifts to us." This idea of universal law aligned beautifully with Mama's beliefs, and soon enough with my own; long after Butterworth had moved to New York to lecture weekly at Carnegie Hall and other ministers took his place in the city, I liked attending Unity Temple services with my mother; there we'd stand, joining other congregants, holding hands and singing "Divine love flowing through me blesses and increases all that I give and all that I receive" as the collection plates passed along the pews. Mama always threw in a twenty- or fifty-dollar bill.

I see now that my mother lived a spiritual contradiction. With a livelihood based on gambling, she could easily slide into worry, into a negative mind-set: "I hope that damn number does *not* come out today." And when she got that way, she was hard to be around. Worry is contagious, and I tried to quarantine myself against it in my room. But Mama really wanted to be a proponent of *positive* thinking. She tried to mitigate that habit of anticipating bad outcomes by becoming a better student of Butterworth's teachings. I often accompanied her to Unity Temple's adjoining bookstore, a cornucopia of New Age thought books, where Mama and I would browse the shelves after the one-hour service; there she'd buy bookmarks and stickers with aphorisms printed on them, such as: "No one can keep your good from you but you" and "We must live from the inside out." She'd always be sure to buy the latest Butterworth book, and one of my treasured inheritances is her collection of first-edition hardcovers by Eric Butterworth, with titles like *Life Is for Living* and *Discover the Power Within You* and the provocative *How to Break the Ten Commandments*.

Just as she admired ministers like Butterworth and Reverend Stotts, Mama had special derision for con men, so-called men of the cloth who duped their poor and working-class followers out of hard-earned money by claiming to be prophets. Chief among them was Prophet Jones. A migrant from Alabama to Detroit in the 1930s, James F. Jones was one of the earliest "prosperity pastors," who went on to head two churches, both with unwieldy yet lofty names: Triumph, the Church and Kingdom, and later Dominion Ruler of the Church of the Universal Triumph. He was known for his gold tooth, two hundred suits, $12,000 mink coat, pastor's robe worth $20,000, outlandish jewelry, and two mansions that he called castles. His entire fortune was acquired from congregants' monetary gifts and donations given to him in exchange for advice and blessings. And despite preaching "morality," he sold so-called lucky numbers for his followers to play. Whenever my mother spoke of this shyster, who was at his height by the time she migrated to Detroit, she seemed angered anew. I could never decide what she hated more, the hypocrisy, how Prophet Jones exploited and took advantage of weak-minded, poor people, or the people who foolishly let him do it.

"One thing I can't stand, it's a follower," she'd say, shaking her head for effect, baffled that people felt they needed an intermediary in their relationship with a higher being: "Why would I need somebody else to talk to God on my behalf?" she'd say. "I can get my own blessings."

Mama was so passionate about the subject she'd sometimes go on a tear, often for an audience of visitors, or during a debate with her best friend, Lula. "I'm not worshipping no man!" she'd say, voice raised. "What's the point of having your own mind? Folks wanna believe in something so bad, they should believe in the common sense God gave 'em."

She did believe that some rare individuals were authentically psychic, especially those "born with the veil," meaning that a part of the birth sac covered their faces at delivery. These people, she said, had visions, and could "see into things," witness the future. If she called someone "gifted," that meant she respected her spiritual powers. She held these women, always women, in high regard; I remember accompanying her more than once to see a psychic, who'd do a reading for Mama and share what "came up" for her. She gave this woman money for her reading, but I don't ever remember Mama asking her for a number to play.

At the same time, she had no patience for those who claimed gambling was an evil force or "against God." Her position was: "Folks need to focus on not breaking the ten commandments that do exist, instead of trying to add an eleventh." This is where she had nothing in common with the men and women who belonged to rigid Sanctified churches, with their strict codes of morality. (More than a few of Mama's customers were "saved" or Sanctified women, who secretly played numbers with her regularly.) Nor did she have much respect for the men and women pastors of those churches. "A lot of those preachers would get up in the pulpit and talk about the Numbers being bad," says Aunt Florence, "but they ain't turn down that money in the plate."

Even still, Mama genuinely believed that ministers or pastors or psychics or anyone who had a true "calling" should not traffic in giving out Numbers; it felt to her untoward, the worst kind of racket, combining religious leadership or spiritual gifts with Numbers profiting. To her, the secular and the sacred shouldn't be in business together.

Aunt Florence agreed with her sister on this: "I don't believe in these little churches you go to, and they up there preaching and then they tell you what number to play," she insists. "God don't work like that."

In Mama's mind, closely aligned with charlatans like Prophet Jones were Spiritualist leaders who ran their own storefront churches. These women, again always women, provided religious teaching and a space for "getting happy," what scholars call "ecstatic worship." In addition to the shouting and clapping and "getting the Holy Ghost," congregants could have their bad luck cured, and also receive numbers to play—services Spiritualist ministers provided in exchange for donations to the church. Some women weren't ministers, rather worked solely as "mediums" within a Spiritualist church or by doing individual readings, again for a fee. These mediums were believed to have the power to either predict a number outright, or divine it by feeling a believer's "vibrations," which "gave off" what number he or she should play. During a church service, congregants who wanted to receive numbers would stand and march single file past the medium, who'd be standing near the altar. She'd dip her hands in holy water, sprinkle the believer, and whisper a number in her ear. In another variation, the medium would lie in a coffin, and as people filed by, she'd give each one a number from "the deceased."

Aunt Florence was less hard-core than Fannie when it came to these women. "Some of them could tell you a number to play," she says. "And some of them could tell you lies too."

By far, the most potent hunch Mama could get was via a good dream. Nothing in her myriad ways to find a winning combination carried more weight than "dreaming up" a number to play. And this was pretty much true for all Numbers players. Nothing was more clear, no sign greater, no hunch more valuable, than what your own subconscious provided while you slept.

Night dreams have always carried deep meaning and power in African-American culture, what Anthony Shafton in *Dream-Singers* calls "a lively tradition." People believe it's a spiritual carryover from Africa that powerfully shapes our way with dreams, that our ancestors and deceased loved ones visit us this way, via prophecy and warning, as a way to help with the real world. For some, this connects to the deep religious aspect of dreams and they believe that going into a dreamlike state, what we call a waking dream, is a form of religious practice, while nightmares are a form of bad spirits; and not being able to wake up from a dream is "witches riding you." No wonder some feel it's the spirit world or God or a deceased loved one who communicates with us through our dreams, blessing us with a certain number to play.

Our household was awash in the language of and belief in dreamed-up numbers. Often, Mama would share her dreams, or speak of one that got away from her because the phone rang, or something else woke her up just as she "was getting to the good part" of a dream.

Often, a typical morning conversation began with Mama asking me, or a sibling, "Dream anything good last night?"

She believed that someone else's dream could be as lucky for her as if she'd "dreamt it" herself. And nothing carried more weight than a child's dream; it's a widely held belief in black culture that children are naturally gifted with the power to divine or predict things, particularly in their dreams.

"Children have no bias or hang-ups and will tell you things that they see or feel," explains my cousin Jewell. "We adults need to have evidence of everything, but kids honestly are in tune with their spiritual selves."

I must have intuited this belief, because I desperately wanted to have good dreams. There was no higher compliment in my childhood world than to be deemed gifted in just this way, to be that girl who dreamed of images and situations and people that translated to the next day's winning numbers. I knew how much Mama valued a good dreamer. Funny thing, I remember sharing dreams with Mama, but not the follow-up of finding out whether or not she actually hit on what I shared.

When Mama spoke of a good dream, she meant one with a definite character, clear symbols and images that could easily be "looked up" in one of the most important books in our home, the encyclopedia-style Bible of every Numbers runner and every Numbers player: the dream book. These books interpreted dreams by assigning three-digit numbers to different symbols, nearly any random image or experience that could appear in a dream, from "ladies' names" to love songs to lizards to laughing out loud.

The first dream book appeared as early as 1862, back when lotteries were legal and whites dominated the playing. After lotteries became illegal and morphed into policy and then into the Numbers, African-Americans were the primary buyers. Apparently more than three dozen dream books have been published from the mid-1920s through the 1970s, but in our home, two dominated: *The Red Devil Combination DreamBook Almanac* and *The Original Lucky Three Wise Men Dream Book*. These were bestsellers, and Mama could easily buy either for a dollar at a neighborhood party store. New editions came out every year, and copies of both dream books, often dog-eared and worn, could be found within Mama's nightstand drawer, as well as the den and kitchen drawers. It wasn't unusual for a customer to pause and ask Mama what something played for while putting in their numbers with her for the day. I have a vivid memory of Mama looking up something in a dream book, her index finger traveling down a row of words, in later years with reading glasses perched on her nose.

The competing dream books didn't agree on specific three-digit numbers for the people, places, objects, animals, events, and experiences listed. Where *Wise Men* listed *fish* as playing for 377 and 637, *Red Devil* listed *fish* as playing for 134 and 436. That made the books no less credible or popular. My favorite of the two dream books was the *Three Wise Men;* I was drawn to the cover, with its woodcut image of three men, one in shadow, all on camels, all waving, a five-point star above them. I found the cover of *Devil* slightly frightening, with its bright red-and-white backdrop against the image of a leaping, mischievous-looking bloodred Satanic figure. Back then I wasn't interested in looking up dreams, but I *was* attracted to the supernatural, which is why I read and reread *Three Wise Men's* introduction. It was wonderfully written by a "Prof. Zonite," a so-called sage who turned out to be a Detroiter named Mallory F. Banks; I liked his mystical language: "Dreams are illusions produced by an involuntary activity of the mind during sleep," he wrote. "In primitive societies it was, and still is, believed that dreams are inspired by the gods— that in sleep the soul of a dreamer visits his friends, and that the souls of the dead come to visit him." Meanwhile, *The Red Devil's* text had a more scholarly bent, less engaging to my young taste: "We might infer relationships between our dreams and secondary elements, such as numbers," it stated in pseudo-seriousness. "The following list combines dream images along with their numeric counterparts...."

Within the pages of these annually updated dream books, you could not only read mystical text and look up specific objects or situations listed in alphabetical order, you could also find astrology guides, yearly forecasts, moon phases, hunches, and holidays—all with assigned numbers to play. You could also find a list of popular fancies, and "daily vibrations" for each day of the week. The essentials of the original text didn't change across the decades with subsequent reprints; nor did the covers of these cheaply made paperbacks deviate from their original images, apart from listing a new date. And despite the fact that policy hasn't been around for decades, the books continued to list not only three digits, but a sequence of three two-digit numbers based on old-fashioned daily drawings from policy wheels. Reading a dream book's list of imagery and symbols is like peering into a window onto *that* time in America, to see what haunted black folks' sleeping *and* waking lives: You could look up three-digits for *lynching* and *negress*, *prejudice* and *white woman*. No surprise that dream books "mirrored a sobering reality," as *Playing the Numbers* put it. And further capturing a time capsule, you could also look up what played for *ice box, looking glass, vaudeville, coal man,* and *odd fellows.* Under automobiles, you'd find among others the DeSoto, the Hupmobile, and the Studebaker.

Dream books weren't only used for interpreting dreams. Like any worthy guidebook, they were there to look up whatever a person might experience while awake. *Wise Men* had a page devoted to *Things You See and Hear*, everything from *getting fired from your job* to *seeing a black cat crossing street* to *see suicide*; another category was called *If You Get*, and under that heading you could find listed, among other things, *a new lover*, *pregnant*, *a telegram*, and *arrested*. Mama and others often would look up loved ones' names to see what numbers they played for.

"Jewell's name plays for one-six-one," Aunt Florence tells me. "And that number was good to me too. I furnished my house on that number."

Charlatan preachers also used dream books. One dream book publisher was quoted in *Dream-Singers* as noting that he "had a run on *Aero* books back in '72 or '73 because there was a minister in Detroit who would have private readings for like twenty-five dollars." Congregants would go into a chapel, only to find a coffin. Its lid would open and the minister would sit up, look at the person, "read" him or her based on his "visions," then use the *Genuine Aero Dream Book* to give that person a number to play. Likewise, the Spiritualist women preachers and mediums would relay messages they received from the Holy Spirit in codes, such as a message recorded verbatim from St. Ruth's Spiritualist Church in Detroit by scholar Gustav Carlson: "When I come in touch with you, all right, a beautiful *cloud* is over you. The spirit brings *cotton* to you. Watch yourself very carefully and you will succeed, said the spirit. A *bridge* is standing before you and you will be successful in crossing this condition." The parishioner would then go to her favorite dream book and look up *cloud*, *cotton*, and *bridge* and play those numbers.

Some people believed in a "scientific" system for figuring

out a winning number. Often, this fell into three categories: those who kept track of which numbers fell on which days across a given year, in order to ascertain a pattern; those who did workouts, or "rundowns," which were specific formulas for figuring out a number; and those who combined the two. Some who claimed to have surefire methods for picking winning numbers advertised their services on the front and back inside covers of the dream books. And folks could buy separate "workout" books devoted solely to various methods.

Aunt Florence explains her own preferred rundown method thus: Take the day's date, for example 6/03, which is 603, add to that the previous day's winning number, say 568. Add those figures together, but don't carry the 1, so that the total of 603 plus 568 would be 161—today's number to play. Or you could continue the rundown another way, by taking the day's date, 603, and adding a 2 to each digit (again without carrying the 1), and adding that over and over, until you see a number that "feels right." It looks like this:

603
825
047
269
481

Or you could add a 3 to each number, and get this rundown:

603
936
269

592

825

Even though Numbers was seemingly a game of chance, with no amount of prediction or skill mitigating its high odds, it's easy to understand how players tried to remove the guess-work from picking a number. After all, many decisions went into each day's play: What combination of three digits to play? Play those numbers straight or box them (so that you'd win any combination that came out)? Which "race" to play, either Detroit or Pontiac or both? Which dream book to use? How much to put on any given number as opposed to another? How long to stay on a number before jumping off and playing a different number? Multiply that by the more than 300 days (minus Sundays and holidays) that a given three-digit number could "fall" or come out in a given year, and it makes sense that folks wanted to take the randomness out of it. Hence the dreams and hunches and prophets and magical aids and run-downs, all designed to thwart those 1,000-to-1 odds.

This explains the close relationship between spirituality and the Numbers. My cousin Jewell firmly believes a hunch on a number is "Spirit talking to you." Similarly, the Numbers are seen by many, particularly self-proclaimed mystics, as directly connected to numerology. Numerology is said to be based not on chance but rather on the belief that numbers are clues to the real, underlying structure of the universe, and that the number of a thing contains the essence of its being. Prof. Zonite, in *Three Wise Men*, devoted an entire page to numerology, describing it as an age-old science in "the study of the law of vibrations." He noted that "One has but to consider his daily life for a moment to realize that either consciously or unconsciously he is ruled by numbers." His dream book also offered "popular numerology vibrations," which included two lists of numbers: the sixteen best boxed and the sixteen best straight.

I was fascinated by this so-called science, and would often sneak and read (it felt like I *should* sneak) my sister Deborah's paperback copy of the 1960s *Complete Illustrated Book of the Psychic Sciences*, purchased by her for $1.25, and which I still have on my shelf. In addition to everything from astrology to domino divination to moleosophy (the study of moles and their meaning) to palmistry, the book includes an expansive section on numerology. Given that every letter of the alphabet also stands for a number that carries its own vibration, a person's full name equaled a "vibratory" number, which was an expression of that person's "developed personality" and a key to her ambition or achievement. I recall Deborah lying across her bed, working out the details of her own personal number, and of our mother's: *F-A-N-N-I-E D-A-V-I-S*, which equals the number 5. According to *Psychic Sciences*, "As a name number, 5 shows independence of thought as well as action...their names literally vibrate the spirit of adventure; without it, they feel lost. If they can apply that dash to their daily work, so that their jobs and surroundings are dramatic, with promise of the unexpected, they may gain real results."

Equally important was a person's birth number, which represented the vibratory influence existing at the time of birth. My mother's birth date, May 9, 1928, equals the lucky number 7. The number 7 is highly powerful in magic *and* religion, called a "complete" number, in part because seven of a thing often makes a complete set: seven planets of antiquity; seven days of the week; seven notes of the musical scale; seven deadly sins and seven virtues; seven colors of the spectrum. (No surprise, 777 also became a popular fancy to play.)

"As a birth number, 7 denotes a scholarly, poetic nature, often inclined toward the fanciful, though persons with this birth vibration are analytical as well," explains *Psychic Sciences*. "Intuition is a strong part of their nature and many such persons are highly imaginative."

As a child, I didn't know about Mama's lucky birth number, nor did I understand the connections among metaphysics and religion and luck and numerology and mysticism and dream interpretation. I just saw my mother's life in the Numbers as magical, which included my genuine respect for the tools of her craft. I was fascinated by the red and green and blue spiral notebooks, yellow legal pads, multicolored pens, adding machines, staplers, ink pads with PAID stamps, white scratch pads, binders, lined loose-leaf paper, and the wondrous old-style, rectangular ticket books complete with receipt numbers and carbon paper. I also loved all of her reference materials, as I was drawn to the pink and blue and gold tip sheets, those softback dream books with crude artwork covers, the payout schedules, the "year in review" listings of fallen numbers. These materials were to me almost like children's playthings, yet clearly grown-up—the paraphernalia of a Wise Woman at work.

One day, I decided to organize Mama's number-running materials, and went through the house gathering everything together into one shallow cardboard box. I was enamored of my own organizational skills and decided to add one final touch: on the side of the box, using bright pink nail polish, I carefully painted in boxy letters MAMA'S NUMBERS.

I proudly showed this to my mother, impressed with myself for remembering the possessive apostrophe. She took one look and said, "You can't put my business out in the street like that."

Looking back, this was *the* moment when I became consciously aware that I must keep my admiration for my mother's work a private experience; before, I'd known to keep her livelihood a secret but hadn't yet formed an opinion of, felt any pride in, what Mama actually did for a living. Now I understood that my pride for her *also* had to be kept secret, as did all the evidence of her work.

Chastened, I took my black Magic Marker and scratched out what I'd painted onto the box; and after that episode, I began shoving things into drawers away from visitors' view. Yet, to my delight, Mama continued to keep all her paraphernalia in that box, which ended up permanently perched atop a Louis XV–style chair in her bedroom. If I looked closely, I could still see the pink letters I'd painted beneath the blackout marker, and whenever I passed by, I'd chant to myself incantation-style: *Ma-ma's Num-bers, Ma-ma's Num-bers, Ma-ma's Num-bers...*

Six

For my tenth birthday, Mama threw an elaborate party, inviting my entire fourth-grade class. A white magician performed magic tricks that actually included a live rabbit, and then made animals out of balloons as we children gathered round. Party guests spread out across the wide expanse of our big blue living room, the Jackson 5's "ABC" blasting while we danced the funky chicken. I wore a deep pink pleated dress that fanned out when I twirled, making me feel like a princess. My classmates sang "Happy Birthday" before I blew out the candles on a dazzling tiered cake designed as a replica of my face. This birthday was a highlight of my young life, marking a shift for me. After months of uncertainty, Mama's prediction had come true: we *were* happy in the new house.

I had no idea that just twelve days before, on the same night I'd watched Michael and his brothers perform on Ed Sullivan's show, the Feds had conducted a gigantic bust on the city's Numbers racket. In simultaneous planned raids throughout the metropolitan area, three hundred FBI agents arrested fifty-eight people at thirty-six different number houses, twenty-nine of them run by blacks. More than half arrested were women.

J. Edgar Hoover called it "the largest gambling raid in history" and boasted that the Mafia-controlled Numbers racket had been "eradicated" in the Motor City, effectively halting $300,000 a day in bets. Hoover bragged that the bust left the twelve thousand to fourteen thousand people who worked for Numbers operators, mostly as writers and runners, unemployed.

The FBI had figured out that the telephone was now the key way bets were placed, unlike back when runners took customers' bets in person using slips of paper; and so they had eavesdropped on calls, tapping sixteen telephones. This allowed the FBI, of course, to trace who calls were placed to. My mother now did nearly all her business over the telephone.

Through those tapped conversations, agents also discovered that the numbers were rigged, to ensure that heavily played combinations didn't fall; Detroit's Italian Mafia reportedly made $18,000 a month supplying the winning numbers to the city's operators—and another $10,000 a month for protection from big hits.

James Ritchie, director of the federal Organized Crime Task Force, declared: "We have stopped every major numbers operation in the City of Detroit. We've got it stopped cold now." Both the *Detroit News* and the *Detroit Free Press* published the FBI's list, naming every person arrested on "alleged numbers operations," including his or her age and home address. All were charged with violating and conspiring to violate provisions of interstate racketeering laws (since winning digits for the "Pontiac number" were by then received by long-distance telephone, rather than a wire service) and were released on $1,000 personal bonds.

John M. Carlisle, a *Detroit News* staff writer, wrote a feature story that ran the day after the bust, meant to explain the Numbers to laypeople. "Maybe there isn't much sense or logic to the numbers game," he opined. "Still it has been a great money-maker for the operators and a get-rich-quick dream for bettors with only loose change in their pockets." His dramatic, one-sentence final paragraph reads: "The roof fell in last night."

Turns out, that high-profile bust didn't stop the Numbers at all, and in fact operators, my mother included, were back in business within twenty-four hours. Still, Mama personally knew some of those who'd been arrested—"all on the operational or ownership level," as the Feds described them—and it felt like too close a call. That was when she employed new security measures: She had a second, unlisted telephone line put in, on which she took numbers. She also began burning the previous month's records in the incinerator, behind the furnace, in our basement. (A bonus feature that Broadstreet didn't have.) She made sure only customers' code names were used to identify them, and that the "key" to those names was kept at Broadstreet, in my sister Dianne's possession (she and her husband had recently moved into the family home.) That way, if my mother ever got busted and police confiscated her betting slips and notebooks, no one else could be implicated by name. She protected her customers' identities as she did her own.

If my mother was on edge about being exposed, I didn't see any signs of it in her demeanor. Is that why I did the unthinkable? One day, in front of Dianne and one of Mama's oldest customers, Miss Bernice (who used to call me Four Eleven, my birth weight), my sister said, "I can't believe it's already the first of the month."

To which I replied, "Yeah, time for Mama to run her tapes."

Using her adding machine, Mama would create a monthly tally of the activity for each book (customers who themselves had people who bet with them)—including all payouts for hits, total money she'd collected and any "bonus" her customers had received. Customers got bonuses if by month's end their particular book or "business" had no payouts, i.e., no hits. This windfall was up to 40 percent of that book's total revenue, and offered as a gift, an incentive for customers to benefit from a given "good month" Mama was having with their particular group of bettors. Because her customers often got 10 percent tips from their *own* customers who hit a winning number, Fannie's monthly bonus was also a generous way to offset that loss of extra money—and to keep bookies happily turning in their business to her.

Mama didn't let on to customers that she was in fact "holding" their numbers, that she and not someone else, someone bigger, was essentially the banker. They thought she was just collecting numbers, a ruse that was necessary for several reasons: first, to thwart those who might try to cheat her by not paying what they owed; if the money was going to a big Numbers man, customers were less likely to mess around with paying. Second, to thwart jealousy; if some of her clientele knew Mama was holding the business, they might stop turning in to her, this woman they viewed as getting "too big." This is why, for instance, my mother eschewed Cadillac cars as too showy, and didn't move to Southfield, a nearby suburb, or to a large house in one of the city's tonier neighborhoods. Also, to thwart busts or break-ins. The subterfuge provided a layer of protection, always important for an illegal enterprise. The less people knew, the better. You're more vulnerable if folks know you're the one coming up with large sums of money for payouts. And police liked to bust the ones in charge. Only the house created these monthly tallies, so when I said Mama had to "run her tapes," I was revealing way too much, putting her, and us, at risk.

It grew deadly silent after I said that. I knew immediately that I'd messed up. Would Miss Bernice tell other customers the truth? Would word spread? Would this make Mama a target? Would she lose business?

After Miss Bernice left ("You mind your mama, Four Eleven!"), Dianne made it clear she had to tell our mother what I'd done, even though I begged her *Please, please don't*. She told me to expect a whipping, something I'd managed to avoid up to then. Reluctantly, I went to my room and awaited my fate. I was so scared I grabbed Rita's Bible, which sat on our nightstand, and opened it to a random page. Why? For heavenly protection? Solace? I didn't yet have a relationship with God in a profound way, but I was desperate in my foxhole. I waited in that room for what seemed like several torturous hours. At one point, my teeth started to chatter.

Finally, Mama entered, closed the door. She didn't have a belt, thank God. She sat on the twin bed opposite mine and said to me, her voice calm: "Why'd you do that?"

I shrugged, eyes watery.

"You know you can't tell something like that ever again, don't you?"

I nodded as my tears fell. She looked at me.

"Okay," she said, finally. "I trust you."

Then she got up and left the room. I felt relieved, confused, grateful, and embarrassed all at once. I know this now: Not being punished for telling our secret that day has everything to do with why, growing up, I never felt ashamed of Mama's vocation. *She* never shamed me. But you can best believe I never, *ever* ran my mouth again. Many years later, Mama said to me: "I know my children, and I knew that with *you*, the anticipation was punishment enough. I also knew you didn't mean no harm. You really do know how to hold a secret in your belly. Always have."

Mama's indulgences continued. One day I came home to find brand-new bedroom furniture, complete with a tall book-shelf, a handsome desk, and a matching chair. On the desk, Mama had placed a brand-new diary, and on the bookshelf she'd placed a book by Louise Meriwether entitled *Daddy Was a Number Runner*. Once I read the novel, about a black girl growing up amid Harlem's numbers trade in the 1930s, I felt deeply comforted to know that a character in a book who looked like *me* had lived my experience.

I decided then that I'd write stories one day. I already had a writing desk and a diary. In fact, I had a role model in my mother, who was working on her own story, one she wrote in longhand with green and black and blue ink in a black binder on unlined paper. She referred to it as "my book." While I didn't know exactly *what* she was writing, I knew that the binder existed, and that was permission enough.

We had a housekeeper, Miss Katherine. She was a black woman who'd migrated from Mississippi, and Mama felt it important to help women like her by giving them work (despite the fact that my mother was convinced Miss Katherine didn't clean our home as thoroughly as she cleaned white and Jewish women's homes). I didn't like how Miss Katherine chewed tobacco, and I once complained to her about it; Mama snapped at me, told me I was to respect all adults. "You are as good as anyone," she said. "But you're better than no one."

Inside the same old brass trunk where I found Rita's letters to God, at the same time, I also found random receipts and invoices, two in particular that confirmed both Mama's wealth and its fragility. One was a "retail installment contract and security agreement" between Mama and Crowley, Milner & Company for custom drapes and valances in "New Kashmir Kelly Green," with matching sheer drapes in "Somoa." The cost for the drapes including installation and tax is $1,295. But she was buying them on installment, and was charged an additional $193 for a "time price differential," as well as 17.75 percent APR on the balance minus her $295 down payment. By the time she'd paid for the drapes, in twenty-four monthly payments of $50, they would have cost $1,700. I always saw my mother as "good with money" and not the type of person who'd enter into what looks like a classic furniture store rip-off. And yet, it makes sense that she was forever balancing her love of high-end purchases with her need to hold on to as much cash as possible. Pay-over-time arrangements made sense, given the nature of a gambler's life.

The other was an application for an "Investors Accumulation Plan" my mother filled out when I was seven. *Fannie*

Drumwright as custodian for Bridgit Davis, under the Michigan Uniform Gift to Minors Act, it reads. She'd applied for a $15,000 plan, with an initial $200 and twelve years' worth of $100 monthly payments to purchase shares of an "Investors Stock Fund, Inc." that would mature by the time I was nineteen. Funny how dry documents can prompt deep emotion. I don't know what became of Mama's application, whether she joined the plan, made a few payments or many years' worth; I don't know what became of the stock, if in fact she ever acquired it. But the thought that she was trying to create a nest egg for my future, that she had that presence of mind and the smarts to do it, brings me near to tears. I suspect that either Mama was cheated out of her money, the stock fund accruing no value, or, far more likely, she needed the money at some point, to pay a big hit, and withdrew the funds. That too is the nature of a gambling life.

Anyway, Mama found a totally different way to secure my future. When I was still ten, Rita fourteen, she gave us each a modest diamond ring she'd purchased at a pawnshop. "Now you don't have to get excited just because a man gives you a ring," she said to us both as we placed them on our fingers. "You can get excited over how he treats you."

That same year, my mother bought another diamond ring. My brother, Anthony, told her that his girlfriend, Renita, was pregnant. They were both eighteen years old, and Mama had asked him what were his intentions. "I want to marry her," he said. On Christmas day, he proposed.

"There was a box under the tree," Renita recalls. "Anthony handed it to me and I opened up this big box, and there was another small box inside. I opened up that box and

155

there was another really little one, and *that* one had my engagement ring." She goes on: "I knew it was really from her." She pauses. "That's my favorite memory of your mother, the Christmas when she gave me my ring. She was so happy for me, you know?"

On New Year's Day 1971, Rita wrote a new letter:

Dear God,

Please help me and do a favor for me and my family. I, Rita Davis, will not worry have positive thinking and have faith in you. My mother Fannie Robinson will be in good health and not worrying about things she have no control over.... Jesus thanks a lot for letting me leave my prayers to the throne of grace.

This can be a year of happiness. If everyone tries.

Thank you,
Rita

My sister knew. I didn't exactly know what was going on, but already could feel that this new year wasn't like the old one. Mama had recently been in the hospital, admitted to control the blood clots that often formed in her leg and were for her a chronic condition, one she treated more like a nuisance. "I suffer from blood clots," she'd tell people in an offhanded way; she sometimes wore compression stockings to help with circulation and prevent swelling, and was prescribed Coumadin, the blood thinner. She felt the medication kept her perpetually cold, and so our house was always blasting with heat. Now I know how potentially dangerous a blood clot can be, but back then Mama never showed much concern. She'd say that short stays in the hospital—to "break up" a clot or prevent it from traveling to her lungs—gave her a chance for some much-needed rest, and when I visited her she never looked sick; there she'd be sitting up in bed in a pretty-colored nightgown and matching robe, sometimes wearing reddish-pink lipstick. Apparently, a doctor had told her years before that whatever she eventually died from, it wouldn't be those blood clots.

The city itself was tense too. To kick off the new year, Detroit's police commissioner formed a new elite undercover police operation called STRESS, which stood for Stop the Robberies, Enjoy Safe Streets. Nearly all the officers of STRESS were white, and of course they targeted "high-crime" black neighborhoods. We saw a steady stream of black "perps" on the news, as well as regular reports of black men killed by police. (By the end of that year, Detroit's police department led the nation in civilian killings, one-third of them committed by STRESS.) I had an eighteen-year-old brother. We were all on edge.

Somewhere in there, I found myself in the car with Mama, her friend Lula, and Jewell. My mother had found out that Anthony was inside a "shooting gallery," and she'd decided to go get him. Why were we girls in the car? I can only assume that there was no one else at home and she didn't want to leave us in the house by ourselves. So there we girls were, in the backseat.

When Mama pulled up to the actual house, Lula kept saying, "Don't go in, Fannie. Don't go in!"

"I got my pistol right here," said Mama. "I'm not worried."

She got out of the car. I watched in terror as she entered through the front door, wearing her soft blue leather coat with the mink collar, hands in her pockets, finger, I was sure, on the trigger; I waited to hear gunshots. Jewell and I began crying, and Lula began praying out loud. Finally Mama burst back out through the door, dragging my brother, Anthony, by the arm to the car, where he slid into the backseat with us. "Fannie, you shouldn't have done that," said Lula.

"The way I see it, I didn't have a choice," said Mama as she took off from the curb.

Here, a soundtrack asserts itself in my memory: Marvin Gaye's haunting concept album, *What's Going On*, climbed so fast up the charts that year that you couldn't avoid those spiritually soulful songs if you wanted to, their pensive, yearning lyrics and lush orchestration spewing from hi-fis, radios, and our car's eight-track. I was a fifth grader walking three blocks up Margareta to school every day, with *Mercy, mercy me, things ain't what they used to be. Nah, nah, nah* . . . playing on a loop in my head.

And then a bizarre thing happened to *me*. I got into a fight at school. With a boy, named Peter Golightly. (And yes, he had a sister named Holly.)

We were in the same grade at Hampton Elementary, shared the same homeroom. Hampton was still in its brief period of integration, as we now lived farther northwest in the city in a more upscale area and whites hadn't fully fled the neighborhood yet. In fact, the elementary school was diverse enough to host a yearly Heritage Day, when we students came to school in ethnic attire that reflected our ancestry. Mama said that her own grandmother had "some Indian blood in her," and dressed me one year in an American Indian outfit she'd rented from a suburban costume shop. The dress was rich brown suede, with fringes along its hemline falling below my knees. Multicolored beads wove throughout its bodice, ropes of chunkier beads hung from my neck, and I wore soft, fringed moccasins on my feet. I liked the way my long, sandy-red hair, parted down the middle, lay snug inside the matching feather headband. I'd just seen *Love Story* and thought of myself as a Native American Ali McGraw. Other classmates dressed in Irish kilts, Dutch embroidered dresses with clogs, and Jewish yarmulkes and prayer shawls. My best friend, Diane, wore a bold-print head wrap with a coordinating skirt, an African princess. I won the school award that year for best heritage costume.

On this day, Peter and I had puppets on sticks that we'd created in art class, made, I seem to recall, of papier-mâché. Peter was really into his puppet, moving it up and down in animated and sweeping gestures. More than once, he put that puppet in my face, playing around. I didn't like that and told him to stop. He didn't, so I smacked the puppet away from my face and it flew across the room. Of course, the entire classroom of fifth graders broke into laughter. Embarrassed, Peter got angry and vowed payback. The rest of the day, word spread about an after-school fight between Peter and me. Fast-forward to school dismissal. I was terrified. My strategy was to just walk home as fast as I could. But Peter was there, taunting me, and an entire gang of kids was following behind us, egging us on. *Fight! Fight! Fight!* Peter yelled things at me, but I just kept walking. He called me a chicken. I kept walking.

Then he pushed me in the back. I stumbled but kept walking. He pushed me again and I knew the way you know something with dread that I had to act. I turned around and flailed my arms in his direction. *Fight! Fight! Fight!* roared the crowd. I think Peter was stunned, actually, that the quiet brown-skinned girl actually fought back. I only remember swinging my arms wildly and fearfully. I wasn't even sure I'd managed to hit him at all. I just wanted him off me, and my windmill approach kept him at bay until someone, I don't remember who, broke up the fight.

Heart pounding, I told Mama everything when I got home. I was terrified that I'd be suspended from school, but she said not to worry, she'd go talk to the principal. Then I told her the boy's name.

"Did you say *Golightly?*" she asked.

Mama knew what I didn't: Peter was the son of Cornelius Golightly, a prominent member of the Detroit school board. (He'd go on to become board president two years later.) That was when our phone rang. Not our regular phone, but the extra line, the unlisted, private one Mama had gotten specifically for her Numbers business, the one she was trying to keep hidden from the Feds' wiretapping frenzy.

Peter's mother was on the other end. She wanted to talk about the fight between her boy and me, but Mama had a more urgent concern: "How did you get this number?" She listened, repeated herself. "I said I want to know how you got this number."

Mama told Mrs. Golightly she had no right to use her influence to get access to our unlisted number, that it was a violation. "I'm a private citizen!" said Mama, adding that she didn't give a damn *who* Peter's father was. They exchanged more heated words. Mama said, "I'll see you in the principal's office tomorrow," and all I could think was *Fight, fight, fight!*

Then Mrs. Golightly asked, "You're a big woman, aren't you?"

"What of it?" said Mama.

"Because I'm not. I'm small."

"Well, for a small woman you sure do have a big mouth!" said Mama before she slammed down the phone.

My mother knew the implication: that she, with her girth, was somehow not the same caliber as the Golightly family, with their classic black bourgeoisie pedigree. Mr. Golightly was a philosophy professor and associate dean at Wayne State University. Mrs. Golightly was a "homemaker," an active member of the NAACP as well as a prominent member of the neighborhood association. And this woman had, by dialing the secret number, encroached upon our family's safety zone of protection.

The next day, we walked into the principal's office, and there sat Leslie Golightly and her son. I was stunned. Peter's light-skinned face was covered in red scratches and welts. He looked bad, and I was unnerved, completely unaware that I'd done that kind of damage. I was unscathed.

Percy Porter, the principal, invited us to sit in the two empty chairs that formed a semicircle in front of her desk. I idolized Mrs. Porter. She was tall, pretty, and so kind to us students. First, she apologized to Mama for the school giving out our phone number. That had been a mistake, she said. Then she asked Peter and me to each tell our side of the story; we did, as the adults listened. I think of that scene now, of the three women in the room that day, all African-American, each in her early forties, two of them migrants from the South, the other from Ohio; one a professional working mom, another a pillar of black society, the other a number runner. I seem to recall Mrs. Golightly implying that her son would never start a fight, that I was the troublemaker, because at one point Mama said to Mrs. Porter: "I tell you what. Pull out their school records and lay them side by side."

My transcript was filled with As and 1s for "citizenship." Turns out, Peter didn't have quite the same stellar track record for behavior. All the students and teachers knew he liked to talk in class. A lot.

What buttressed my self-defense was that our fight took place on Birchcrest, the street I walked down each day to get home from school. Peter lived on Muirland, only five minutes from my house. But that day he'd passed by Clarita, the street he should've turned down toward his own home, and stayed on Birchcrest. This was proof that I was trying to avoid a fight while he was inciting one, by following me home. My fondness for Mrs. Porter leapt to a new height when she said, "I think it's clear you initiated this altercation, Peter, and I believe you should apologize." He did.

When I think about the courage it took for the principal of our elementary school to admonish a school board member's son for starting a fight with me, a working-class girl whose parents had no real influence, I'm awed anew.

Meanwhile, I recall my father's delight that I'd "whupped that high-yellow boy's butt"; Daddy was convinced that the playful shadowboxing I used to do with him as he taught me to make a fist, jab at the air, do some fancy footwork had paid off. Honestly, I wasn't even sure I'd thrown a punch, let alone landed one, but I reveled in Daddy's praise.

There were no more busts by the Feds that year, and I remained oblivious to potential risks our family faced. I was fixated on becoming an auntie. That spring, Mama threw Renita an elaborate baby shower, which produced mounds and mounds of impractical, exquisite gifts.

"Girl, too much of everything," recalls Renita. Mama's friends went all out for Fannie's first grandchild, giving her daughter-in-law exquisite blankets and pillows and silver rattles and hand-knit booties and linen baby gowns. "Everybody was trying to outdo everybody else," says Renita. "But that's how much they all loved her. You could see that they showed their love for her through all those beautiful gifts to me."

I was the one who told Mama that Renita's water had broken. As Renita stepped out of the car on a hot July night and waddled toward the hospital doors, she turned back to us and said, "I hope it's a boy"; it was. Given that she and Anthony were both so young, Mama stepped in to help care for Anthony II, or Tony as we called him, while paying for Renita to attend college in Texas. Meanwhile, Anthony worked for Mama, as he'd done since we moved from Broadstreet, helping out with the business. He and Renita lived in a small flat nearby.

Dominant among my memories of that time is the layering of sounds: Mama's voice as she greeted a customer on the phone: *Morning, Miss White, you ready for me to take your numbers for the day?* followed by her repeating numbers as she recorded bets in her spiral notebook; or her warmer, relaxed tone as she chatted with a friend, troubleshooting or debating or discussing a good number to play. In between, the ringing phone, loud and incessant like high-pitched cicadas in season. Sometimes it was two phones from our two different lines, ringing in unison. Always in the background, TV voices talking at us in ongoing one-way conversations, from morning newscasters to the ads' announcers to midday game show hosts: *The Price Is Right*'s Bob Barker, *Let's Make a Deal*'s Monty Hall, and eventually, *Wheel of Fortune*'s Pat Sajak, their deep male voices luring jubilant contestants with chances to win refrigerators and vacations and oh my God, a new car! (Mama never watched the soap operas that dominated major networks during daytime programming. They bored her.) Punctuating the TV sounds and those ever-ringing telephones, and Mama's constant phone talk, were Tony's cries and coos adding a layer of daycare chaos as he banged pots, broke things, played with annoyingly loud educational toys.

On the weekend, another group of sounds—different ones coming from the always-on TV with its programming of cartoons, *Jeopardy!*, *The Newlywed Game* and the never-to-be-missed *Soul Train*; this accompanied by the squeals and laughter of three *new* children in our house, ages two, four and seven, cousins by marriage now spending every weekend with us: my stepfather's nieces and nephew cared for by Mama because their own mother was in need of relief, her nerves bad. And with my oldest sister, Deborah, now helping to run the tapes, the *rat-a-tat-tat* of the adding machine punctuated by a trill every time she hit the Total button. In all this cacophony, the doorbell would inevitably ring, with either a sibling or relative or customer dropping by, a delivery made or a family friend paying a visit, often poised to ask for a favor. And amid these competing noises, Mama's confident voice, wrapping up a week's worth of business with customers:

Listen, Miss White, Burt will be around to collect later today. You know what your bill is, don't you? Oh, I can tell you. Wait, hold on a minute. Grabbing a loose-leaf binder lying nearby, she'd open it, go to a divider tab marked with the customer's code name, flip to that page, figures moving down the loose-leaf paper, inside vertical columns Mama had created with a wooden ruler. End-of-the-week totals would be written in green or, if money was owed, red ink.

Okay. I got your credit page from my record book right here, she'd say into the phone. *Your total was six hundred fifty dollars high, minus your thirty-five percent, which brings it to four twenty-two fifty low. And you had a hit on four-six-nine for fifty cents, so that leaves you owing a hundred seventy-two fifty. You got that? Now, what's the best time to come around? 'Cause you know Burt can't be coming out too late, bad as it's getting out here.*

I often heard this symphony of competing sounds through my bedroom door, plopped on my bed reading *Jonathan Livingston Seagull* or my sister Dianne's copy of *I Never Promised You a Rose Garden* or *Go Ask Alice;* or writing in my new diary as I hid out, seeking solitude.

Amid the busyness of her daily life, turns out Mama sought something too. I found a GED test she'd taken on July 26, 1971, just a week after becoming a grandmother at forty-three. This test confuses me slightly, because Aunt Florence says Fannie definitely graduated from Pearl High School back in Nashville, but nevertheless there it is, scores and all. She passed easily. She ranked in the eighty-seventh percentile for reading and the seventy-third percentile for math, which doesn't surprise me. She lists her age as ten years younger than she actually was, something Mama often did. I used to think it was vanity, and there was certainly that, but I now believe she feared aging, as if she knew that time was running out to live the fuller life she'd once envisioned for herself, rather than just the one she found herself living.

In summer of 1972, as I graduated from Hampton Elementary and Rita from Mumford High, Motown graduated to another level of success: the homegrown record company synonymous with Detroit and "the sound of young America" announced plans to move its headquarters to Los Angeles. Even though the *Michigan Chronicle*'s front-page story quoted the company's general manager as saying the move was "simply a matter of sound business judgment, economics and logistics," it was a major blow to black Detroiters. A rumor began that Berry Gordy had been "run out of town" by the Mafia. This claim was never proven and isn't really rational (why wouldn't the local syndicate keep Gordy and his lucrative business in Detroit, making money for them?), but the rumor gained traction because it was easier to believe *that* story than the harsher, simple fact that Detroit's crown jewel had been snatched away by a sexier, richer, sunnier place. Emotions ran so high after the announcement that black disc jockeys boycotted Motown music on the radio (except for Stevie Wonder's) for months. I didn't notice, as I was listening to soft rock on Q-93, my friend Diane and I obsessed with Chicago's "Saturday in the Park."

Yet in October of that same year, Berry Gordy's movie division released an homage to Billie Holiday, *Lady Sings the*

Blues. The film was the first of its kind, an extraordinary experience for black Americans and black Detroit specifically. Yes, folks were upset about Motown's move west, but that was *our* hometown girl up there on the big screen, in all her black-diva glamour, and with her stellar acting chops and pretty singing voice. I was twelve and so loved that film that I convinced Mama to take me to see it, then convinced Daddy to take me to see it again. When she received an Oscar nomination, Diana Ross still belonged to us. And now that folks could see what its film division was pulling off in Hollywood, how mad could you be at Motown?

Besides, another seismic event had just hit Detroit, one that had an equally reverberating impact on the city, and eventually our family: Michigan's legislature passed a proposal allowing voters to decide whether they wanted a state lottery.

This referendum had history. As far back as 1937, the question of legalization had been raised, and across the next three decades bills were introduced, the issue debated in the black press, polls taken, letters to editors written, and persuasive arguments made both for and against. I suspect that the 1970 raid led by Hoover had a lot to do with swaying elected representatives' decision, as that bust revealed just how lucrative the city's Numbers racket was, with its estimated $94-million-per-year revenue—money all taken in by local Mafia and black Numbers bankers. By that point, police estimated that a hundred thousand people, or one in every fifteen Detroiters, played the Numbers daily. Legislators surely reasoned that the state should capture all that money wagered, rather than leave it in the coffers of two of society's most despised groups.

No surprise that once legalization was on the table, law

enforcement staged more raids on illegal Numbers, arresting more operators, but curiously not any Mafia-related ones. The highly respected African-American judge George Crockett Jr. released twenty-seven black defendants, declaring later in an interview with *Jet* magazine, "There seems to be a tendency for the law to work one way for the poor and the Black and another for the wealthy and the white."

Two months before the vote, the *Detroit Free Press* ran a three-day series on the Numbers, its front-page headlines capturing the accepted narrative of what the Numbers was: NUMBERS RUNNERS SELL DREAMS TO POOR; THE SYNDICATE, DISHONESTY REPLACE GOLDEN ERA OF NUMBERS; and NUMBERS TODAY: A TOUGH JOB, i.e., asserting that Numbers players were impoverished victims of a massive scam, made worse by Mafia control, all for a game that had already experienced its heyday. In truth, many people hit the number every day; and my mother and other bankers on her level—those with several books in their business, and all men except for one other woman—were at that moment maintaining a brisk livelihood as number runners. The big bankers were millionaires.

The staff writer of the *Free Press* stories, Tom Ricke, showed his take on Numbers in an early paragraph:

Since the early 1900s, numbers men have been making billions of dollars selling people the chance to dream of having money.

The writer went on to patronizingly make a claim that has no statistical basis:

Most of the people who play numbers are black. It's always been that way. It started in the ghetto and is still there. It's the only way for many to get a sum of money and it is a habit for many others that started when they bought dreams to help them through empty days.

The price? Whatever a person can scrape together each day. For that money, he buys a thousand-to-one chance of getting 500 times the amount he bet. But it's more than that. He has purchased a thought—the right to think all day long about what he is going to do with the money if he wins. And that makes it easier to get through each day. Just the thought of it.

Ricke's point was a deceptively clever one: Playing the Numbers was understandable—who doesn't dream of striking it rich?—but doing so illegally, where the Mafia controlled the three-digit winners, was a fool's errand. Those thousands of blacks who played the Numbers were, effectively, dupes in need of protection from their own poor choices. His series of articles included anecdote after anecdote about black men and women who'd lost all their money playing, or had blown their winnings on foolishness, had been lured by preachers who promised, for a hefty donation, "blessed over" winning numbers. According to Ricke, number runners' primary customers were allegedly mothers on welfare, boosters (professional shoplifters), and "high" dope dealers.

"Numbers is a terrible thing for a lot of people," a man named "James," who'd been collecting numbers for thirty years, was quoted as saying. "The more they bet and lose, the longer they bet. They think each day is the day they will hit....A numbers player is a fool."

Mama took offense at those claims. "I don't have no customers like that, who bet up what they can't afford to lose," she said. "And no damn way would I let somebody gambling up their rent and food money play numbers with me. Not if I knew about it."

Research done by the scholar Felicia George has since proven Mama's experience to be the norm. Most black people who played Numbers weren't spending money they couldn't afford to lose; many of them were *not* poor, rather working and middle-class folks with disposable income, a piece of which they chose to spend on playing the Numbers the way others spent extra money on eating out or buying cigarettes or going to the movies or betting on horses. And people often hit just enough to make it worth their while to gamble. More to the point, numbers players *enjoyed* it.

Never mind that whites played the Numbers too. According to the *Detroit News,* an estimated thirty thousand Detroiters played the numbers in 1970, but when the (largely white) suburbs were included, that number rose to a hundred fifty thousand—a stat omitted from Ricke's story. To Mama, the only "fools" were those who didn't see that with this referendum, Michigan legislators were trying to wipe out the largely black-run Numbers and replace them with a fully state-controlled numbers operation. "Sometimes, it's hard to get black folks to see the truth," she'd say.

But the argument that the Numbers preyed on poor blacks, that the game was by and large exploitative, was a strong one and didn't need to be rooted in truth. It was rooted in a racist narrative that had long cast African-Americans' gambling habits as morally deficient, a belief shared by a significant number of upper- and middle-class blacks. Legalizing lotteries would supposedly root out the criminal element of number running, making it legitimate and, by extension, respectable.

Cue the state's lottery game.

Even Judge Crockett, who'd released all those black defendants, was pleased that voters might decide to legalize the Numbers. "Maybe this will get rid of the numbers business and make gambling a state monopoly," he said. "Then the proceeds, hopefully, will be used to underwrite projects for social change, such as hospitals, schools, and recreational facilities."

What an ironic rationale, given that Numbers men were historically the very ones who provided the black community with programs and facilities and resources that the state neglected to provide. By the late 1960s and 1970s, these men (and yes, women) directed their largesse toward black organizations like the NAACP, funded black political candidates' campaigns, and sustained vulnerable social programs, all to further African-American progress. My mother contributed to these very causes, while she also regularly sent money to upstate prisoners, hired out-of-work young black men, and donated to the beloved but beleaguered college for low-income blacks, Shaw College at Detroit. Moreover, she patronized black businesses almost exclusively. These contributions add up, have a cumulative effect; how naïve to believe that once the profits made by informal Numbers were taken out of the hands of black operators and turned over to the state's coffers,

Michigan's elected officials would miraculously start meeting African-American residents' needs.

"The Numbers man is no longer a community leader," proclaimed Ricke, who went on to quote "Sam," who had grown up in a number-running household which he described as a friendly gathering place. "But that's over now," Sam lamented. "The dope houses have taken over the neighborhoods and the people aren't as friendly as they used to be, and neither are the numbers." (There has, by the way, never been any association between Detroit's drug trade and the Numbers.)

The strategy worked. With a steady drumbeat of negative press about the Numbers—Ricke's series chief among them—coupled with city and state officials' demonization of number runners, public perception against this decades-old underground lottery coalesced, alongside the desire to usurp it. No surprise that on May 16, 1972, voters chose by a three-to-one margin to amend Michigan's constitution and end the 137-year ban on lotteries. Turns out, nearly 80 percent of blue-collar suburban whites voted for the lottery, as did those in rural counties, as well as large numbers of both white and black Detroiters—proving that gambling itself was not what the majority of Michiganders opposed. The option to bet on numbers out in the open was the real lure.

Michigan was, it turns out, part of a wave of states that promoted legal lotteries as a form of "tax rebellion," an easy way to raise revenue without imposing additional taxes on residents. This too was rooted in race-based policy, as states' conservative Republican legislators and governors fueled resentment in their white suburban and rural constituents, who didn't want their tax dollars going toward "inner-city" schools for public education, nor urban social programs. Nine states legalized lotteries from 1967 to 1974, with the obvious intent of capturing some of that Numbers money for their own coffers.

"Even if you lose, your money is going for a good purpose rather than an evil purpose," proclaimed William T. Cahill, then governor of New Jersey.

After the vote, how did Mama feel, she who had doggedly built her business, risked arrest, paid out large sums to winners, kept money circulating in the community, used her proceeds as a consumer, lender, employer, and philanthropist? Maybe she felt some vindication, since the decision to legalize lotteries proved that the Numbers had, all along, been a legitimate business that just happened to be illegal. This I do know: she believed her livelihood was not under threat. Everyone in the business was confident that the Numbers would continue running, right alongside the legal lottery, and that plenty of black folks would stay loyal to them. Mama felt certain her own customers would stay loyal to *her*. She seemed, more than anything else, resigned after the vote. I heard her say, "Well, we already know that when white folks want to do something bad enough, they can just create a law to get away with it."

That August, Governor William Milliken signed Act 239, the Lottery Act, into law. I was an oblivious twelve-year-old focused instead on my sister Rita going off to Fisk University in Nashville, where she got to be around our kin from both sides of the family. I was a little jealous about all the fanfare of her departure. And then I missed her. Yet, Rita's leaving home totally shifted the dynamic in the household in a surprising new way: Mama and I grew closer.

As much as I'd loved being a daddy's girl, once we moved,

he wasn't around for me to spend my free time with, and with Rita gone, I naturally found myself spending more time with Mama. As a preteen girl, I *wanted* to be around my mother more. Besides, the new house was designed in a way that made it easier for us to interact, none of the upstairs vs. downstairs living that took place on Broadstreet. Mama and I would go clothes shopping together at Southfield's Northland Mall, spending most of our time in the gigantic four-story Hudson's department store, where we always had lunch. We'd both order Hudson's famous Maurice Salad, with its strips of ham, turkey, and Swiss cheese atop iceberg lettuce, covered in the yummiest lemony mayo and Dijon dressing I've ever tasted in my life. Some evenings, I'd stand over Mama as she sat on her bedroom's chaise lounge, part her hair with a fine-toothed comb and scratch her dandruff, then oil her scalp with DuSharme hair cream. She liked that.

By far, one of my favorite rituals we shared was watching classic films together. Every weekday afternoon the local Channel 7 station, WXYZ, showed *The 4:30 Movie,* and I looked forward to it as an after-school treat. Each week focused on a different actor's or actress's movies, and I'd sit next to Mama in the den with its red and black decor, the phone ringing intermittently as she took folks' numbers, and hungrily watch those old movies, many in black-and-white. I seldom had to fill in Mama on what she missed during a call, because she'd seen most of them already. I wonder now, did Mama first see *Back Street* with Susan Hayward, and *A Raisin in the Sun* with Sidney Poitier, and *The Misfits,* Marilyn Monroe's last film, while sitting in that movie theater back in the day, me in her arms, girding herself against bad luck? Once, the late, late show aired a double feature—1934's *Imitation of Life,* starring Louise Beavers, which Mama had seen as a child, and 1949's *Pinky,* starring Ethel Waters. "You need to see these films," Mama said, emphatic, and so I stayed up into the early morning hours watching them back to back. These were "race dramas" about a light-skinned black woman passing as white, with disastrous consequences. In *Imitation of Life,* the daughter even disowns her mother. I understood the twin messages I was expected to take away: Be who you are. Honor your mother.

As the last one of her five children still at home, I was also more attuned to Mama's professional concerns; at some point that fall, I could feel a shift. It's not that I actually knew that soon these new lottery tickets would go on sale; but I felt something, maybe even felt Mama's growing anxiousness, because I took a newfound interest in the family business. I started helping to spot hits, Mama showing me how to refer to that day's four different winning three-digits and carefully check to see if I found those exact combinations, straight or boxed, in customers' plays. If I did so, I'd circle the hit in red ink. She explained how important it was that I not miss a hit, because an overlook was bad for business, as it cut into her reputation for running an operation "on the up and up," as she put it. She never wanted to appear begrudging of customers' good luck.

I took the job of looking for hits seriously. In fact, it was a task suited for me, a bit like the puzzles and board games I enjoyed. Also, if Mama was busy, I sometimes took customers' numbers over the phone, repeating each back to them as I'd heard her do for years. I also started calling customers each evening to give them the day's winners: *Hi, Miss White, this is Fannie's daughter, Bridget. I'm calling to give you the number.* For this task, Mama paid me twenty dollars a week.

Two weeks before the first lottery ticket went on sale, authorities went hard after the Numbers. State and local police raided the Twenty Grand Motel, owned by Eddie Wingate. Police arrested twelve people, and alleged that the Twenty Grand—a favorite lounge for my adult sisters and their friends—was the headquarters for a $9-million-a-year operation.

That chill in place, the first green lottery tickets went on sale to the general public for fifty cents each on November thirteenth. Even an oblivious seventh grader couldn't miss all the hype over the new state lottery. The daily newspapers and newscasts reported "the richest state lottery in the nation" heavily and positively, and my mother watched all the coverage. Here's what she did: she bought several tickets, becoming one of a stampede of Michiganders who purchased over five million tickets in that first week. "Might as well," she said. "Might as well."

Eleven days later the Michigan state lottery, with extraordinary fanfare, held its first drawing at Cobo Arena in conjunction with the venerable Detroit Auto Show, complete with Governor Milliken's attendance and "lottery ladies" in elegant dresses selecting the winning numbers.

Mama got lucky. Her ticket was a winner, allowing her to enter the state's "supersize" drawing: first prize was $200,000, second prize was $50,000, and third prize was $10,000. The entire family was anxious and excited as Burt drove Mama to the secretary of state's office, where she had to place her winning ticket in an envelope and drop it into a clear globe alongside ten other semifinalists. I distinctly remember the feeling that our lives could really change if she won, that she'd never again have to worry about getting hit hard, because the money always would be there, endless. When the winners' envelopes were drawn, Mama had won $10,000, not enough to change our lives, but clearly enough to pad her reserve for those large payouts when customers hit—and enough to keep intact her reputation as a lucky woman.

Michigan's lottery pulled in over $135 million in gross sales in its first year. Yet it was a game most black folks played as an extra treat, the way people today buy a Mega Millions lottery ticket when the jackpot climbs into the stratosphere. Meanwhile, the day-to-day operations of the Numbers continued in full force. For those who collected and booked the Numbers regularly, and those who banked them, it wasn't a game at all, but rather a daily business. Besides, the state lottery was just once a week, and you couldn't pick your own numbers. *That* was the Numbers' edge.

Still, another series of Numbers raids and arrests by local police soon followed. Around this same time I became friends with another seventh grader, Sarita Williams, whose father, Paul, was one of Motown's original Temptations. By then, Paul's downward spiral was in rapid spin, mere months before he apparently committed suicide. I visited Sarita in their sprawling upscale house in Palmer Woods. What I saw was a home in disrepair. The toilet wouldn't flush, the carpet was soiled and peppered with cigarette burns, the automatic garage door wouldn't open, and the hot tub in the back was filled with algae and small dead animals. I felt a kind of vertigo, witnessing the decay of prosperity. I thought of what my father had once said to me: *You can survive a fall from the basement. Falling from on top is what kills you.* Later, in our kitchen, I recounted everything I'd seen in vivid detail to my mother, who clearly heard the anxiety in my voice.

"They've just had some really bad luck lately," I explained to her.

Mama, who was frying catfish, said, "That's not bad luck. That's a squandered opportunity." She turned to me, eyes boring into mine, spatula aloft, and said, "I would never let that happen. I would never go backwards."

As soon as she said this to me, I felt relief, confirmation that our comfort was not simply born of luck, based on a given day's number. It was strived for, built and sustained by my mother's efforts and yes, pride. *We* would never lose everything, because she would make sure we didn't.

But now, in the early days of Michigan's brand-new lottery, it wasn't clear yet just how much harder her job had become.

Original lottery tickets, 1972 and 1977

Seven

Fannie and Burt, date unknown

Mama and I are shopping inside Bonwit Teller at Somerset Mall in Troy. A saleswoman approaches us. "We have some nice things marked down on the sales rack," she says, gesturing with a sweep of her arm.

My mother eyes the white woman. "Did I ask you what was on the sales rack?"

The woman mutters an apology and steps away as we continue shopping. Once we're done, Mama seeks out the same saleswoman and hands her our selections to ring up, their full-price tags dangling.

"Cash or charge?" asks the saleswoman as she stands before the register.

"Charge," says Mama, and flips open her Louis Vuitton wallet to reveal a plethora of credit cards, the array in full view of the saleswoman. She runs her fingers past the Carte Blanche, Diners Club, Saks, B. Siegel's, Jacobson's, and Hudson's cards and pulls out her Bonwit's.

The saleswoman studies the card, looks up. "Could I see some ID, please?" she asks.

"Sure," says Mama, and she pulls out her driver's license, Blue Cross/Blue Shield medical card, and Social Security card and hands over all three. She has pulled out her checkbook, about to show that too, when the saleswoman holds up her hand to stop her.

"Oh, that's okay," she says. "Really, this is sufficient."

"You sure?" asks Mama. "Because we can call my bank if you like. Or your manager."

The saleswoman shakes her head vigorously as she hands back Mama's multiple forms of ID. She tries to make small talk as she rings us up, but Mama has very little to say. We take our Bonwit's bags adorned with their signature violet bouquets and leave the store.

I've seen variations of this scene play out often with my mother, and every time, I've watched closely. I never cringed from embarrassment over all the fuss, because I knew the point my mother was making. Still, those scenes made me feel a certain kind of way: First, I loved that she, as this black woman, had her own credit cards in her maiden name—*Fannie M. Drumwright*. I loved that she bought what she wanted when she wanted it from any part of any store she wanted. I loved that she had her own money and ran her own business. And I could tell that *she* loved it too. I didn't actually know back then that she was one of only two Detroit women banking the Numbers. But I knew enough to know she was unique, that none of my friends' mothers were like her. This fascinated me because I was also newly interested in her *as* my mother.

And so I took note. Mama was making sure, without a

doubt, that these saleswomen, that all people on the outside, acknowledged her value. She demanded it, in fact, and I was beginning to understand that her secret profession was part of the reason. She had something to prove: *Because I'm a brown-skinned black woman, you think you're better than me; and if you knew what I did for a living, you'd look down your nose at me. Well, I'm going to* make *you respect me.*

This sense of gravitas permeated my mother's entire life, with friends, business associates, her own siblings, us. As approachable and helpful as she was, she invited a kind of decorum from others, a hint of formality. People of all ages, men and women, watched their words and their behavior around her. People didn't curse or raise their voices around her.

Now I see how she commanded respect as a woman, and there's no question she was a feminist. But back then I wouldn't have called her that. Yes, it was the seventies and I had a subscription to *Ms.* Magazine, an obsession with *The Mary Tyler Moore Show,* and a devotion to Marcia Ann Gillespie's "Getting Down" column in *Essence.* But despite seeing my mother daily pushing against expectation and assumption, I associated feminism with white women. Besides, I didn't witness any contradiction or struggle or "balancing act" in her quest to be both homemaker/mother and business owner. When many years later I read Toni Morrison's comment that "Black women seem able to combine the nest and the adventure...they are both safe harbor and ship; they are both inn and trail. We, black women, do both," I felt she was describing my mother.

Meanwhile, I was more influenced by the Black Power movement, enough to briefly wear my hair in an Afro, or a

Natural as we called it, which I created by an elaborate process of applying lotion to my hair, then curling it with twisted strips ripped from a brown paper bag. I was swayed by the catchy TV commercial airing weekly during *Soul Train* that showed a man and woman sporting perfect Afros as background voices sang, partly in Swahili: *Watu Wazuri, use Afro Sheen! Beautiful people, use Afro Sheen!* Yet more often I joined my mother in the basement salon of Miss Evelyn, her hairdresser, where we'd both get our hair press-and-curled.

Too, I often accompanied my mother on visits to her girlfriends' homes, these funny, hardworking, and ever-supportive women who always knew about my latest achievements in school. (Mama apparently bragged about me, but never in my presence. That was her way.) She had a special relationship with each friend, and none more special than the one she shared with Lula. Although Mama didn't believe in godmothers (*No one is gonna do for you like what I can do, so what's the point?*), Lula was Rita's unofficial godmother. As Mama's closest friend, she came over nearly every day. Many, many nights Lula would fall asleep on my mother's bedroom chaise lounge until Burt came to bed. He'd wake Lula, walk her to the side door, watch as she got into her car parked in the driveway, and wave as she backed out, headed for home.

I also sometimes went with my mother to the bank, watched as she requested the help of a particular bank teller or manager, always an African-American woman whom she had a working relationship with. Mama would hand the woman a mixture of cash and checks to deposit, all collected from customers, some of who paid their Numbers bills with portions of their pension and Social Security checks. My mother needed a banker to accept these signed-over third-party checks without question.

Other times, she'd rely on her friend Miss Lucille, who owned a check-cashing business with her husband, LaVert. Any checks that the bank wouldn't accept, Miss Lucille would cash for Mama. More important, Miss Lucille could help Mama out with cash flow. If Mama needed to "get up the money" for a big hit, she could turn to Miss Lucille for a large sum to borrow; they had a close friendship built on trust, and Miss Lucille knew Fannie was good for it, would return the money within a couple of weeks, if not a couple of days. I enjoyed visiting Miss Lucille, because she also loved beautiful things, and her home was a display of wondrous tchotchkes and furnishings. She collected elephant figurines, often showing off the newest addition to Mama and me. Miss Lucille was also a heavy Numbers player, but she didn't turn in her numbers to Mama. This was how my mother kept healthy relationships with her close friends; she didn't let them play Numbers with her. "I'd rather have your friendship over your business any day," she'd say.

It worked. "Fannie was my mother's best friend, outside her bridge club members," confirms Miss Lucille's son, Eric. "Something good always happened when the two of them got together."

One of my mother's most vital friendships was with Pearl Massey, the only other woman in Detroit known to be a major banker for the Numbers. They didn't share customers, but they did have each other's back. Given that both women dealt with significant amounts of cash, each could borrow from the other when she had a cash-flow issue. She and Mama could discuss the vagaries of the business in a way neither could with anyone else. I liked when we visited Pearl for this reason alone, to hear my mother open up about her challenges in a way I never otherwise would.

With my own dawning awareness, I began to notice my mother's double allure, one secret and one out in the open: while many folks saw her as a wise and nurturing maternal figure, with great instincts about human nature and people's character, a way of helping others with their problems, and a generous spirit, these same people didn't even know she ran Numbers. Meanwhile, for others, she had a special aura specifically *because* she ran Numbers, and she was seen as successful, and yes, lucky. (Of course there was overlap, with some people part of both of her worlds, doubly admiring her.) As I matured, I realized that I knew of no man or woman in the Numbers business, or outside of it, quite frankly, who was lauded that way, which made me believe Mama wasn't just liberated; she was powerful.

"She was a big honcho!" is how Renita, Tony's mother, puts it. "I didn't understand that at the time, but that's what she was."

I also paid more attention to the way people were drawn to Mama, wanted to be in her orbit. "Sometimes, I'd be in the area and I'd go over to see if you were home," recalls Stephanie, my close friend since junior high. "And even if you weren't there, I could just slip into what was going on. It was easy to get sucked into your house, anyway. You sit at that kitchen table and the next thing you know, somebody is coming in and this and that is happening, and your mom might say, 'Can you go get this thing for me?' You felt needed, and a part of things.... It was just a comforting feeling to be in your mom's presence."

Many folks came over just to sit at our kitchen table and listen to my mother dispense advice, what one friend called "a little counseling clinic." My sister Rita's high school friend Jill put it this way: "She could help you think yourself out of a situation. Your mother was one of those people that knew just enough about everything."

She was certainly a lifelong learner, thanks to her voraciously reading books, magazines and the daily newspaper; she not only watched the local and national news each night but also *Face The Nation* on Sunday morning. She had genuine interest in politics and current affairs; as she put it, "I like keeping up with the news." This largely contributed to her deft debating skills. Mama's political views were a blend of progressive and conservative, and her views on racial matters could aptly be summed up in her assessment that "All black folks should be in therapy at the government's expense."

Another distinction of my mother's was that she didn't judge others based on what they looked like or where they came from or what impediments or disabilities or imperfections they had. She welcomed all different kinds of folks into her life. "That taught me a lesson," recalls Stephanie. "Certain people we sometimes shy away from, but your mother had a variety of people coming through, who could be totally free and at home and embraced and accepted."

Having such a cool mother made *me* feel special. Plus, she was married to a man who obviously adored her, and I liked that fact too. Whenever he traveled to out-of-town golf tournaments, my stepfather would send Mama postcards, always signed *Your Loving Hubby*. And sometimes Burt playfully patted my mother's behind, or pulled her to him in a bear hug, landing a sloppy kiss on her cheek. She'd act like she didn't have time for such horseplay, but it was obvious she was flattered by her husband's sexual attraction for her being put on display.

Mama was also, however, no-nonsense. As her children, when she told us to do something, we did it. One of her favorite Bible passages to quote was "Honor thy mother and thy father and thy days will be long." Given this, my siblings and I had an understanding. If one of us faced a crisis or problem, our goal was to work it out among ourselves. "Don't tell Mama!" was our go-to command to one another. To be clear, we all knew that if we needed real help, she'd be there to do whatever she could. We knew that. But if we could solve the situation on our own, we did. That's because none of us wanted to disappoint her. In fact, on those rare occasions when I did have to confess to her something I'd done wrong, the most bruising thing my mother could say to me was one simple sentence: "I'm disappointed in you." I'd cry for a day.

Sometimes, she'd get angry and "go off" on someone she felt deserved it. This didn't happen often, but my mother had a sharp tongue coupled with a quick mind and no one wanted to be on the receiving end of that. Curse words came easily to her lips. ("I got to say it the way that makes sense to *me*.") What could *really* set her off were liars, anyone trying to get over on her, and greed—folks trying to take more than they deserved, or what didn't belong to them. "Ooh, that thing has really unnerved me," she'd say. "I don't like being around people I can't respect."

She revealed herself mostly by what she liked and disliked, by what she embraced and what she disdained; and she seemed genuinely unconcerned with what most people thought of her, or as she put it, "I don't give a damn." The one thing Mama often said about herself was "I'm very sensitive." This statement had a twofold meaning for my mother, and she expected everyone in her life to deal with her accordingly. First, it meant, "Watch your mouth. You're not gonna just say whatever you feel like to me." She let you know that her feelings could be hurt by your words, and "You took it the wrong way" was not a good defense. "Maybe you said it the wrong way," she'd shoot back.

Also, she used her sensitivity to pick up on social cues, a skill she prided herself on, and one she felt too many others lacked. "Some people aren't sensitive enough," she'd say.

As a young teen, I thought Mama was scared of virtually no one and nothing. I'll always remember the day she got a call from Renita saying that my brother, Anthony, had taken her car and now Renita's own crazy brother, Dwight, had threatened to "go out looking for him" and teach him a lesson. Mama grabbed her .38 pistol and drove over to Dwight's house to confront him. Burt, Rita, and I jumped into Burt's car to follow behind and try to stop her.

"Girl, I got out of Dodge when I seen her pull up," recalls Renita. "'Cause just from being around her you wouldn't know it, but *I knew* she was tough."

When we arrived, Mama was standing before Renita's brother, hand in pocket, clearly gripping her gun. "Nigger, you lay a hand on what's mine," she told him, "and I'll kill your fucking ass!"

"You got no problem with me, Mrs. Davis," said Dwight, backing down. "None."

Anthony then pulled up in his wife's car, and when he refused to hand her the keys, Mama was so angry she began beating Anthony with her hands, which made my sister Rita jump in to stop her. Frightened by it all, I began crying, and according to what I wrote in my turquoise one-year diary, "lost my best pair of earrings!"

My diary from those junior high days is filled with praise for Mama. In between excruciating detail about a boy I had a crush on, my experiences attending Patricia Stevens Modeling School, visiting Daddy on weekends, being part of a modern dance group, attending church youth group functions, and my first after-school job at a nursery school called Timbuktu, I also show lots of gratitude for my mother. After a shopping spree: *I got a good momma and I love her like mad.* When I realized my mother was paying close attention to my behavior: *Really, I want to impress my mother. I love her!* After she chastised me for something, and that made me cry, and *that* upset her, I wrote: *She really is a precious person and I love her to all ends.* And in another, exuberant entry: *I found an exciting new friend. My mother! Today I was laughing and joking with her as if she were my best friend! Actually she is my best friend.*

When I was thirteen, just as an interminable six-week public school strike finally ended, my mother made possible one of my most treasured experiences: she took me to see *the* Josephine Baker perform at Detroit's Fisher Theatre. "She's a legend and you should see what a legend looks like up close," Mama told me about the woman who went from the slums of St. Louis to become the toast of Paris, the first black sex symbol of the twentieth century. I was invited up onstage, alongside other young people from the audience, to dance with Baker during her finale; even though I was startled to see the sixty-seven-year-old singer up close, as she'd looked much younger from my seat, I was thrilled nevertheless. Afterward, I became fascinated with the legendary performer, pulling the *World Book Encyclopedia* off our den shelf to learn more about her. I found inspiration in her life and started toying with the idea of bigger possibilities, of ways I might reinvent myself as a black girl, dream big.

Suddenly, Mama seemed pretty ordinary by comparison. La Baker was the exotic one, and very much unlike Mama—famous, talented, mother of a rainbow tribe, once-sexy topless dancer, Parisian. Today, the parallels are obvious to me: Mama, like Baker, took stock of the life she was born into and used her skill set to reinvent herself, become someone who hadn't existed before. But back then all I saw as a young teen was inspiration to leave home, explore new places, really become *somebody*. I began to see that, compared to a citizen of the world, being a number runner meant being trapped at home all day; you were tied to a schedule that could begin at the crack of dawn, when a customer would call to put in her numbers before she "heads out fishing," until late evening after the number came out and you needed to check the business for hits. It dawned on me that Mama only got one day off a week, Sunday. And the rough patches in her business could last for a while, with all the stress and household tension that came with them. My mother lived constantly with the fear that too many big hits back to back would put her "in the hole," as she called it, from which she'd have to dig herself out, i.e., start from scratch to build up a cash cushion.

I found out that Momma has been hit for $10 in the last two days, I wrote in my diary barely a month after seeing Josephine Baker perform. *That's $5,000.00 dollars. . . . It scares me. This has been a tough year for Momma. Sometimes I wish we weren't in Numbers cause this way, we don't get a steady paycheck. But then I ask myself do you want to give up your luxuries along with the Numbers? And the answer is "no."*

These stresses came as I was also feeling the hormonal effects of puberty. My diary reflects this complicated dynamic: *Momma and I went through it again,* says one entry, about my being late for school yet another time: *She kept saying, "What more can I do?" Anyway, I know I better not be late again, cause she won't stand for it.* And in another entry: *One minute I love my mother and everything about her, the next thing I know, her ways urk me!* And from December 1973: *Momma and I got into it again. She called me a liar and after a few words she says, "Well, I just made a mistake. Do you want me to say I'm sorry and take it back?" I said, "No, if you think I'm a liar I don't want you to apologize." I wasn't mad at her by then. . . .* On New Year's Eve of that year, I wrote: *What's going on around here? Is it me? Is it her? It's her. She's so tough and mean right now.*

I was certainly more judgmental of her: *I'm so mad at my mother for not letting me see* The Exorcist! I lamented. *Everybody else gets to go, but not me. I think she's just acting that way to impress Carol Ann's mother. They both try to act like model little mothers. Bull Crap! I'm gonna ask her again!*

This was also when I developed an obsession with Richard Pryor, shortly after my cousin Curtis took me to see the concert film *Wattstax*, which included Pryor's stand-up performance. I carried a picture of him in my wallet and regularly rifled through my sister Deborah's record collection, sneaking and listening to Pryor's stand-up albums, filled as they were with "blue humor," half wanting to get caught. I never did.

Despite my quasi-rebellion, it would take yet more to shake off my mother's generosity. And some good spells did appear just in time to mitigate the rough patches. *I think '74 will be better financially for this family,* I wrote with confidence. Things did pick up enough for me to get my own telephone line (with an easy-to-remember number: 861-8666). Also, that spring my mother treated me and my cousin Lisa to a Washington, DC, trip to visit relatives; I recall this sophisticated teenager, Joanie, who sat with boredom watching *The Sound of Music* in a movie theater alongside us and her mother; later she took me and Lisa with her to hang out on the lawn of the Washington Monument. There she danced to the Isley Brothers' "Summer Breeze" with other cool-looking teens, the sun setting behind them, this giant obelisk reaching into the sky; she was dazzling, a pot-smoking black hippie in a flowy midi dress and velvet choker, and as I watched Joanie, with her perfectly round Afro, I thought she was the freest spirit I'd ever seen, not unlike a modern-day Josephine Baker. Was this when I started formulating a way to live a life far from the Numbers and from Detroit? Inspired by that visit, I returned home and began writing my first fictional story, in cursive, on one of Mama's lined legal pads used for the Numbers. I don't recall the story's plot, or its title, but I still remember its first line:

The scent of cherry blossoms permeated the air as Percy Jordan walked along the streets of Washington, DC. I read Mama the entire fifteen-page story, which I referred to as "my book"; she nodded her approval.

As I was fantasizing about leaving home, Detroit was getting its first black mayor amid enormous excitement and expectation. Diana Ross flew in from California to perform at Coleman Young's inauguration, and Young was promising a new era for the city, what was being called *economic revitalization.* Black folks, meanwhile, were genuinely excited about the idea of black political control in a majority-black metropolis; and the word *renaissance* got thrown around a lot, given that the massive Renaissance Center, conceived by Henry Ford II, was already under construction downtown.

And in other good news for the city, as the mammoth RenCen was rising, busily employing thousands of workers, a federal appeals court had just ruled that in order to achieve racial balance and desegregate public schools, some black students in Detroit must be bused to the suburbs, and many more white suburban students bused to Detroit. The judge noted that the district boundaries, drawn along racial lines, were unconstitutional. His ruling meant that integration, rather than racial isolation, was on the horizon. We needed it. In the few short years since I'd won the Heritage Day award, white flight had been so complete across Detroit that such a day of diversity would be impossible to pull off. But now, white residents, many of whom had fled the city after the 1967 uprising, would find it far harder to abandon Detroit financially, psychologically, and literally, since their children would be enrolled in its public schools. To avoid that fate, whites would have to move deeper into suburban or rural townships, much farther from Detroit proper, and its industry.

Sadly, within months of Young's taking office, the Supreme Court agreed to take on the case, Milliken v. Bradley, and in a landmark decision described by a public policy scholar as "one of its most villainous," determine the fate of urban schools across the nation. The highest court in the land overturned the earlier ruling and upheld the city's segregated school districts. Of course, white businesses and residents and investors found incentive in the ruling to keep their resources focused on the surrounding suburbs. This while urban Detroit was already facing economic decay, with its auto industry feeling the brunt of the OPEC oil embargo. Hence, Mayor Young's efforts toward renewal and equality for the city's black residents were both thwarted. Young himself later admitted: "I knew...that my fortune was the direct result of my city's misfortune....I was taking over the administration of Detroit because the white people didn't want the damn thing anymore. They were getting out, more than happy to turn over their troubles to some black sucker like me."

Those disappearing jobs were not coming back. Folks *needed* to hit the number. And it didn't help that during his inauguration speech, Young made the famous comment that would haunt him throughout his mayoralty: "I issue a warning to all dope pushers, rip-off artists and muggers. It's time to leave Detroit—hit the road. Hit Eight Mile Road. I don't give a damn if they are black or white, or if they wear *Superfly* suits or blue uniforms with silver badges. Hit the road." Because Eight Mile Road divided the city proper from the suburbs, many white folks believed he was telling *them* to get out of black Detroit.

Amid the upheaval, rumors spread that the state might launch a daily lottery game, and lottery commission officials in Lansing didn't deny it: "The Bureau continues to analyze the possibility of a daily lottery operation which might, *as was hoped by some when we began operations, provide direct competition for illegal gambling*," stated the Bureau of State Lottery's first-year report. Yet, at the same time, there seemed no urgency to change what worked: "The Lottery's primary objective," noted the report, "is revenue." And there was plenty of revenue. By the end of its first year, the state lottery had sold over 271 million weekly tickets across the state, including in rural counties. The Michigan lottery lauded itself as the most successful of all state lotteries, one that operated with "integrity and dignity." But despite the legal lottery's obvious success, many black residents held to their beliefs that Mayor Young would protect the city's Numbers racket. Young was born and bred in Detroit, raised in its culturally rich Black Bottom, a former vocal union boss, and a fierce defender of the city's African-American traditions and culture. He'd most likely once played the Numbers himself.

But even a sympathetic mayor was no match for the drumbeat of unprecedented coverage and support by the press, and by the lottery commission, that worked to portray the lottery as the positive alternative to the Numbers. Gone were the exposés on how Numbers gambling was a fraudulent evil, indulged in by poor, ignorant black people. Now the *Detroit Free Press* and other newspapers lauded the state's lottery betting. Stories of winners were pushed by the lottery bureau itself, to prove the lottery was fair, and of course to encourage ticket sales. Profiles featured the first million-dollar winner, Hermus Millsaps, a white man who worked for Chrysler, described as "an excellent winner." The second million-dollar winner was a forty-seven-year-old Greek immigrant named Christeen Ferizis, who didn't speak English and had come to America with her husband eight years before to "get rich."

Despite its looming presence throughout those early years, Mama didn't reveal any major concern about the legal lottery. Our lifestyle remained intact. She was, in fact, now officially raising her toddler grandson. His father, my brother, Anthony, was struggling with his heroin addiction—in and out of a private drug treatment program that my mother found for him. Tony's mother, Renita, decided the best place for her son was with his grandmother. "I just wanted better for Tony," she explains. "And I knew he would get it from her. She exposed him to things that he would never have been exposed to had he been with me." She adds: "He's everything I wanted him to be, and it's all because of her, really." Tony certainly had the best back then: educational and imaginative toys from F.A.O. Schwarz—a stuffed horse and buggy with actual reins, which Tony furiously pedaled up and down our driveway, comes to mind; stimulating activities and fun trips; and attendance at a quality preschool called Buttons and Bows.

Mama also continued to travel with my stepfather, Burt. When they vacationed in Aruba, she sent me a postcard that read, *Hi, wish I could stay longer. I like it very much. The weather is so nice, 86 degrees and it stays like this. I am going on a tour Monday. Aruba is an island in the Caribbean controlled by the Dutch. Love, "Mama."* She spent some of that vacation working on her book and, of course, shopping. Mama returned with a pretty fourteen-carat tricolor gold braided necklace and matching bracelet, which she gave to me. (I was astonished that gold could be yellow *and* white and rose.) Also during that time, she and Uncle John bought a horse together, paying $1,500 for the Thoroughbred; soon enough, Mama won $10,000 "right quick and everything," as Uncle John put it. He and Fannie enjoyed watching their horse compete at Hazel Park Raceway before eventually selling it. I remember a photo of brother and sister in the winner's circle, standing before their horse, Uncle John also its triumphant trainer.

Mama also wasn't done beautifying our home. I recently found among her belongings a telegram sent from a saleswoman at Wiggs Furniture store in Bloomfield Hills, who resorted to writing because the main telephone line was always busy, an occupational hazard in our household in the days before call waiting. She wrote:

Dear Mrs. Drumwright:

I do believe you are the busiest gal in town, as I simply cannot get through on your phone....Please call me at your convenience, and I will be happy to help you. Your furniture is to be shipped in 3 weeks.

Polly Garland

My mother had decided to redecorate and transform our living room into a blue oasis. She removed the gold carpet and the furnishings that had followed us from Broadstreet and replaced it all with powder-blue walls, sky-blue custom drapes offset by pale blue sheers, and royal-blue carpet flecked with shades of midnight and cobalt. She chose a sinewy cerulean crushed velvet sectional sofa with circular button pillows; a cream coffee table with a cushioned top in the same color as the sofa; a light blue French Provincial desk and matching chair; cornflower-blue-and-white-striped Louis XV chairs; and a baby-blue Tiffany-style floor lamp.

"Ah, the blue living room," sighs my cousin Lisa. "Everything in the whole room was blue, which kind of sounds tacky when I think about it, but when I picture it, it was very elegant and regal and timeless." Lisa ponders how my mother might've pulled it off: "Where she developed this sense of style I don't know. A lot of black folks who had first-generation money during that time, they chose things that were gaudy, overdone. But her style was sophisticated and understated."

I loved our sprawling blue room, found it both calming and bold, a perfect extension of Mama. That signature living room was not unlike our home's unique exterior, with its giant picture window and its gray brick against black-and-white double front doors, giant circular brass knobs in their centers (reminding me of the mansion doors in *The Beverly Hillbillies*). The house stood out from the rest of the modest redbrick houses on the block, and to me it gave us yet another layer of distinction.

The best indicator that her business remained secure was Mama's continued giving. And during those years, my cousin Lisa says, *she* was a prime beneficiary. Her example involves one of the key ways my mother showed her generosity, via gifts of clothing.

"I was twelve or thirteen, and I'd hit puberty," recalls Lisa. "I'd had a bad case of chicken pox, and had a lot of scars, and a lot of acne; and my hair wasn't right and boys didn't like me. I felt ugly and insecure. It was not a cute time." She pauses. "And your mom took me shopping. She bought me my first real outfit that I loved." Lisa remembers that it came from Bonwit Teller or Saks. "And it was a white cotton summer pantsuit with all this fancy embroidery on the lapel and the yoke of the jacket, and on the back of the pants; and she got me a pair of those sandals that strapped all the way up your legs. It was my first semi-grown-up girl outfit."

Lisa goes on: "During that same shopping trip there were some cottony jeans that I liked and I picked them in let's say, navy blue, but she ended up getting me the blue, the red, the yellow, like four colors of the same pants, and I was like, 'Oh my God, I'm going to be so sharp!' There was no regard for price or anything; she just let me pick out what I wanted. And she didn't make me feel like, 'You better take care of this, now don't get it dirty, you know how much this cost, dah, dah, dah,' which was the situation at home."

Looking back, Lisa realizes it was no coincidence that Aunt Fa, as she and her siblings called my mother, took her shopping for a new outfit just when her parents' marriage was collapsing and she, a pubescent girl, was in desperate need of attention and affection.

"She always had a way in her, not direct, but some indirect approach to soothe me," recalls Lisa. "And make me feel like, 'I am special, and I'm going to be special.'"

It was a special time in many ways for my family, with me and Tony living at home with Mama and Burt; I have memories of trips up north, the four of us going to apple-pick, do overnight stays in my cousins' camper trailer. And the rich pop and soul tunes of the era provided a perfect soundtrack. Even though everyone was losing their mind over the Jackson 5's "Dancing Machine" after Michael did the robot on *Soul Train*, I preferred the slower songs that, as a brooding teenager, resonated with me: Elton John's mournful "Don't Let the Sun Go Down on Me," the sensuous crooning of Minnie Ripperton's "Loving You," with its risqué line, "Making love to you is all I wanna do," and especially Stevie Wonder's lyrically complex singles. Stevie's mother lived on the same block of Greenlawn as Lisa's family, and she and Lisa's mother were friends; she gave Aunt Gladys an early release of Stevie's masterful album *Fufillingness' First Finale,* and I spent many days at their home listening to the funky "Boogie On Reggae Woman" and the more political "You Haven't Done Nothin'" blasting from the living room stereo. But my favorites were Stevie's somber songs: "Heaven Is Ten Zillion Light Years Away" and "They Won't Go When I Go."

Josephine Baker died in spring of 1975, the morning after an extraordinary comeback performance in Paris, just as I was completing ninth grade. I saw her sudden death as a sign, a cautionary tale of time running out, of needing to define what I wanted to do with my life. When I entered Cass Technical High School that fall, I was no longer helping to take customers' bets, or calling them to share the winning numbers each evening, or looking for hits. I was too busy, either at school, where I was on the newspaper staff, or at my part-time job at Winkelman's department store at the mall, or hanging out with friends, often at parties. I was decidedly *not* interested in the family business, and it was easy to distance myself from the Numbers. The world was too big for that life. I had other plans, as I half-jokingly wrote in my diary: *I could make modeling a career if I wanted to. But I'm going to be a phyciatrist (sic). I never told you this, dear Diary, 'cause I can't spell it!*

I always had some activity or event or rehearsal after school—pep rally, bowling team, *Technician* staff meeting, fashion show rehearsal—which my sisters viewed as a ploy, a way to be too busy either to help out with the business, as they all did, or to do household chores. They weren't wrong. I liked socializing and having new experiences away from home, "out ripping and running," as Mama called it. But she let me be. She never said "It's your job to help with the business." She didn't really need my help, with other family members and hired help around, but the point was that she decidedly let me steer clear of the Numbers, while supporting my love of school. "She acts like the doors of Cass Tech can't open if she's not there," she'd say about my spending so much time at school. I could tell in the way my mother said it that she approved, was proud of me.

I also preferred to largely ignore our family business because I was becoming more aware of its negative connotations. I hadn't read those derogatory articles in the newspaper, but I *was* listening to what others were saying. My friend Stephanie once told me: "Our neighbors are into the Numbers, and I can't stand them. They're into illegal stuff, yet they think they're better than everybody." She had no idea, and of course I kept quiet. And one of the most popular songs of the era was Harold Melvin and the Blue Notes' "Bad Luck." A verse from that song went, *Played a number 'cause that number's hot. But the bookies get you for every cent you've got. Bad luck! That's what you got, that's what you got.* I hated the implication that my mother was in any way ripping off people.

While I wasn't interested in the Numbers per se, I *was* interested in the ancillary world created by the Numbers. The best example of this was that in eleventh grade, I chose to write a major research paper on dreams. I was obviously interested in dreams because of the central role they played in our household, but I knew I couldn't reference our ubiquitous dream books. I turned to my sister Deborah, known for her brilliance. She thought my topic was great and gave me her copy of Freud's *The Interpretation of Dreams,* but the late-nineteenth-century language was a bit over my head.

More helpful was Mama's book *Edgar Cayce on Dreams.* She was a fan of Cayce, known as "America's sleeping clairvoyant," who gave "life readings" and taught followers how to understand their unconscious dream worlds in order to gain greater happiness. He was at the height of his popularity throughout the first half of the twentieth century, and so Mama grew up hearing and reading about him; interestingly, he was also a "mystic" healer with his own occult philosophy. Mama was among the millions who believed Cayce was truly gifted, using his abilities to diagnose and help tens of thousands of sick people; yet he never really profited from his gift, and that only enhanced my mother's admiration for him. From her paperback copy of *On Dreams,* I quoted Cayce for my research paper: "In dreams, people experience for themselves every important kind of psychic phenomenon, and every level of helpful psychological and religious counsel." I also used Mama's *Complete Works of William Shakespeare,* with its gilt-edged pages and attached red-ribbon bookmark, to recount the famous dream scenes in *Macbeth, Romeo and Juliet,* and *A Midsummer Night's Dream.*

But the majority of my research came from a set of books on our den bookshelves' top shelf: *Man, Myth and Magic: An Illustrated Encyclopedia of the Supernatural.* This twenty-four-volume collection, published in 1970, covered every possible topic, including the obscure: exorcism, Indian snake charmers, hypnosis, tarot, demonology, UFOs, zombies, paganism, telekinesis. These books captivated me in part because their dark subject matter also slightly frightened me. Each nine-by-twelve-inch black-bound hardcover volume had color illustrations throughout, and very provocative cover art. The cover that I clearly remember was a scary funhouse image of a girl's face and breasts, eerily distorted as multiple dark eyes stared out at you. These books' popularity is perhaps not surprising, given that fascination with the occult was a real craze in the seventies; yet, I admired my mother, and still do, for owning the *Man, Myth and Magic* collection. Her willingness to explore the occult flew in the face of her own and nearly all her friends' Christian beliefs, and that seemed brave to me, that she apparently saw no contradiction between her own faith and the supernatural world. (Her livelihood, after all, was based on a game of hunches and premonitions.)

In fact, Mama's influence was all over my schoolwork. For

my econ class, she let me bring in all her credit cards, which I taped to a poster board as part of an oral presentation on the "Pros and Cons of Revolving Credit." Senior year, for my television production class, I recorded a "how-to" show on making a witch's potion, complete with Mama's lucky candles, a cauldron she'd found for me at an estate sale, and my on-air script material taken from her *Man, Myth and Magic* encyclopedia's entry on witchcraft.

Another defining experience of my teen years was the elaborate, fun Sweet Sixteen party Mama threw for me at the Radisson Cadillac Hotel downtown. She had given me an option: a new car, or a party. Daddy was incredulous at my choice, but I chose the party because, as I told him: "I can get a car anytime, but I'll only be sixteen once." I planned every aspect of the party myself and wore a sky-blue spaghetti-strapped silky Qiana gown with a ruffle across the V neckline. Nearly a hundred guests attended, and my cousin Curtis was the official photographer. I had four hostesses—including two cousins, my oldest friend, and my closest friend—a DJ and a sheet cake with blue roses that I cut to the tune of Average White Band's hit song "Cut the Cake."

I begged my father to attend my party, but he claimed he had "nothing to wear." Truth be told, he'd become something of a recluse over the years, restricting himself to the nearby party store, the check-cashing place, and a neighborhood grocer. I knew without it being said that he didn't feel as though he fit in my mother's world anymore, he who had long since moved from Broadstreet and now lived in a small flat, on a modest disability income. Besides, Daddy had no desire to be in the same room with Burt, Fannie's new husband.

(Even though she'd been married to my stepfather nine years by then, my father always considered himself her only real husband.) I was sad for him, sad that my wanting him there wasn't enough to get him to come. But I didn't fully understand just how usurped he felt until days later. I showed him the write-up about my party in the society pages of *The Michigan Chronicle*. He squinted at the small print and read out loud, *"Bridgett Davis, the daughter of Mrs. Burtram Robinson and John Davis, was surrounded by all of her favorite people Saturday, May 22, at the Detroit Cadillac Hotel when she celebrated her Sweet Sixteenth birthday."* He looked genuinely surprised. "You had them put my name down?" he asked.

"Of course," I said. "You're my father, aren't you?"

He looked over at me and nodded, and that was when I saw it in his eyes, the fear that I'd claim another man over him as my father. I want to believe I hugged Daddy in that moment, as we stood together in front of the party store where we bought extra copies of the *Chronicle*. I'd like to think we spent the rest of that day together.

I often chose time with Mama over Daddy. Apart from our movie-watching and shopping and hair-scratching rituals, I looked forward to going out to eat with her, another of our favorite pastimes. In fact, vivid in my memory is one of our last mother-daughter outings before Rita returned home: visiting the brand-new Fairlane Town Center mall in Dearborn and dining at Olga's Kitchen, a new kind of eatery where you could get a souvlaki-style sandwich filled with seasoned lamb or beef and wrapped in Olga Bread (a sweeter, chewier, and softer version of traditional pita). We added to that curly fries and a delicious Greek salad with feta, and Olga's Kitchen quickly became our favorite place to eat. Olga was a friend of Mama's friend Miss Lucille, who introduced the two women to each other. It was fun to dine and have the restaurant's namesake come over to our table to personally greet us. I knew too that Mama admired Olga, felt a kindred spirit with this Greek-American woman who had, like Mama, launched her own successful business against the odds. But of course, Olga would never know that she and Mama shared a similar story as entrepreneurial women.

My mother did not discuss sex with me. But she did give counsel indirectly. Just as she'd placed a complete set of books about puberty on my bed when I was eleven, as a way to prepare me for menstruation, she now had her way of making sure I got some sex advice. She'd use that well-worn phrase, "Why would a man buy the cow if he can get the milk for free?" and add that "gals gapping open their legs" are loose and "too easy" and never get a man's respect. I took to heart a comment she made within my earshot around the time I entered high school: "The way I see it," she said, "anyone who thinks she's old enough to be doing it is old enough to figure out how to protect herself." I took this as implicit permission to get birth control, which I did from the Planned Parenthood in Southfield.

She also gave out some choice advice on men. Three things my mother said stayed with me throughout my own years of dating and relationships: (1) "Any time the King of England could give up his throne for a woman (Edward VIII and Wallis Simpson), don't ever let a man tell you what he can't do for you." (2) "Pick a man up out of the gutter and clean him up, every time he looks at you, you'll remind him of that gutter." (3) "You don't need to change for a man because if he loves *you*, he'll love whatever you're into."

During one of our times together, when I was seventeen, my mother talked to me about the business in a candid way she hadn't before. She said that she'd been turning in most of her books to Mr. Taylor, the big Numbers man, and she was ready to once again take back the business in order to increase her profits; but now she wanted to employ all her children in the daily operation, give us each a salary, perhaps even open an actual office outside the home. My responsibilities would take no more than two hours a day, she promised. I responded with total support, despite my actual lack of interest in the Numbers. I knew that if my mother was asking for my help, she needed it. And I was anxious to do whatever I could to take some of the pressure off her.

Funny, while my mother most likely did take back her business, become "the house" again, she never did follow through on getting the outside office, nor did I start officially working for her. Instead, Rita decided to return to Detroit rather than stay in Nashville, which she'd done briefly after graduating from college. My sister took over helping out, from taking folks' numbers over the phone to running tapes on the weekend to looking for hits. I was probably relieved, but what I remember is the jealousy I felt once Rita and Mama resumed their close relationship. Everyone always spoke about how tight they were, what a devoted daughter Rita was to our mother. They were seen as alike in so many ways, both born under the zodiac sign of Taurus, with similar tastes and similar points of view; and both of them could captivate listeners in the way they told a juicy story. Rita and Mama were engaging and funny and entertaining to be around. I was a moody Gemini, quiet, introspective, in my head a lot. I felt that the experiences I'd shared with Mama in Rita's absence now seemed unimportant, as though that part of her personality wasn't the real her. Even our ritual of watching old movies disappeared. The local Channel 7 TV station had shifted the time by thirty minutes and now aired *The 4 O'Clock Movie,* too early for me to get home from school. Even on the days I was free to share that ritual with Mama, she seemed not to be interested anyway.

Yet on an ordinary March day, as I was washing dishes, I looked out the kitchen window and saw Mama pull into our driveway behind the wheel of a brand-new canary-yellow Sunbird. As soon as I saw it, I knew that car was mine. I'd spotted it at Porterfield Wilson's Pontiac dealership on Livernois (just a couple of blocks from our home) when Mama and I were together and made mention of how cute it was. When Lula noted to Fannie that she'd told me to choose between a party and a car, Mama said, "The other morning, I watched her stand at the bus stop across the street in the freezing cold for over an hour, trying to get to school; that fool didn't even come back in the house; I figured somebody like that needs a car." I loved my Sunbird, with its white leather interior and sunroof, and I tooled around in that car for many years.

Two weeks after my seventeenth birthday, five years after the weekly lottery had been legalized, the rumors finally came true: on Monday, June 6, 1977, Michigan's Bureau of State Lottery introduced a new game called the Daily, effectively a carbon copy of the Numbers, i.e., a complete and wholesale rip-off of the informal lottery that black men and women had created, developed and grown into a multimillion-dollar underground enterprise. Unlike with the weekly lottery game, now players could select their *own* three-digit number, play it straight or boxed, with drawings every day, six days a week, Monday through Saturday. And the payout odds were, just like with the Numbers, 500 to 1, so that a fifty-cent bet on a number played straight could get you $250, and $1 could get you $500. The state also allowed a winner to "play today and cash in tonight" for all winnings up to $550, at any Daily sales location. This made the state's quick payout competitive with the Numbers'.

There'd been warning signs that this day was coming. Michigan's lottery commission had claimed when the lottery became legal that their weekly drawings weren't trying to compete with the "daily, quick action numbers racket," yet ticket agents surely hoped the state *would* be competition. In a photo from 1972, a smiling black woman holds her lottery tickets, standing in front of a party store sign that reads: THE LEGAL NUMBER MAN ... LOTTERY TICKETS.

As similar as the two games were, the biggest distinction was that the Daily winning number was broadcast live each evening at seven-thirty on WWJ-TV, Channel 4.

On day one, the three-and-a-half-by-two-inch tickets for Michigan's new Daily game went on sale at 300 computerized sales terminals, all within a ninety-mile radius of Detroit. Suddenly, everywhere you turned, you could buy a "Daily 3" ticket—at a party store, drugstore, gas station, bar, or liquor store, at the airport, and from vending machines. Lottery officials heavily promoted the state's competition to the Numbers in the major newspapers with full-page ads, using rip-off slogans: "Got a Hunch? Play the Daily" and "Pick Your Own

Number and Play." One ad even offered suggestions: "Play your birthdate, telephone number, bowling score, or street address. It's your choice." The lottery's hip new slogan was: "Every Day's a Play Day." And the state made sure it was easy to play: you could even buy tickets up to six days in advance.

Turns out, black folks *liked* playing the lottery. It did take away the stigma and worry of gambling outside the law, since you could now play your numbers right out in the open. It also pulled in some religious people who rationalized that a game sanctioned by the state couldn't be a sin, now could it? More importantly, it gave myriad players relief from the widely known fact that certain illegal numbers were fixed by the Dagos, i.e., the Mafia. It alleviated the fear that a winning number could be changed at the last minute, or "cut" (its payout reduced), or a hit left unpaid. As one man told a reporter: "You know when you win because you can watch it on TV with everyone else."

And the very first week of the Daily's existence, Skippy's Candle and Incense Company craftily published and distributed *Skippy's Lucky Lottery Dream Book* (copyright 1977), which flew off the shelves of party and novelty stores all over the city. From the beginning, sales of Daily tickets averaged an astonishing $1.3 million a week.

Now I wonder, did Mama see this coming? Because if she had, would she have bought, just months before, a brand-new car for me? Our phones rang a little less that summer—just as I'd set my sights on a private women's college five hundred miles away.

PART III

Living Takes Guts

Eight

Daddy (John T.) on Broadstreet, 1960s

In the early weeks of the state's bright and shiny new Daily
game, most of my mother's customers did remain loyal to her,
as she'd predicted. The state required you to pay taxes on your
winnings; Fannie did not. The state required you to bet at least
fifty cents on a number; with Fannie, you could play for as little as a quarter. The state demanded cash on the spot for each
number played; Fannie allowed her good customers to play
on credit and pay at the end of the week, and even offered
a discount. State lottery winnings above $550 required filling
out a claim form and waiting for a check in the mail; Fannie
paid off big hits in cash, the next day. Besides, she had genuine
and often warm relationships with the people who turned their
numbers in to her; Fannie asked about your health, your children, your latest dream. She trusted you, and you trusted her.

Black folks had many, many reasons *not* to trust the government. Few believed that the state's revenue from Daily
ticket sales would make its way from Lansing back to Detroit.

That certainly hadn't happened so far with the weekly lottery or with the plethora of one-dollar Instant Games. The nearly $300 million in lottery revenue that already fattened the state's coffers had gone into Michigan's "General Fund," and Detroiters assumed those resources had largely benefited the state's suburban, Upper Peninsula, and rural citizens. Why would the new lottery game's profits be any different?

Better to play your numbers with Fannie. At least those dollars circulated throughout your own community.

By the end of 1977, the Daily had reached $2 million a week in sales; clearly, my mother saw some of her customers siphoned off, saw others dividing their gambling budget between the legal and "street" numbers, as they were now known. Still, many folks were creatures of habit and loyalty and continued to play their numbers with Fannie.

Besides, the state was no match for the social component of the street numbers. My mother had a circle of friends and acquaintances that had grown wide and deep over the years, thanks to her life in the Numbers. A range of folks from, as they say, all walks of life came through our home to play with Mama. A few of her customers were my favorites. I had intellectual discussions with Carlos, a schoolteacher who quoted philosophers; I learned French phrases from Peter Gunn, a mechanic who'd become fluent while stationed in France as a soldier; and I discussed vintage designer fashions with Beverly, who'd been a well-dressed, high-class "lady of the evening" in her youth.

My mother entered the new year—her twentieth anniversary as a number runner—with her core customer base intact. I now suspect she was nervous, but she didn't show it, at least not to me. At the time, my sole choice for college was Spelman, the premier black women's college in Atlanta, and I'd already been accepted through early admission. Spelman's tuition was twice that of in-state schools such as the University of Michigan and Michigan State, yet it didn't even occur to me to ask Mama whether my choice was affordable. I'd never had to ask such questions, and Mama didn't bring up the costs, so I assumed I'd be going to Spelman. She even suggested I consider other private schools. "You're getting letters from all these top-notch colleges," she noted. "You could at least apply to some of them."

But I'd made up my mind, and I entered the new year anxious to leave home and get to Atlanta. It didn't matter that I'd never set foot in that particular Southern city. Detroit was dubbed Murder Capital USA in the 1970s for a reason: In 1977, there'd been 853 murders, a rate that had quadrupled in a decade. Added to that were over 3,500 reported "forcible" rapes and a staggering 23,900 robberies. On the one hand, I felt somewhat inured from the city's violence, caught up in my sheltered teenage life, which largely revolved around listening to the great seventies music spilling out from everyone's cassette players and radios. (I distinctly remember my cousin Jewell playing Steely Dan's *Aja* album on the record player in her small bedroom, hipping me to this astonishingly groovy white band.) I hadn't even known, for instance, about the "Livernois Incident," a near-riot narrowly averted just two blocks from my home the summer before tenth grade, when a white bar owner shot a teenage black boy in the back of the head for tampering with a car in the bar's parking lot; the bar owner was taken into custody for the murder and released on a $500 bond, which prompted hundreds of protesting blacks to pour into the streets, some setting the bar on fire before Mayor Young stood atop the hood of a car and calmed down the crowd.

Yet the fact of the city's high crime rate found its way into my everyday life. Whenever I pulled into our driveway, I followed the required ritual of tooting the car horn so my mother could come to the side door and watch as I got out of the car and entered the house. I never, ever walked Detroit's streets after dark. And I remained relieved that my mother carried a gun in her purse, and had another in the house, because I believed she needed them. She often said, in response to why she didn't want me out late or going to a specific area, "It's just too dangerous out there." I felt this pervasive sense of danger ever lurking, confirmed by gruesome local news reports as well as the curfew imposed one whole summer requiring "all people under eighteen in before 10 p.m.," with police patrolling neighborhoods to enforce it. I never felt I could fully relax or feel truly safe in Detroit, and I was ready to say goodbye to all that.

Honestly, I was *also* ready to be away from ringing phones and the daily tension in anticipation of customers hitting the number. I wanted to feel free from a life tied to a three-digit fate, and graduating from high school was my ticket out. Mind you, until then there was much to look forward to: senior trip to Toronto, graduation photos, and of course prom. I was determined to find the perfect dress.

As soon as I received the proofs of my graduation pictures, I took them over to Daddy's. As he looked at each pose, I noticed that he had to sit very close to the lamplight, the high blood pressure having worsened his vision. He was now wearing thick prescription sunglasses, both to offset the glare of bright lights and to help him see better. He chose a double-exposed image of me, the one with both a front view and a side profile; I ordered that one in eleven by fourteen, as he requested.

Before my graduation photos came, Daddy was admitted to Ann Arbor's VA hospital. Having suffered with hypertension his entire adult life, he'd once told me that his doctor seldom bothered to check his pressure levels using a regular cuff, that was how high his baseline numbers were. Besides his doctor's advice to avoid too much salt, little was done to treat my father's condition. Now Daddy's pressure had quickly accelerated, causing dizziness and difficulty breathing, and he'd taken himself to the hospital. On one of my visits, he told me that he'd had two mini-strokes since being admitted. I didn't see how this could be true—*Who gets worse when they're in the hospital?* I thought in my naïveté—and I tried to quiet him. He got upset and yelled, "Listen to me! I'm telling you, I've had two strokes!" Looking back, it haunts me that I didn't do anything with that knowledge, didn't advocate for him and demand proof that the doctors aggressively treat his condition. Back then doctors only managed to control 10 percent of all patients' hypertension, and studies now show that African-Americans, who suffered more frequently and severely from the disease, got inferior treatment in hospitals overall. I recall how a nurse said to me, "He's a very sick man. Why didn't someone encourage him to lose weight, with such high blood pressure?" More guilt.

If it was up to anyone to do more, it was me. I'd spent every day of the first nine years of my life with Daddy, sharing a close intimacy: sleeping atop his back; his saving the last swig of Pepsi-Cola for me; sticking out his arm and pointing to each scar as he told me the story behind it. After my parents' divorce, I spent many, many weekends with my father, playing cards and Chinese checkers, watching favorite TV shows, going to the movies, walking hand in hand to the corner store—still a daddy's girl and in many ways the center of his world. But I was now in deep denial. When Rita asked would I go on my senior trip to Toronto as planned if Daddy was still in the hospital, I said, "He won't be." She said, "But what if he doesn't get better?" I said, "He will." She let it go.

On another visit to the hospital, Daddy pulled me close to him and said, "Be a good girl." I nodded my promise. Then he said, "And tell Fannie that I love her." Again, I nodded.

Two days later, on a cold, wintry evening in March, I called home from my salesgirl job at Northland Mall and asked Rita, "How's Daddy doing today?"

"About the same," she said. "When are you coming home?"

"When I get off work," I snapped. It seemed like such an unnecessary question.

But as I pulled up to the house that evening, too many cars were parked both in the driveway and out front, along Seven Mile Road. As soon as I opened the front door, my aunt Florence greeted me in tears, pulling me into her arms. More arms grabbed at me, my sisters' all at once. "He didn't make it," said Dianne. "John T. didn't make it."

That night, I wept in my bed for hours, Jewell handing me

Kleenex and, grieving herself, unable to say much of comfort; I cried until I was weak with exhaustion. Suddenly, I remembered the scrapbook I'd created when I was a child, capturing a spring of playing card games and tic-tac-toe with Daddy during my weekend visits. *I will begin this book by showing you the numerous amount of games my father and I played in the year 1971,* I wrote. *We began playing dots...* I taped pages into the scrapbook, showing a plethora of tic-tac-toe and Chinese Dots and S.O.S. games played. (*Daddy loves S.O.S. So do I!*) Atop one page I wrote, *Then we fell for Gin Rummy 500. We love 500 so much we decided to keep a record of all the games we play.* I filled the scrapbook with our game scores, one column headed with my name, the other with *John.* I won a lot, and when we didn't finish a game, I noted why below the score: *We quit, so nobody won.* Candid Camera *is on, and we want to watch it.* And: *We had to stop because* Flip Wilson *is on.* And: *We stopped to watch* The Greatest Show on Earth. On another scrapbook page, this one capturing a score that included a third player, a family friend named Gregory, I wrote: *We didn't finish because I had a stomach ache.* On still another I recorded the time: *At 4:05 in the morning.* I noted too that we played on Mother's Day 1971, yet I didn't mention that it was also my mother's birthday that year.

On that night when Daddy died, I quickly rose from my bed and scoured through my closet until I found the green-covered scrapbook on a shelf, held it to my chest, and rushed into the living room, where my mother sat with a circle of visiting relatives and friends. Crying, I thrust it at her. "What do I do with this now?"

She was startled as she paged through the scrapbook,

unaware until that moment that I'd captured my childhood visits with Daddy this way. "Save it," she told me. "It's really good you have it."

"I just hope he knew how much I loved him," I blurted out, suddenly stricken with recent memories of every time I chose to talk on the phone with my boyfriend instead of spending time with Daddy, every time I promised to come over and then let my social life get in the way, every time I gave Daddy a late Christmas or birthday gift out of carelessness.

Mama looked up at me, and as I write this I can still feel her dark eyes on me, her voice steady. "He knew, Bridget. He knew. How could he not?"

My aunt and uncle joined in to reassure me, as did Mama's best friend, Lula. *He loved the ground you walked on. You were his baby...Crazy about you...No doubt in hell that he knew you loved him. Don't you never say nothing like that again...Honey, wasn't nobody closer to her daddy than you. You were his life.*

Their words just made me feel worse. I was devastated, my grief thick and impenetrable. I felt I'd failed my father somehow. And when I found the letter I'd written to him when I was eight, tucked inside his wallet and worn with age, I cried uncontrollably.

In the days that followed, my sister Deborah and I hovered over Mama's blue desk and together, his oldest and his youngest, wrote a tribute poem, "In Remembrance of our Daddy":

You were our father, so gentle, loving & strong
Your grasp on life made you tolerant of its wrongs
The simpler things of life never made you sad

Despite the occasional lonely hours you might have had
There never was a crisis you couldn't joke your way
  through
So you kept on smiling, no matter what beset you
Though now we wish sometimes you had, our time you
  never demanded
You knew we had our own lives, and for that you were
  understanding
The everlasting impression you inscribed on our hearts
Is so intense, that for us, memories of you will never
  depart

The funeral procession left from our house on Seven Mile, and I remember my stepfather, Burt, standing on the porch, watching as we all entered the limo. "I turned to him. "Are you coming?" I asked. "No, Chicken," he said. "You don't need me there. I'll be here when you get back."

At the funeral, Mama holds me in her arms, and I bury my head in her soft bosom throughout the entire service, wanting to crawl into her lap. I am seventeen and six inches taller than her, yet my mother holds me tight like a baby, pressing her arm tighter around me every time I sigh.

But when we view Daddy's body lying in his white casket, dressed in a white suit, Mama stands off to the side, tears falling. Stunned to see her cry, I go up to her, and she says, "Nobody even thinks about how I feel."

When my graduation photo chosen by Daddy arrived, I couldn't bear to look at it. I gave it to my brother, Anthony.

Several days later, in my journal I wrote, *I dreamed about Daddy last night…he looked at me with those eyes. I think about his eyes all the time. That searching, rambling, wandering look they had when he was in the hospital. It was as if he was really trying hard to show us he was okay, really trying hard to make it—to live for us.*

With signs of spring after a long, hard winter, Mama decided to treat Rita and me to a weekend in New York. It was our first trip to the Big Apple, and I fell in love with the city immediately. I'd learned about New York from watching Robert Redford and Jane Fonda's *Barefoot in the Park* as a young teen, and had decided I'd eventually live in one of those crazy walk-up apartments with bizarre neighbors, very near Washington Square Park. Now, in New York for three days before I left for college, Rita and I got to see our first Broadway musical, *The Wiz,* went dancing at a disco, walked for hours through the Village, and shopped along Fifth Avenue. On one of our shopping sprees, we passed by a stunning dress undulating in a store window: slate and light gray with small pink roses, the dress had a belted waist, a blouson bodice, and a split up one side. Its fabric design was exquisite, shimmering in the light with raw and refined silk stripes, gold threads woven throughout. The dress cost $350, more than I'd ever spent on one item of clothing. When I tried it on, it fit perfectly, and I called home to ask Mama's permission to purchase it. "That's your spending money," she said. "Spend it how you see fit." I bought the dress. For the longest time, the running joke with my friend Stephanie was that I was the only girl she knew who managed to pick a prom dress you could actually wear beyond prom night. I did wear that dress again and again for years.

Only much later did I learn that Mama had divided up Daddy's modest life insurance proceeds by first giving some to his two older sisters and then sharing the rest with us, his two youngest girls. It made me deeply fond of that silk dress in a new way, knowing where the money came from. And it offered some odd comfort when I actually did move to New York, knowing that Daddy had, in the way he could, helped me experience for the first time this city that I loved.

High school graduation picture, 1978

Nine

Spelman College graduation, 1982

After the initial shock of those early weeks, I found myself reacting to my father's death with anger at the world, furious that one of the most loving relationships in my life had been taken from me; and I was in terror that that hole would never be filled. I withdrew, wanting to escape from everything and everybody that reminded me of who I'd lost. That included my mother. I distinctly remember one of those endless June days before high school ended: I had come home from somewhere, and didn't say hi to Mama as I passed by her bedroom en route to my own. She stopped me and said, "Oh, you call yourself not speaking to me? Let's see who can go the longest not speaking; let's see who needs who first," and she refused to speak to *me*. Of course, the next day I needed lunch money from her. I apologized, and having made her point, my mother handed me a twenty-dollar bill, no hard feelings.

Yet, hard for me to admit now, when I left home in early July 1978, accepted into a special prefreshman summer program at Spelman, I did so in stony silence, rejecting Mama's offer to accompany me to college, filled with what my family called "her attitude" and what I later harshly described in my journal as my "evil, selfish and secretive" ways. Mama said nothing to me about my demeanor. She must've known that I was suffering from a paralyzing grief. Now I can see that I was depressed, but at the time I simply had a pressing new reason to escape Detroit—to leave behind the place where I'd lost my father. I decided, rashly, that I also wanted to leave behind my name. Having again changed the spelling, I changed the pronunciation, no longer wanting to be called Bridgett, (BRIDGE-it); I wanted to be called Bridgétt, with the accent on the second syllable (Bridge—JET), the way Aunt Gladys, Lisa's mother, pronounced my name. (As a preteen, I'd already changed the spelling from its original B-R-I-D-G-I-T to B-R-I-D-G-E-T). Mama didn't object and actually helped me legally change the spelling. But she never called me by my new name.

My departure that summer coincided with the first anniversary of the state's Daily. Lottery officials celebrated the milestone, crowing that by the end of the year, the thousandth Daily sales outlet would be licensed. ("Play today—Cash tonight!" was the bureau's newest promotional slogan.) When I returned home after four weeks on a magnolia-filled college campus, I was blithely indifferent to Mama's Numbers operation. To my eyes, nothing had changed: she still took in folks' numbers, checked the business, collected her money, and paid out hits. I did work long hours at Winkelman's that final summer month, using my pay to buy a wardrobe for life at Spelman, where fashion mattered. Interestingly, I didn't ask Mama to buy those clothes for me, as she'd always done.

When it was time to return to college, Mama drove me to the airport. Before I boarded the plane, she handed me a fat envelope with *L-22*, a customer's code name, scrawled across the front. The envelope was stuffed with bills, easily a month's take from one of her biggest books.

"Try to make this stretch," she said. "I'll send more when I can."

I'd never heard my mother speak quite that way. *Try to make this stretch. I'll send more when I can.* That was when it dawned on me: while I'd been home, our telephones hadn't rung as much as usual. When I got to campus, I went straight to the financial aid office and requested a work-study job. I was given one in the student newspaper office.

Years later, Rita told me what was actually going on when I left home that late-August day in 1978: "Mama's business was really down, I mean *really* down," she said. "But she didn't want you to know that."

As it happened, Mama traveled to Las Vegas for a nine-day vacation the day after I left for school. She was joined by Burt, Rita, Jewell, Aunt Florence, Uncle Gene and her friend from childhood, Mariah. I was invited too but turned down the offer, to be at school for Freshman Week. I later regretted my decision, because that trip became a touchstone they all spoke about with fond and animated memories. "They were like kids," recalls Jewell about our parents in Vegas. "I never saw them! They were gone all the time. They'd come knocking on the door at three in the morning asking, 'Did you eat?' 'Yeah, we ate.'"

My mother loved Las Vegas, visiting it several times throughout her life. Ironically, gambling was a small part of its lure for her. Mostly she enjoyed the live shows, and over the years got to see Cher, Diana Ross, Sammy Davis Jr., and many others perform. "You have not seen an entertainer perform until you've seen one put on a show in Vegas," she'd proclaim. When she did gamble at the casinos, my mother chose a set amount of money to wager on blackjack, roulette, or the slot machines, and when that cash was gone she left the floor. Conversely, when she won, she got up from the table, turned in her chips, returned to her room, and napped. Her motto was: "The only way to win in Vegas is to know when to quit."

The Vegas trip, planned and paid for months in advance, came along just as the Daily lottery was roaring its way to $4 million per week in sales. Meanwhile, Mama had paid for everyone's hotel and airfare. "We were not out of a penny" is how my uncle Gene described it more than thirty-two years later. "She paid for everything." That included everyone's tickets to see Liberace perform at Caesars Palace. Could Mama afford that trip? Even if the legal lottery was hurting her business, she would *not* have wanted it known that she was struggling and unable to keep sharing the good life with others. Of course they took the trip.

That first semester, I found a college filled with girls from upper-middle-class black families, girls who'd grown up in leafy suburbs, many who'd gone to predominantly white schools, some who'd chosen Spelman for a new "black experience." I felt like the only girl on campus from a working-class, urban background and a public high school, whose parents hadn't gone to college, let alone pledged sororities and fraternities. I was no legacy. ("How could any of you have parents who didn't go to college?" asked my English professor, Millicent Jordan, herself from an illustrious upscale African-American family. She was genuinely incredulous, but I was left feeling humiliated.) And when my new friend from Los Angeles, Heather, asked to borrow my navy silk Calvin Klein pleated skirt and matching blouse, I didn't dare tell her I'd bought the outfit from a booster back in Detroit. Yet, throughout those first weeks of college, whenever I heard the disco queen Gloria Gaynor belting out that 1978 anthem, "I Will Survive," I couldn't help but think of Mama. She wasn't "educated," but she knew how to stay alive. Still, I definitely made sure to keep Mama's profession a secret from my college classmates. I did not want my two worlds colliding.

The irony is not lost on me that while I was working hard to make sure no one at my beloved college knew what my mother did for a living, she was struggling to maintain her livelihood largely so she could keep me enrolled there. My high school friends, also children of working-class and lower-middle-class parents, all attended in-state schools—Michigan State, University of Michigan, Western U, Eastern U. I was the only one of us who "went away." I knew I was an exception, and I worked hard to fit in. I also worked hard to leave that other, secret life behind.

And then barely a month into my fall semester, Mama got carjacked. A driver bumped her car from behind, and when she got out to investigate, the carjacker hit her on the side of her head with a pistol, knocking her to the ground. And then he stole her car. The robbery so shook us up that Rita and I flew home from Atlanta shortly afterward to be with her. (Rita had just begun an MBA program at Atlanta University.) Whatever misguided anger I'd felt dissipated long before we boarded the plane. For the first time in my life, I was forced to consider the improbable: the possibility of losing my mother. *I realize how lucky I am that she's still alive,* I wrote in my journal. *If she'd lost her life, I'd be saying "If I had just told her..." I don't want to wait until it's too late...I want to tell Mama that I love her. I've never said that to her. She's never said it to me, either, but I know. She knows too, but I still want to tell her.*

"A lot of stuff changed after that," recalls my nephew, Tony, who was seven. "You didn't see a gun prior to that. After that, a thirty-eight was always visible in her purse. And she started carrying bigger purses. I remember that."

While back in Detroit, I noticed so many orange lottery terminals that it was staggering. In one party store on Six Mile Road, I watched as a man in his twenties bought $120 worth of tickets for the week. It was suddenly clear to me that for young people like him, the street numbers evoked no warm memories or sense of loyalty. Placing their bets with the state simply made sense, both modern-day and convenient.

I also noticed Mama's glass jars, once filled with gleaming coins, now empty. "It was impossible to tell exactly how much the state-sanctioned lottery took business away from the illegal numbers," writes Felicia George, the scholar, but clearly my mother was facing the biggest threat yet to her livelihood.

So she fought back.

When I returned home for Christmas break, I discovered a major shift: Listening to Mama doing her business over the phone, I didn't hear her say to a customer, *Morning, Darlene. I'm calling to take your numbers,* as I'd heard her say for my entire life. I heard her say, *Morning, Darlene. Will this be for the lottery or for the Numbers?*

My mother had done her own market research and learned from folks that yes, they really liked how the lottery's numbers got announced publicly, so that everyone found out the winners at the same time. But customers also told her they didn't like giving the state their money, even though they grew more and more nervous about the alternative. Could the Numbers' bankers pay off hits? Phones across the city quit ringing: the Daily had cut into so many runners' profit. One mini–grocery store on the east side, Chene Trombley Market, sold well over a million dollars' worth of Daily lottery tickets that year, to six thousand people a week; and more important, the store paid out over $850,000 in winnings. Perceived by players as a lucky spot, the mini-grocery proclaimed itself the number one agent in the state in lottery sales *and* payoffs. A feature story in the *Detroit News Magazine* noted that the store's owner, with his "friendly Slavic face," had "every right to…enjoy his 'big daddy' role, given that the license he'd been granted by the State of Michigan was garnering him up to $50,000 a year in commissions." This prompted many business owners to open up party stores *specifically* to sell lottery tickets, only adding to the competition Mama faced.

"The Daily Lottery Game is the pride and joy of Michigan's Bureau of the Lottery," proclaimed that same article, with the reporter bluntly declaring that the lottery was "a state sanctioned version of the numbers racket," adding that its growth had been "phenomenal." The more the lottery impinged, the less people felt they could trust the Numbers; the less they patronized them, the weaker street Numbers became.

Given this reality, Mama had a brainstorm: offer customers options—to play the lottery with her, play the traditional Numbers as always, or play a combination of both. She later said that the idea came to her while on that trip to Las Vegas. She was standing at a roulette table, watching the dealer rake in players' piles and piles of chips, when it dawned on her: *You can never beat the house.* Another thought quickly followed: *If you can't beat 'em, join 'em.* Why not make the state and its Daily the new operator for her Numbers business?

In a very short time, Mama did away with the street's winning numbers altogether and exclusively used the lottery's Daily winners. My mother's shift was a brilliant move, as it relieved her of the need to derive one set of three-digit daily numbers from a convoluted calculation based on horseraces *and* it eliminated the ability of syndicate men to "fix" another set of three-digit numbers. She also made her business more alluring by becoming more competitive: she started offering a higher payout than the state, paying 600-to-1 winnings compared to the Daily's 500-to-1.

Also, with the Daily, for all its bells and whistles, you could never win more than $3,000 at a time. Folks wanted the chance to win big. Mama said she'd watched closely in Vegas as cashiers in cages took in tens of thousands of dollars on the casino floor but also handed out wads and wads of cash. The house always wins in part because it can pay out with ease the occasional large win. That fact is the lure (something Mama knew well from the days when she wasn't her own banker). She figured out a way to allow larger bets than she'd ever accepted, for as much as $15 or

$20 on a given three-digit. She figured, let people have a shot at winning $9,000 or $12,000.

I witnessed with fascination how my mother did this, in a new household ritual unfolding before me: Burt made daily trips to the nearby party store to buy lottery tickets, essentially using the State of Michigan as insurance against Mama "getting hit hard" on a particular number, i.e., making the state her "backup" bank; this was the very backing she had once depended on big Numbers men to provide. Burt came home each day at dusk with his pockets full of lottery tickets, pulling them out, these long paper accordions purchased before the 7:08 p.m. cutoff, and dropping them onto the kitchen table. And each evening at exactly 7:28, conversation abruptly halted, Mama shushing us and holding her breath as we all turned to watch the TV, waiting until the local news anchor announced that day's Daily 3. Another shift: Mama didn't have to check the business to find out if anyone might've hit. Our phones now rang within seconds, with a customer who'd also just learned from TV what digits were winners calling to "let you know I put in today's number." My mother now checked the business—the rundown of numbers played—largely to *confirm* a hit, rather than to see who hit. Essentially, customers called in their numbers as usual; the only difference was that the winners were provided by the state and announced on TV each evening rather than by the old methods of racetrack calculations and syndicate selection.

Soon enough, all number runners adopted this approach, which saved Mama's business and our livelihood. I returned to Spelman for the spring semester and promptly moved off campus with my dorm roommate Nikki into an apartment in a new complex called Bordeaux South. My mother helped me furnish the place and paid my rent for months in advance, enough proof for me that she knew how to survive, stay alive, and thrive.

As the eighties rolled in, Mayor Young was left in control of a 63 percent black-majority city suffering from an inadequate tax base, too few jobs, and swollen welfare rolls, which the new president, Ronald Reagan, was determined to slash. Yet while Detroit's population had dropped from its 1950 height of 1.85 million people, the city still boasted well over a million residents. Young lobbied hard to bring casino gambling to the city, a dream he'd had since taking office, as he saw it as a way to create jobs and offset Detroit's dying tax base while making the city a major tourist destination. The question was placed on the ballot, and for the second time, voters said no. Ministers lobbied hard against it. Detroit was a Numbers gambling town, true, but this was different: the fear of commercial sex and yet more drugs killed Young's casino dreams. And in another destabilizing development in the city, Chrysler Corporation found itself on the verge of bankruptcy, an unthinkable outcome for a Big Three auto company. Mama, liking the way its new president, Lee Iacocca, lobbied Congress for a bailout, decided to invest in the company. Chrysler's value was nil, but that didn't bother her. "It has nowhere to go but up," she said, acquiring shares of its common stock.

This was also when my mother vigorously returned to her philanthropy and began helping several young women get through "rough patches," including my cousin Lisa, who'd also chosen to attend Spelman College. Her parents' bitter divorce had jeopardized the family's financial status, and despite loans and grants and work-study and a part-time job off campus, Lisa couldn't pay the balance of her tuition. She'd called her father, explained her predicament, and asked for five hundred dollars; he told her he didn't have it. There was a new wife, and new responsibilities. This meant Lisa wouldn't be allowed to take her finals and would have to drop out of school. Heartbroken, she called Aunt Fa and lamented her plight. She says my mother said to her, "Are you kidding me? How much? That's not a problem. There's no question your bill will get paid."

"I remember thinking, *Wow, I mean wow.* Her just doing that for me with no lecture, no guilt trip, no martyr type of attitude, no sense of 'you owe me,'" recalls Lisa. "And I was so upset about my dad not being willing to help me, and she said, 'Well, you don't know what's going on with your dad.'"

Mama had also helped Lisa's older sister, Leslie, go back to school by taking care of her little boy; she did the same favor a few years later for my childhood friend Diane, caring for her infant daughter, Brittany, while Diane completed her master's degree.

"She said, 'Who's gonna keep that baby?'" remembers Diane. "And I said, 'Mrs. Robinson, I don't even know right now.' And she said, 'You bring that baby over here.'" Diane says she offered to pay Mama, but my mother told her, "You're not paying me to do nothing; just bring that baby over here, and don't even think about taking that child anywhere else."

When Diane came to pick up her little girl each day, "She was clean and she was happy," recalls Diane. "And more than a few times, she was rolling around with a couple other little babies."

My friend Stephanie has her own story: She'd moved to New York and was struggling, unhappy, living in a cramped one-bedroom with a roommate she didn't get along with. My mother visited us both, saw Stephanie's situation, and later sent her "a little piece of money," as she called it—five hundred dollars to help her move into her own place. "I never said to her, 'Oh, I'm overwhelmed,' says Stephanie. "But she could see, and just the fact that she offered that encouragement, that extra help that my own mom wasn't able to offer, was such a sweet thing to me."

My mother deeply wanted us all, Diane, Lisa, Stephanie, me, and other young women she cared about, to pursue our education—and yes, if need be find a life outside Detroit, which had become unrecognizable from the Motor City she'd migrated to three decades before. While I remember two black street gangs, the Errol Flynns and the BKs, when I was growing up in the seventies, Detroit had now entered into what local criminologists refer to as one of the most violent eras of crime in American history, with hundreds and hundreds of gang-related and drug-trade homicides. The former head of Detroit's DEA, Robert De Fauw, quoted in an exposé by journalist Scott M. Burnstein, said of that time: "The streets were decaying, people were fleeing the city in masses and the dope peddlers took over what was left."

Further terrorizing residents was the notorious Devil's Night, a uniquely Detroit phenomenon of a largely harmless tradition run amok. Since the late 1970s, each year on October thirtieth, vandals set fire to buildings "for fun." That number had grown exponentially year by year to include hundreds of fires throughout the city, prompting watch groups to patrol their own streets that night. Meanwhile, into this morass the State of Michigan introduced the Daily 4 lottery game, in which a player must match four winning numbers. That meant much higher odds but also much higher payouts: $5,000 for a $1 bet, versus the Daily 3's $500 for the same $1. Mama was confident that this new four-digit game would have no impact on her three-digit-based Numbers business. It was an extra gambling option, sure, but it was hard enough to hit the three-digit, she insisted. People wanted better odds than the Daily 4's 10,000-to-1.

The following spring, I graduated from Spelman. It was such a communal celebration that even Buddy, our upstairs tenant, flew to Atlanta to join in the festivities. Shirley Chisholm gave the commencement address. As the first African-American woman to run for Congress, and also for president, her campaign slogan had been "Unbought and Un-bossed." Mama enjoyed her speech, later telling us all at my graduation dinner, "You know what I really like about Shirley Chisholm? She didn't wait around for somebody to accept her. She just accepted herself."

Did the state's latest encroachment weigh on my mother's mind, prompting her to begin thinking beyond the Numbers business? Shortly after graduation, I mentioned to her that my friend Elliott was struggling to find backers for a local production of *Purlie,* the Tony Award–winning "spirited black musical" based on a play written by Ossie Davis. My mother surprised us all and announced that she'd like to invest in the production. While I'd spent my previous summers since sophomore year away from home (working in Atlanta, interning in New York, and traveling through Europe), I committed to staying in Detroit that summer and coproducing *Purlie* with Rita (*Davis & Davis Productions*).

The musical, set in the Jim Crow era, premiered at Detroit's venerable Music Hall Center. Our local production starred Ruben Santiago, billed as "a New York actor!" Later adopting his mother's maiden name, Santiago-Hudson would go on to become an accomplished actor, playwright, and theater director. In fact, Santiago-Hudson wrote and directed *Lackawanna Blues,* an off-Broadway play and later a film—his tribute to a spirited and loving surrogate mother who ran a boardinghouse in 1950s and 1960s Lackawanna, New York. (My nephew Tony loved the film version of *Lackawanna Blues,* always said the woman at its center, Nanny, reminded him of Grandma.)

Purlie was a family affair. I can still see my brother Anthony sitting in the theater in his suit and tie, looking handsome, Rita greeting guests in the lobby, Mama waiting quietly in a front-row seat; I remember thinking, *We're a family that does cool stuff.* (My favorite line from *Purlie*: "It sure is fun being colored, when ain't nobody looking.")

"Your mother was down for it, and that was rare," says Elliott, who brought the musical project to her. "We were in our early twenties and yet she had the vision to invest in someone so young; she was into giving people opportunities to pursue nontraditional things that at that time in the early eighties, black folks didn't do." He adds: "And I think it was more about that than 'I'm going to get a return on my dollar.'"

Sadly, Mama didn't get *any* returns. We weren't as successful as we'd hoped, with the result that Mama's total investment in the production—the entire $15,000—was lost. As inexperienced producers, we made lots of novice mistakes: gave away too many comps for the ten-day run; chose a union-house venue that cost too much and was too large to fill, didn't do publicity soon or widely enough. I tried to put a good spin on this flop, saying how we "brought art to the masses." Mama said that was ridiculous, no comfort at all. "Don't try to make it into something that it's not," she snapped. "Sometimes you win, sometimes you lose. And we lost."

Our financial loss came just as law enforcement raided a large street Numbers operation in the city. Twenty-one locations in Detroit and the suburbs were found to be part of a $60-million-to-$80-million-a-year Numbers ring owned and operated by the local Mafia, not much smaller than the $90-million-a-year operation J. Edgar Hoover's sting had uncovered twelve years before. In this 1982 bust, Mama and other midlevel operators were again spared, but it showed that years after the Daily was introduced, and just months after the four-digit launched, law enforcement was hell-bent on protecting the state's interest.

That fall I went to stay with a boyfriend in Atlanta, happy to escape our family's theatrical-debut defeat. My mother never brought it up again, nor blamed anyone else for the financial loss. Her staunch belief was that just as you should never loan money you need back, you should never gamble money you can't afford to lose. I suspect she saw her younger, risk-taking self in us when she signed on to the project. But I felt awful about our defeat. Several weeks later, I escaped farther, and for longer, by leaving for a year on a post-college fellowship, one that allowed me to travel to Nigeria and Kenya to study African women working in media. My experience with the continent was culturally shocking and life-changing and I wrote many letters home to Mama, some as long as fifteen pages, to share details with her. (*Your letter was so interesting. I really did enjoy reading it, and I think that is what helped me to get out of the hospital,* wrote my mother after getting my long-awaited first letter from Nigeria, just after she'd suffered another blood clot.)

When I returned home the following year, I shocked everyone by deciding to live on Broadstreet with my sister Dianne and her husband, George, who'd moved into the house several years before. I assumed I could because it was the family home and there was plenty of space, so I didn't have to ask permission. Broadstreet was my right. (I later learned that Dianne was initially unhappy about this.) I stayed in my childhood bedroom, which was both comforting and odd. "This is the same bed John T. used when he lived here," said Dianne, knowing it would comfort me to sleep where our father had once slept. Sadly, in that time I saw firsthand the dysfunction of my sister's marriage, her husband's excessive drinking, irregular work, staying out late. But I also got to see my brother a lot. He and his wife, Renita, had broken up years before, and Anthony, who was living nearby, came over nearly every day. I also got to share my favorite books with Dianne, giving her my copies of Alice Walker's *The Color Purple* and Toni Morrison's *Song of Solomon* and Gloria Naylor's *The Women of Brewster Place* to read. Driving around in my stepfather's giant white-with-red-interior Lincoln Continental, I hung out with my junior high and high school girlfriends and enjoyed being back stateside, reveling in this brief respite before I had to figure out what to do with my life. On a whim, I took a graduate creative writing class at Wayne State University, submitting a revised version of a short story I'd written in college to the campus literary magazine, *Wayne Review.* That story won an award for best story by an Afro-American writer. ("I sure wish there were special awards for the best white person's short story," a white male student said to me.) The story, entitled "...And Deliver Us from Brown," was loosely based on my mother and stepfather's relationship, and I credit that award with launching my professional writing life. Too at Wayne State, I reencountered a classmate from elementary school, William James. Also a writer, he was visiting us one day, sitting at our kitchen table, when my mother asked him, "What's the name for a book that's based on the truth but is still fiction?" He told her the term was *roman à clef,* and Mama carefully wrote the phrase on a piece of paper and stuck it to our refrigerator with a magnet.

That was also when I played a special three-digit on a hunch, and hit. My sister Dianne and I had been hanging out all day, running errands, and three different times I saw 788, Mama's pet number. I saw it on a car's license plate, as the number on a dry cleaning ticket, and as the cash register total after a store purchase. "I'm gonna play a number today," I announced to everyone. While Dianne knew what the number was, I didn't tell anyone else. My sisters and my brother and my mother all said, "I'm in," and each gave me money to play the mystery number at a party store for them too. "You never play the Numbers, so if *you* have a hunch, it must mean something," said Mama. She was right. The number came out that day, straight, and we each had it for "good money," among us winning several hundred dollars.

During that time my mother began hosting fabulous poker

parties. Those marathon card games would start on a Friday night and not end until Saturday afternoon. "You had a smorgasbord of people at the table," recalls Tony. "Plant workers, numbers people, teachers, a lawyer...Everybody felt comfortable coming to Grandma's to play, because it was always the same group of people, no outsiders."

Those card parties were also an extra source of money for my mother and Uncle Gene, who as hosts shared the "cut," or a percentage of every pot. They'd have three tables going at one time, two in the living room and one, higher-stakes poker game in the den. Folks would play the lower-stakes games to win enough money to compete at the big table. It was a *thing*, punctuated by yummy food, free-flowing liquor, lots of jokes, laughter, Mama as hostess.

I would come to treasure that moment as part of a magical eight months when I was twenty-three, living in my hometown, surrounded by family and old friends. Using the proceeds from my hit, I soon left home to do a newspaper internship in Gainesville, Georgia, and later take a newsroom job in Atlanta. It felt good to be making my own money, to be living self-sufficiently. Beyond a few weeks one summer, I never did return to Detroit to live.

Turns out, the four-digit was taking hold and gaining massive popularity, to my mother's surprise. The lure of such high-paying wins was too strong. Also, players actually believed they were supporting education, as the state began earmarking lottery revenues for its School Aid Fund. (What ticket buyers didn't understand was that the twenty-nine cents of every dollar of lottery proceeds set aside for Michigan's school fund translated to less than five hundred dollars per student.) Although Mama wasn't saying so, Rita was the one who told me that the four-digit was cutting into the business in a big way. I thought this latest usurping by the state was so unfair, yet another attack on my mother's hard-earned livelihood, and it made me wish for the first time that she had other options. Complicating matters, Mama said it was too much effort, and unwise, to change her business so drastically. Everything she knew about the Numbers was based on a three-digit system—from the payouts to the percentages to the dream books. Besides, the idea of having to pay out a whopping 5,000 to 1 was daunting to my mother. It required a far, far bigger reserve than the three-digit payouts, and she knew it could lead to a far quicker wipeout.

"She's really being stubborn about it," said Rita. "It's not like her, to *not* do what she needs to do to make it."

I had another point of view: I believed that after nearly thirty years, Mama was simply tiring of the hustle and grind. I'd noticed how the hair around her temples had thinned, how her smooth complexion had faint age lines, how the gray hairs on her head had multiplied. "When does it end?" I lamented to my sister. "Will Mama ever be able to build up a nest egg so she can stop? Everyone deserves to retire."

"That's true," said Rita. "That's true."

Of course my mother saw the passing of time, faced head-on the price paid for decades of work in a precarious and stressful business, one where the competition kept mounting. Now, as a young adult, I was beginning to grasp the greater extent of her sacrifice. I had to admit this to myself, despite what the Numbers had made possible. And that she'd had other dreams. In fact, over the years she'd enrolled in a couple of college courses, with a desire to someday open a home for the aged. But she could never devote the time needed, because running the Numbers is an all-consuming job.

Many times, Mama said to us, "I'm doing this so you don't have to." I took that to heart. She also would often say, "Don't thank me. Just take advantage of the opportunities I made possible, and that'll be all the thanks I need." I was thinking about that when I applied to Columbia University's Graduate School of Journalism. Mama was happy for me when I got accepted, and oh so proud. I was pleased too; I felt my admission to Columbia was the best way to show her my gratitude. I really believed, still do, that she found comfort in my success.

In the summer of 1984, months before I applied to grad school, Michigan's lottery officials introduced yet another new and alluring game: Lotto, with its cumulative, multimillion-dollar jackpots. I'm sure Mama would've found a way to come up with the money to pay for Columbia. But I didn't dare ask. I'd seen the news, and Lotto was a whopping success, setting a national record in first-week sales of over $3 million. I'd *also* seen the plethora of four-digit dream books now sold in local stores. I didn't even discuss the cost with my mother. I happily took out a $10,000 loan to pay for the tuition not covered by scholarships.

By then, my own work had taken me into a world of college-educated professionals, upscale lifestyles, whiteness. And when I returned home for visits, I reentered the world of the Numbers. My two worlds never collided, until the day I announced in class that my favorite book was Louise Meriwether's *Daddy Was a Number Runner,* the novel that had validated my own lived experience. A classmate, Suzanne Kay, who happened to be the daughter of the iconic black actress Diahann Carroll (whose Barbie-doll likeness I'd owned, and whose hairstyle inspired my mother's wedding-day chic), looked at me quizzically and asked, "What's a number runner?"

I was silent. I could not, would not explain the meaning of that vocation to this rich black girl in front of our white classmates, inside the hallowed walls of an Ivy League institution. Yes, I'd spent my life keeping the secret both out of necessity and because I didn't want Mama to be judged. But this was the first time I ever felt *embarrassed* by what my mother did for a living.

After grad school graduation, I was working as an intern at the Detroit bureau of the *Wall Street Journal* when the house on Broadstreet was set on fire by an arsonist and badly damaged. Mama had only truly owned the house for four years. Mr. Prince, who'd sold her the house, had waited until she'd paid for it in full to sign over the deed, "given pursuant to and in fulfillment of a certain land contract between the parties" in 1982. After twenty-one long years, Broadstreet had finally truly become ours.

Her name was on the deed, yet Mama had put my brother-in-law, George, in charge of paying the homeowner's insurance, since he and my sister lived in the house as their own. Unbeknownst to anyone, he'd deliberately let the coverage lapse. Mama pondered what to do with Broadstreet, now uninhabitable without a costly renovation, and with no insurance money to pay for the work. She did briefly toy with the idea of slowly renovating the house, and I remember going with her once to an antiques shop that sold original, refurbished materials and watching her look at costly stained-glass windows and French doors. But we left the store without her purchasing anything. A complete restoration was just too daunting a prospect; and it was obvious her heart wasn't in it.

Besides, she was again fighting to save her business. Mama finally acquiesced after years of vacillating and began taking the four-digit lottery alongside the three-digit. She had to, to stay competitive. So many other number runners were accepting four-digit bets that Fannie's customers were leaving her, even loyal ones who figured it was easier to play all their numbers, both the three- and the four-digits, with one bookie. A cottage industry for the four-digit had already sprung up and thrived—not just dream books, but tip sheets and new rundowns and even psychics who now miraculously envisioned numbers with four figures.

I recently found among my mother's possessions a numerological rundown from that time, provided by Dennis Fairchild, a radio host of a program called *Thank Your Lucky Stars;* Fairchild had, in his own handwriting, figured out the personal-year numbers for my mother; Burt; me; Rita; my nephew, Tony; my aunt Florence; and my mother's older sister Alice, all for 1987. Mama's personal-year number was 4, which meant: *Like the four corners of the earth, this is a year of developing new monetary foundations. Be practical and logical and don't financially over-extend yourself.* Fairchild added: *Most people leave a 4-year with more money in the bank than they enter it with.*

For me, it was odd, once again, to hear the shifting cadences of Mama's voice as she wrote down a customer's bet: *Three-eight-nine-two for fifty cents, uh-huh, 8-1-4-5 for a dollar, okay, and 2-9-9-6 boxed for a dollar.* This came as I was in the throes of pursuing my own career, moving to Philadelphia to become a newspaper reporter for its award-winning daily the *Philadelphia Inquirer*, affectionately called the Inky. (Mama drilled me on a list of most commonly misspelled words as we rode to the airport for my interview, helping me prepare for the newsroom test I'd be given.)

During this time, Mama also threw her energies into steering her grandson as best she could through the ever-increasing dangers for a black teenage boy in mid-1980s Detroit. The city was in the throes of the nation's crack epidemic, so a young man or woman now had to avoid drugs and getting caught in the crosshairs of drug-related shootings, as well as the relentless police brutality for which Detroit was notorious. As Robert De Fauw, the local DEA's former head, put it: "With cocaine in the mix, things got pretty chaotic. Life was cheap." And drug lords, the most famous among them a fifteen-year-old called White Boy Rick, made hundreds of millions of dollars.

It shatters me to fathom how drug dealers changed Detroit, hurt so many people, some I'd known all my life. This is why I've always loathed comparisons made between illegal lotteries and the drug trade. As if all "illicit" enterprises are equal. People often say that the head of a drug cartel could, with better opportunities, have been the CEO of a *Fortune* 500 company, and the same is often said about major number runners. I certainly believe that to be true of my own mother. But that's where the comparison ends. Selling chances to win a lottery obviously has no similarity to the whole-cloth destruction of lives, families, and communities that selling hard drugs leaves in its wake.

Some have said that number runners preyed on people's gambling addictions; I reject this claim. As someone who grew up going to the racetrack often, thanks to my horse-trainer uncle, I've seen up close the adrenaline rush folks get from gambling; so yes, I'm clear what that particular addiction looks like, clear that folks who need it will find a way to gamble on *something*. But I'm equally aware of how certain forms of gambling are indulged without denigration and allowed to thrive within certain sectors of society (horse betting, for instance, gets a free pass, as do Catholics' bingo nights at church). This makes me wary of the charge that Numbers had a negative impact on the black community. If there *were* disadvantages, if some folks gambled too much, and if others spent coins and dollars on the Numbers that could've gone to more so-called honorable means, then in my mind that is completely offset by the invaluable ways Numbers money *was* used. I've also seen firsthand how outsiders, i.e., whites and Arabs, maintained businesses in Detroit's black neighborhoods as store owners and landlords and *never* reinvested that money made off African-Americans in our community; many number runners not only launched legit businesses that provided vital services, but that Numbers money stayed in black neighborhoods, those dollars turning over many times.

Still, how *did* my mother manage to run a cash-based business amid the Wild West–style shootings inflicted upon the city during one of its most notoriously dangerous eras? And how did she do it, given that her enterprise *was* decidedly underground and therefore couldn't rely on protection from "the law"?

One way was to hire a brawny and brave young man named Buster to handle her collecting and payments "out in the street."

"He was like an enforcer," recalls Tony. "Because he was

big, with a broad chest, big shoulders, stood about six foot three inches, had a big mustache and goatee. Always in leather, wore a bebop hat."

While Buster might've "had a record," as they say, maybe served time in prison, he was not an actual enforcer for my mother. He did do an important job for her, though, and what I remember most about Buster is his loyalty to her, and how he was ever respectful and reliable. For her part, my mother was both grateful for Buster's service and happy to give him a job when few others would bother to even give him a chance.

Soon enough, Tony turned sixteen just as the Daily celebrated its tenth year and lottery sales reached $1 billion. With his driver's license and a brand-new white Camaro compliments of my mother, Tony also started collecting payments and delivering payouts. "I'd be out driving with my friends," he says. "And I'd tell them I had to stop off and pick up some money from one of my grandmother's 'rental properties.' I might have an envelope with ten thousand dollars in it, and my friends never knew."

They also never knew that Tony carried a gun: a .380 automatic given to him by his grandmother.

"What did she say to you when she gave it to you?" I ask, learning this fact for the first time.

"There wasn't a bunch of talking," says Tony. "She said, 'Come straight home.' I would always tuck it under my seat, just in case anything went bad in between going and getting home. You know, they used to do a lot of kidnapping back in the day. It wasn't like I was walking around the street with it. You know I've never been a hothead. If I was going somewhere at night, or was going to pick up some money, I had it."

Tony also took charge of burning old Numbers tickets and notebooks in the basement incinerator, destroying evidence every week or so. His primary job, however, was to go daily to the nearest party store to buy lottery tickets for the numbers that customers had "loaded up on," or played heavily. "I went all the time," recalls Tony, because given the 5,000-to-1 payouts on four-digits alone, no way could my mother risk getting hit for ten or twenty dollars on a number without playing it herself legally to help pay for the hit. Of course, she often played a number for more than she needed to cover a potential hit. A windfall provided extra reserves.

It was rare, but every now and then a number would get by my mother, and she'd miss the fact that several bettors within her business had actually played it.

"I do remember her getting hit hard one time," says Tony. "She had all of us counting the money, trying to figure it out." Adding to the pressure was Mama's payout policy: winners got their money the next day by noon.

With the possibility of such big payouts, my mother also needed to verify folks' claims of having played a certain number. While she didn't have to do it with most of her customers, my mother did tape-record a few, those she felt might lie to her. She used a little circular wire device that attached to the phone's receiver, and after a week she'd destroy the tape. In time, Mama took advantage of the newest technology and had people fax their numbers to her on a machine that sat in the back bedroom—a perfect approach, since the faxed document itself provided paper proof of who'd played what for how much.

Throughout that treacherous decade, my mother was

determined to keep Tony out of trouble, sending him to a total of five different schools—private, public, charter, and Catholic—in an effort to keep him "on the straight and narrow" toward high school graduation. Tony *did* stay out of trouble, and he says it's largely because he never wanted to add more stress to his grandmother's life.

"I remember in high school, I would go out with my friends and do whatever. But when it got to be twelve o'clock, I'd be home," says Tony. "My friends would be like, 'Dude, you're crawling home like a kid?' I'm like, 'It ain't about being a kid. She's worried.'" He knew Grandma wouldn't relax until he was in the house. "She'd hear the door open," he says. "And she'd be good."

One day, a young man, a stranger, knocked on our door. He told Mama his name was Michael Terrell, that he'd discovered her vacant house on Broadstreet through the Registry of Deeds, and wondered would she be interested in selling it to him?

"I'd tried to call first," he now says. "But I couldn't get through. The line was always busy. The records showed your mom's name and where she currently lived, so I just took a deep breath and drove by the house on Seven Mile and rang the doorbell."

My mother told him about the fire damage. He said that as a carpenter, he'd specifically been looking for a fixer-upper for himself and his wife and three-year-old son. It was just the type of old, spacious Colonial he wanted, big enough for a growing family.

"I'd driven by the house, and I thought the neighborhood was like a little oasis," recalls Michael. Also, he'd studied architecture and design alongside carpentry and immediately recognized Broadstreet's potential. "I saw that beautiful house and I said, 'Oh man, this is it. If I could get this, I'd be a happy man.'"

My mother listened as Michael explained that he taught woodshop and mechanical drafting at Mumford High School, stressing that he believed he had the skills to restore the house to its former glory. She nodded. Then she said, "You're Seventh-Day Adventist, aren't you?"

"It was out of the blue," says Michael. "I thought, *This lady must be psychic or something,* and I said, 'Yes ma'am, I am.'"

"I could tell from your mannerisms, the way you present yourself," she said. "You're so polite." My mother then told him she'd consider his offer, but first she had to be sure that no one in the family wanted the house. Two days later, she called him back and agreed to sell Broadstreet for $8,000.

"I thought, *Eight thousand dollars for a house that size?*" recalls Michael.

When my mother found out Michael and his family were staying with his sister in crowded conditions, she told him that the apartment above us on Seven Mile was vacant, and that while he was fixing up Broadstreet, they could live there for a reduced rent.

"You're a nice young couple with a little boy," he says she told him. "And you're trying to do something with your life. I want to help you."

Michael and his family moved in. "It was just nice, like being with family," he recalls. "It wasn't like she was the landlord. Little Mike could go downstairs and sit with your mom, or Rita. It was just a comfortable situation, and nurturing.... It was like having my mother downstairs."

During those few years when Michael and his family lived right above her, my mother was in the throes of maintaining a business now fully dependent on the state-sanctioned lottery. She was taking more bets for four-digit numbers than for three-digits, and business was flourishing again as a result. Basically, more than a decade after Michigan had tried hard to usurp the street Numbers with its Daily 3, number runners like Mama were relying on the state's Daily 4 to sustain those very same street Numbers, by infusing their business with new energy, new opportunities for players to win big, and a surefire way to keep more of their money, tax-free. Nice irony. And it was now an open secret that number runners were using Michigan's daily three-digit and four-digit winners for their own purposes.

"We've talked about it but nobody has figured out what to do," lamented a lottery spokeswoman in 1989. "We can't walk up to a bookie and say, 'How's business?' There's nothing I could say that would have any impact." In fact, in another sweet irony, the Wayne County prosecutor said that the legal lottery "may have diminished public perception that playing the Numbers is wrong."

This is why Tony remembers those gleaming jars inside the glass-front kitchen cabinet again teeming with quarters and nickels and dimes, silver change available to him whenever he wanted. "I had it down to a science," he reminisces, smiling. "I knew that a handful of quarters was twenty dollars."

With the decade winding down, my mother was now sixty. I'd just quit my newspaper job and moved to New York to be a freelance writer; I was twenty-eight, the same age she'd been when she migrated to Detroit. I decided to write about Mama. In fact, I had a deep need to write about her. I wanted to highlight her parenting style, her generosity, her wisdom, her way of living. And there was something else.

The 1980s had not been good to our family. Three times tragedy struck. In 1982, my thirty-five-year-old sister, Deborah, in the hospital to control her high blood pressure, suffered a heart attack from a pulmonary embolism and died. Four years later, my thirty-three-year-old brother, Anthony, was shooting pool at his neighborhood bar, the Blue Room, when he and another man got into an argument. Anthony saw that the guy had a gun, and when he ran out, the guy shot him in the back. He made it all the way home but collapsed and died on the steps. (My mother forbade my sisters to tell me about Anthony for twenty-four hours, because she knew my grad school thesis was due that day.) Eight months later my thirty-seven-year-old sister, Dianne, who had never revealed to us any domestic abuse in her marriage, was shot and killed by her husband in a murder-suicide after she told him she wanted a divorce.

I still don't know how my mother survived that trauma, how she managed to move forward. She told me once, "On the hardest days, I promise myself I'll cry tomorrow." I saw her in such grief, and yet she was still present for those of us who remained, still invested in our lives and our wherewithal. I told myself *that* made her worth writing about, and set out to craft a compelling profile of Mama by leaving in the tragedies but leaving out the Numbers. In my notes I scribbled, *What makes my mother special is her strength, and her unselfish love.* But my story— pitched for a Mother's Day issue—was rejected by the editor of *Detroit Magazine,* because, in his words, I hadn't "fully exploited" my story.

I knew why he said that: I hadn't captured the depth of my

mother's pain after the cumulative heartbreak caused by Deborah's and Anthony's and Dianne's deaths. When I'd gingerly asked about her feelings, she told me, "I still can't talk about it." I realized then that I didn't *want* her to talk about it, certainly not for publication. Truth be told, I didn't even want to write that particular story. I just wanted to write about *her*. The losses she'd faced as a mother had presumably given me an angle. Yet I knew she was worth writing about even before my siblings died. And I knew her livelihood was at the center of that worth. But she was still actively running her business, which of course was a secret. I now understood that I couldn't just tell one part of her story; I'd have to wait until I could tell her whole story.

In a new note to myself I wrote: *Interview Mama.*

I never did.

Rendering of Broadstreet

Ten

Detroit, 1990

October 27, 1989

Hi Mama,

I just came in from teaching and found the package you sent. You don't know what a difference it makes.

That $900 will be my bill money for November and December—so I can hold off on a part-time job a little longer.

I think that by the beginning of the year, things will get a lot better.... Next week, I have an interview for a full-time teaching position in journalism at a 4-year, Manhattan college. The position's not 'til September '90, but it would be great to get it. That means a good salary and benefits. Believe me, I know that since I quit my job a year ago, it's been a strain on you. One more thing to worry about. But, there's nothing like being unhappy with your life. For the first time, I really feel good about what I'm doing....

So for now, it's rough and it seems like it's not paying off. But it will. And when it does, I can start doing things for YOU. I try not to take for granted anything you do for me—because I know it's not because I deserve it. It's because you want to do it, or you don't mind. Ever since you brought me home from the hospital to French-Provincial baby furniture, I've been this very privileged and spoiled little girl. When my classmates didn't even know about places like Saks and Bonwit Teller's, I was wearing trench coats and size AA shoes and expensive dresses from those stores. I remember everything.

Because you're so good to me, I've always wanted to make you proud of me. All you ever had to do was look like you were disappointed in me and I would start crying. I'm still that way. I like to do well in school and win awards and stuff for myself of course, but also because I love to see that look on your face. That's the best feeling in the world, to know you've pleased your mother.

This time, I know I've really asked a lot—paying my rent, my American Express bill, giving me money in Detroit, sending me even more. Buying me a whole new wardrobe.

I used to think I could one day pay you back. I know that's impossible. The only thing I can do is make you prouder of me than you've ever been. And be as good to my own daughter whenever I have one.

Thanks for being so generous. And for making it easy for me to ask for money when I need it. You never make me feel guilty or selfish or greedy.

I hope you know how much I love you.

Your baby,
Bridgett

PS: I got the new Carte Blanche card. The most I'll use it for are occasional dinners and a new book once in a while (maybe treat Stephanie to a meal now and then!).

I recently found this letter in my mother's brass trunk. I wrote it when I was twenty-nine years old and she'd just sent me the same amount of money her parents sent *her* when she'd migrated north all those years before. "She used to worry about you all the time, especially in New York, trying to survive that jungle," my friend Diane confides in me. "But she really wanted you to be able to make it."

Weeks after I wrote to thank her, my mother was diagnosed with diverticulitis—pouches had formed in the walls of her colon that had become infected and inflamed. I grew up seeing both the enema bag dangling from a hanger in the bathroom, and the small bottle of Senokot laxative pills on her dresser. But I made only a vague connection between constipation and diverticulitis. This condition was, she assured me, treatable with antibiotics and a liquid diet. Yet when I came home for Christmas, I saw how much pain she was in and asked why the treatment wasn't working. "They're running more tests," she told me.

I returned to New York, and to an offer for the professor job, at Baruch College. My mother, clearly pleased, said she'd pay my Brooklyn rent for the next nine months until the job started, help I desperately needed. Shortly after, I learned the fuller truth: my mother had a tumor on her colon. She'd insisted no one tell me this fact before I completed my interviews for the new job. *My mother has a tumor,* I wrote in my journal. *Serious? Cancerous? Life-threatening? We don't know, but my instincts tell me it's not. Still…my mother has a tumor.* Later, I admitted: *I don't want to write about Mama because I can't. I can't deal with the possibilities.*

In early March 1990, as I was sitting at Rita's dining room table in her house on Evergreen Road, she told me: "Mama has cancer."

It turns out my mother had been diagnosed with colon cancer several weeks before, but she'd again insisted that the others spare me. While she couldn't bear to tell me herself, she still made everyone else wait until I was back home and could learn the news in person. Then she had my sister do it.

I remember it as an out-of-body experience. The words *Mama* and *cancer* in the same sentence didn't compute. That was something that happened to other mothers; mine suffered from blood clots. I got up from the table and moved to the kitchen, suddenly thirsty. I stood at the sink, just letting the water run. "*My mother has cancer. My mother has cancer,*" I repeated in a low voice, to make myself comprehend. But I couldn't.

Mama soon had the cancerous parts of her colon removed. We all waited in the hospital's waiting room for several excruciating hours for her to emerge. When it was over, the doctor told me that he'd not only removed much of her colon, but had also given her a hysterectomy. He felt he'd "gotten all of it" and was optimistic about her prognosis. As he spoke to me, Aunt Florence and my cousin Jewell stood nearby, and I asked him to step away so we could speak in private. I didn't want him to say too much in front of them because my mother had sworn us, her children, to secrecy. We were not to tell *anyone* that she had cancer, not even her sister. My move away really wounded Aunt Florence, and she yelled out, "I don't need to hear what any damn doctor has to say about *my* sister! I listen to a higher doctor. God is the only one whose diagnosis I care about!"

My mother definitely used secrecy as a form of protection; even Burt didn't know for months after the diagnosis. I see sparing someone by withholding a painful truth now, with distance, as a gesture of love. But did her secrecy also keep her from benefiting from the widest possible treatment options? "If I'd known sooner, I would've taken her straight to Mayo Clinic," Burt later told me. Secrecy also prevented Mama from enjoying a community of support. Today, we handle a cancer diagnosis with openness and receptivity to loving, widespread empathy. My mother believed, like so many black people of her generation, that cancer was something to be ashamed of, a failing of some sort, and definitely to be hidden. To her, it wasn't like dying nobly from, say, a "weak heart."

She was also a very private person. She didn't want "everybody down South" aware of her cancer. She knew that if her baby sister living up North in Detroit knew, everyone from back home, in Nashville, would know too. Her pride made that an intolerable option. She wanted to retain her dignity, and that meant her privacy. Compounding it all was Mama's inability to deliver bad news. That itself must've felt to her like a failing. Fannie prided herself on helping to improve others' situations, as a deliverer of *good* news. For this complex tangle of reasons, Mama swore us to secrecy, made us complicit.

Still, we were optimistic. For seven precious months she seemed fine, and life moved forward: Tony graduated from high school, and a new young woman in need of nurturing and guidance entered Mama's life. Beatrice was Michael Terrell's nineteen-year-old sister-in-law, newly arrived from the Dominican Republic and now living in the space above our family on Seven Mile with Michael, her sister, and their mother. "Mrs. Robinson would check up on me," says Beatrice, who now goes by Vatrize. "She heard our really loud arguments and one day she just sent Tony upstairs to get me." Vatrize spent the night and awoke that next morning to find my mother in the kitchen, preparing her breakfast. "She was wearing white, and she was going through the cabinets," recalls Vatrize. "And I remember I felt such gratitude for this person who didn't know me; yet I could feel her love for me." After that, my mother let Vatrize stay downstairs with her, offering her a safe haven and kindness. "Somebody caring for me for no reason?" says Vatrize. "I had never experienced that in my life."

We were encouraged by my mother's interest in Vatrize, because helping others was her thing, and we saw it as life-affirming. We were equally pleased that she began a regimen of healthy eating, paying a nutritionist to prepare "wholistic" meals filled with roughage, and taking vitamins and supplements, having ended the liquid diet. During my visits home, we all went out to dinner, shopping, and on car rides along the Detroit River. One of my treasured photos was taken during that time: Mama in the middle, Rita and I flanking her. Mama is wearing her grandson's leather jacket and her hair is in crinkly natural curls that I've styled for her; she's looking at the camera with an expression that says, *I'm still here.*

Yet there were signs. For one, she started talking about wanting another grandchild, uncharacteristic for her. *And why is Mama talking about how beautiful babies are and still asking me about J?* I lamented in my journal that summer, not seeing the larger meaning at all. *Now I understand what makes being 30 such a hard thing for a woman.*

That fall, as a new assistant professor, I was featured in the college's student newspaper, the *Ticker.* I sent the article to Mama and she had it laminated, began showing it to everyone who dropped by, including my friend Diane.

"She cherished your accomplishments, and she was so proud of you," Diane tells me. "Doing what you wanted to do, and being able to survive New York doing it? In her eyes, that was really standing up to something. That was truly making it."

But nineteen days after that article ran, Mama entered a different hospital, and a different doctor performed another surgery, to remove "adhesions," essentially scar tissue from the original surgery. No one used the word *recurrence,* despite the fact that she remained in the hospital for over three weeks and was told she'd likely have "light" chemotherapy to kill the remaining cancerous cells *lurking inside her,* as I phrased it in my journal.

At the start of the new year, 1991, I wrote: *Knowing*

Mama's spirits are up has had an infectious effect on me. If she can be strong and optimistic, I know I can. In early April, during one of my visits from New York, she began receiving chemo, and I could certainly see the toll it was taking on her. *Mama just came home from the hospital,* I wrote. *She's taking a bath. She looks tired, older. She has lost weight, is smaller than I've ever seen her. And her hand is dark from the chemotherapy; her hair is shorter (was it cut?).*

Frightened, I'd bark, "Go to bed, Mama!" if she started to nod out around me. And I launched into a rabid regimen of positive thinking. *This is the time for my faith to increase, for my belief in God to strengthen,* I declared. *I have no doubt that God heals, that she can recover fully. I believe. I will affirm her good health daily. And I will pray for her nightly. I want her to put herself in the flow of healthiness; I want her to be positive.*

Because my mother had introduced me to positive thinking, I felt justified. Wasn't she the one known for believing things could get better if you just got your mind right, and trusted? When I came to her for advice, overwhelmed by some crisis, she'd often say, "Nothing is so impossible it can't be overcome," and then tell me to sleep on it, before quoting Scarlett O'Hara's last line in *Gone with the Wind:* "After all, tomorrow is another day."

I convinced myself it was my duty as her daughter to do what you should never do to a cancer patient: put the onus of her recovery on her, making my mother feel it was her job, her *responsibility to us* to remain positive so she could get better—the implication being that if she didn't heal, it was because she was just not being positive enough.

She was back in the hospital a month after her first chemo treatment for a second round. That hospital visit lasted two weeks, during which I didn't return to Detroit. Rather, the day after my thirty-first birthday, two days after my mother returned home from the hospital, I went to St. Thomas with a friend for five days. I told myself that I was going to a peaceful place by the water to meditate, to get into the Flow and send all the positive vibes and energy I could out into the universe, so that Mama would get better. I was trying to be a true student of Unity, and the teachings of Eric Butterworth, who wrote that the best way to help a loved one heal was to "Try to go apart in some way, and get yourself centered." He even stressed that "Being removed from close proximity with the one who is hurting may be an advantage, for you may not be tempted to react emotionally to the appearances. . . . If the consciousness is high enough, you should be able to pray for one on the other side of the world as effectively as one on the other side of the room, perhaps even more effectively."

What I now know is that I was shirking my responsibility to help care for my mother, and sending the message to her and everyone around her that I was selfish and insensitive; after all, while my sister Rita and my stepfather, Burt, lovingly tended to and nursed her, I was vacationing on a beach in the Virgin Islands. During a conversation we had over the phone after my trip, Mama made it clear how she felt with four simple words: "I'm your mother too."

When she said those words to me, I gripped the telephone receiver as tight as I could and cried wracking tears of remorse. But I did so in silence, determined that she wouldn't hear me crying. Of course she heard the silent sobs on my end of the phone. "I know you better than you know yourself," she used to say to me. Now, with those four new, bruising words, *I'm your mother too,* she'd pierced my shame, and my extraordinary fear of losing her. I was devastated that I'd disappointed her. Yet I didn't say, "I'm sorry, Mama." Instead, after I cried those silent tears, I complained to Rita that Mama was "tripping," that she expected too much, that she should understand that I escaped to St. Thomas to "meditate on her spiritual wholeness." Rita, in her infinite grace, only said to me: "I think your vacation was just poor timing."

But I clung to the belief that my mother was the problem, even as my anger at her morphed into new forms of insensitivity. It pains me now to see what I wrote weeks after our phone call: *Thoughts again of Mama. I'm less annoyed. More saddened. She needs constant reassurance that people love her, yet she doesn't really know how to show love herself.* My denial was deafening.

Meanwhile, Vatrize was there, and she saw how much weaker my mother had become. "She had a walker," says Vatrize. "And because she and I had gotten really close and I wasn't working anymore, I was around her a lot. I'd do little things for her, help her get up, or get something for her....I do remember one day she was in a lot of pain, and she was trying to bear it. I just sat with her the whole time."

Throughout their time together, Vatrize had sought counsel from my mother, who'd encouraged her to think about her own future and what she wanted. Soon enough, Vatrize decided to move to Long Island for a fresh start and went downstairs to say goodbye. "Mrs. Robinson was really sick that day," she recalls. Vatrize sat on the chaise lounge beside my mother's bed, quiet for a while before she finally said: "All right, well, I'm going to go." My mother looked her in the eye, and Vatrize says her last words to her were: "Whatever you do, remember to respect yourself."

I spent a week at home that summer and gained only slightly more self-awareness: *I learned a lot,* I wrote in my journal. *I learned that I need to get re-accustomed to Mama's ways, that her negativity bothers me and that I get on her nerves too. With my holier-than-thou attitude. I want her to learn to release things, but I have to stop fussing at her about it. When she slept through an entire day, I missed her. And I was concerned.*

Still, I wasn't really confronting the severity of my mother's illness, in part because Rita and Burt were caring for her day to day in Detroit, while I lived and worked in New York. When she experienced a six-month run without more treatment, I convinced myself the chemo was working.

Adding to my willful denial was the fact that Mama wasn't talking about her illness and remained steadfast that we say nothing to no one. But people knew *something* was very wrong. It didn't take a lot to figure out that her symptoms— surgery, weight loss, tiredness, repeated hospital visits, hair loss—connoted the big C. Still, her belief was that if you could see she was sick, that was all you needed to know. If you wanted to be there for her, support her and even help care for her, why would you need to know the details of her illness? Why would you need to know her diagnosis and prognosis? To my mother, no words needed to be spoken for you to do the right thing by her, whether you were family or a close friend.

Oddly enough, I'd never actually heard Mama talk about

death, except to say "Dying is easy. Living takes guts." Nor did I know her beliefs about an afterlife. The founders of Unity believed in reincarnation, or rather "re-embodiment," but I'd never heard her talk about coming back. Nor did she believe in the old folks' religious philosophy that you'd get your rewards in heaven, "in the by-and-by." And she really didn't care what people would say about her once she was gone.

She wanted to be appreciated in the here and now. "Give me my damn flowers while I can still smell 'em," she'd often say. She hated the idea that people who didn't really know her, or had been two-faced or jealous or backstabbing (all of which she encountered in her line of work), would flock to look down on her in a casket. This combined with my mother's disdain for black folks who went to funerals largely out of curiosity, just to see how the deceased had been "laid out" or "put away." She'd say, "Bury me facedown so I can tell all those nosy niggers to kiss my ass."

With her health declining, Rita took over the business. My mother, so sick, did not resist; besides, she knew her customers were in good hands with Rita, who ran the Numbers well. Luckily, Rita kept Mama's loyal customers even while the state provided yet more lottery options. In addition to the eight existing "draw" games and a plethora of ever-increasing instant "scratch-off" games, a brand-new draw game called Cash 5 was introduced. (It was replaced eight years later by yet another game.) While only the Daily 3 and Daily 4 mimicked the Numbers, the myriad other lottery games were, in a sense, competition.

Only in looking back do I see that my mother was confronting her own mortality by trying to prepare us for a life without her: She began lecturing Tony about becoming more responsible and taking advantage of every opportunity she provided, because "I won't be around forever." And one day, she called and gave me the gift that would release me from a lifetime of immobilizing guilt: "I thought about it," she said to me. "And I wasn't there for my mother when she was sick. I didn't move back to Nashville because I knew my sisters would take care of her."

On one of my visits home, Mama did a private reading for Rita and me from her "book," or as she now called it, her roman à clef.

As we sit with her at the kitchen table, she opens the black three-ring binder, the same one I've glimpsed my entire life but have never seen inside, and with reading glasses perched on her nose announces the title: *617 Crawford.*

Mama recites the words she's written in a low yet confident voice.

> *As the bus rolled along the Kentucky road nearing the Tennessee borderline, many thoughts filled the mind of Rose Miller, fifteen years old, beautiful, pregnant and running away from home. Thoughts of her family kept coming back. What was her mother going to say when she discovered her gone? Would she call the police in right away or would she give her time to come back? Rose had an argument with her mother just yesterday, when her mother found out she had skipped school.*

She reads it all to us that day, the story handwritten across decades in green and blue and black ink, all in her lovely cursive, each capital letter a flourish, moving across forty-three pages.

It's the story of Rose, a fifteen-year-old girl who after running away from home finds her way to Minnie, the madam of a genteel, well-run whorehouse at 617 Crawford Street in Nashville. There Minnie treats Rose like a daughter, helping her get a safe abortion with the aid of a black woman doctor, and allowing her to stay at 617 as her personal assistant, rather than a prostitute. Minnie helps Rose finish high school and "becomes her benefactress," paying for her to attend Vanderbilt University to study nursing. Eventually, Minnie teaches Rose how to run the business, and when Minnie becomes ill, Rose cares for her. Minnie dies, "the darkest day" of Rose's life. Rose inherits Minnie's business, which she decides to close down or sell as soon as she completes nursing school. The whorehouse, coupled with Minnie's generosity, has given Rose a chance in life she'd never otherwise have.

Mama's way of seeing the world shone out from this story: the young woman setting out for a more inviting place, determined yet unprepared for what she finds; the older woman who helps her out; an underground enterprise run with integrity and expertise, and also caution, which gives myriad people new opportunities.

Mama used the power of luck, as Rose fortuitously ends up at Minnie's house of ill repute because the cabdriver takes her to 617 Crawford, assuming she's one of Minnie's new "girls." And the title reflects the symbolism Mama saw in a three-digit house address (her childhood home had a three-digit address: 410 Wingrove), and of course she knew what three digits from a house address could do to change a life, given what 788, taken from her own Detroit address, had done for her.

I now suspect that the story's plot turn, Minnie's illness, was influenced by my mother's own illness: *She had long noticed that Minnie...had been going to the doctor quite frequently....Rose had a feeling that Minnie was hiding something from her. But she did not ask questions. That she also learned from Minnie. Never ask personal questions and never pry....If they want you to know something important they will eventually tell you.*

We spent Christmas '91 in Las Vegas, a family trip that was Mama's idea. She joined me at a blackjack table on that first day, and I let myself think that this was like old times, when she was the luckiest person I knew. It was her one good day in Vegas, and the last thing we ever did together, just the two of us—gamble.

That evening at dinner, I greedily told my mother about my plans to shoot a feature film, hungry for her usual support. She nodded, tried to listen, but when I escorted her to the hotel's bathroom, I stood by helplessly and watched as she pulled out a vial of morphine and took a dose.

We shared our gifts with one another on Christmas morning, trying to act normal. She gave each of us cash. I gave Mama a navy knit pantsuit with tiny silver rhinestones, in a small size that I had to force myself to buy, because I couldn't believe that she, who'd always been plump, could actually fit into it. ("Well, now I know," she'd announced on one of her better days, as she stood before us in Rita's size 10 dress. "The way to lose weight is to not eat.") She stayed in bed for the rest of the vacation, sleeping through the days. When she needed to get up for any reason, my stepfather carried her in his arms.

It turns out my mother wanted a refuge from the onslaught of people who would've certainly come by to visit had she been at home for the holidays. She didn't want others to see her so gravely ill, still wanted to retain her dignity. She flew to Nevada with her family for privacy. But Rita and I didn't see the trip for what it was. We saw her desire to take a trip at all as a sign of our mother "getting better." So when she slept every day, it made us upset, antsy, restless. We decided we couldn't bear to stay for the entire ten days, announcing that we were returning home early. Rita and I were impatient, complaining, puffing on cigarettes. In a rare moment of anger, my stepfather scolded us. "How could you think about leaving Vegas when this was something your mother wanted us to do together as a family?" He knew what we did not. The doctor had given *him* the prognosis for his wife of more than twenty-two years.

I did not write about my mother in my journal for five and a half months. Rather, I busied myself with the goal of "making her proud" by working exhaustively on a screenplay and a novel and full-time teaching, even as she was receiving radiation treatments. On Mother's Day 1992—the day after her sixty-fourth birthday—I wrote: *Mama's illness is a cloud, a time-bomb over my head saying, "Hurry up! Be a success!"*

That day I sent my mother two dozen white roses; she loved white because it was "the color of purity." Our house on Seven Mile filled with flowers and plants, a plethora of friends dropping off bouquets and arrangements as a way of saying how much she meant to them. "It's like a florist shop in here," reported Rita. "Flowers are everywhere." She said Mama took the bouquet I'd sent her and brought it back to Tony's bedroom, placed it on the nightstand, then lay down on his narrow bed. "She just wanted your flowers near her," said Rita. For a long time I comforted myself by imagining my mother enjoying the white roses' fragrance.

Twelve days later, Rita called me at daybreak. First she said, "Happy birthday." Then she said, "Mama was just rushed to the hospital with a faint heartbeat. They say she may not make it through the day."

I boarded a plane that morning and braced myself for what I might find when I landed. But I prayed that Mama wouldn't die on my birthday. When I think about it across the distance, perhaps there would've been a sad but apt symmetry to her life ending on the same day that mine had begun—given that my birth had marked the family's good fortunes, and given all she'd done to make my life so good. There might have been something resonant and meaningful in that. But of course I was terrified that every year on my birthday, I'd also be marking the anniversary of my mother's death.

Mama didn't die that day. In fact, I got to spend a week with her in the hospital, sleeping in a chair beside her bed each night; I never left the room. Late in the week, out of the blue, she called out to someone, "Wait for me, I'm coming! I'm coming!" Then she paused and frowned, realization setting in. "Oh, I can't move my legs," she said. "I can't walk." Seeing her face in that moment destroyed me. Another day, she suddenly began reciting random combinations of numbers, her voice strong: *"Two-nine-five, three-eight-six, and four-three-two...."* But beyond those two outbursts, she said nothing those days, not quite unconscious, but under heavy morphine sedation. In between the stream of visitors, I clung to the pleasure of waking up throughout the night to watch Mama breathe, prepared to stay like that, the two of us in a quiet togetherness, forever.

One day, long before she became ill, Mama, Rita, and I decided to figure out our personal numbers, based on which number recurred the most in each of our lives. Rita decided that her number was 4, because she was born in the fourth month, her name had four letters, and she was the fourth child in the family. I decided my number was 7, because I was the seventh member of the family, my name had seven letters in it (before I added an extra *t*), and in a nod to numerology, the numbers of my birth date equaled a 7. Mama decided her personal number was 9 because she was the ninth child in her family; she was born on May ninth, the full name that everyone called her as a child, Fannie Mae, had nine letters in it, and the date she bought Broadstreet—April 15, 1961—equaled a 9. (I secretly told myself that this also meant that Mama, a good witch, would—like the cats that are witches' supernatural familiars—have nine lives.)

On day seven, the day of my personal number, Mama began making a loud wracking sound when she breathed. Mercifully, the nurse told us she needed to clear our mother's lungs and made us leave because the procedure, she said, could be "upsetting" to the family. But when we returned to the room, Mama was completely silent, yet opening and closing her mouth, clearly gasping for air. It was hard to witness, and Aunt Florence pulled me into the hospital corridor. "Listen," she said to me. "She's holding on for you. Let her go, because she's suffering. Just let her go." I cried hard in that hallway before I reentered her room, leaned into her ear, and said, "Mama, you can go. I love you, and I'll miss you, but I understand. You can go."

I held her hand. Her mouth relaxed. She died shortly after, squeezing my hand with surprising strength just before she took her last breath. The date was May 29, 1992, a 9. In her story, Mama had written: *Aunt Minnie had taken sick and went into the hospital. She died on the 29th of May.*

We stayed with her for a while, and when we left, my family and I assured one another that Mama's passing had been both peaceful and beautiful, with her surrounded by loved ones, what she would've wanted.

It was during the car ride home that Burt told me, "I waited ten years to marry her. She was the love of my life."

"When she died, half of me died with her," says Aunt Florence. "Because when she was living, I didn't have no kind of worry. None whatsoever. Fannie knew how to take care of everything." And then it dawns on her, how well Fannie kept her secret: "You know what? As close as we were, God is my witness, I didn't know my sister had cancer until she was dead."

I took home from the hospital Mama's stylish black hobo-style leather purse with gold studded designs on the front. I held it up to my nose, sniffed its perfumy smell. It smelled like her. It still does. Inside her purse, the things she carried were a combination of quotidian and indulgent, expected and surprising. She carried two Bic pens, a pair of tan hospital footies, a bobby pin, and a Dentyne gum wrapper; in its own Ziploc bag, she carried loose credit cards: Optima,

Sears, Saks, Jacobson's, Michigan Bankard Visa, Discover, and an American Express in her grandson, Anthony Davis's, name. She also carried a green checkbook for American Express Centurion Bank's line of credit, its ledger recording checks written to "Cash" for $1,000 and $500, and another to "Bridgett Davis" for $1,000.

A small purple wallet brimmed with business cards for an antiques store in Washington, Michigan, that sold "Leaded & Beveled Glass Doors & Windows"; Dr. Kadro, her surgeon (on the back of which she'd written Tony's Atlanta telephone number); an artist in Utica, Michigan, who specialized in watercolor and egg tempera paintings; a college planning coordinator/consultant (for herself, perhaps); and Special Touch Nails (with appointments for a manicure one week and a pedicure the next). Inside a green Italian-leather wallet, she carried her driver's license, with its date of birth making her ten years younger, and certificates of insurance for three different autos: a 1991 Chevrolet Camaro (Tony's); a 1989 Oldsmobile Cutlass Supreme SL (hers), and a 1984 Mercury Marquis (whose?). She carried a receipt from Jacobson's for a purse and four pairs of shoes totaling $569.92, and the rest of her credit cards: American Express Gold, Carte Blanche, Michigan Bankard MasterCard, Comerica MasterCard, Winkelman's, Lane Bryant, and American Express Platinum. In there too was Unity School of Christianity's Airplane Blessing. (*This is God's airplane. His intelligence is in every part of it. I rest secure in His protecting presence, and all is well.*)

In a side pocket of her purse, written on large scratch-pad paper in her own handwriting, she carried a rundown combination of two different four-digit numbers she planned to play, and for how much:

```
1112—2.00
1211—3.00
1121—7.00
1101—2.00
1110—2.00
0111—2.00
1011—2.00
1101—50—50
1121—50—50
```

She also carried a Lotto ticket for five plays, totaling $5, dated February 26, 1992. I suspect that was the last lottery she played.

The funeral was packed with hundreds of people. I wore a brand-new white skirt suit, its jacket lapel trimmed in faux pearls, which I promptly gave to Goodwill afterward. During the family hour, as we greeted visitors, a woman came up to me and grabbed my hand. I'd never met her. She said she was a psychic, and that late one night my mother had phoned her to say she was dying, and to ask how her children and grandchild would fare in the years ahead, without her. "I told her not to worry, you'd all be fine," this woman said to me. I thanked her. Reverend Stotts, Mama's beloved pastor, spoke movingly, I'm told, sharing rich details about my mother's special place in the world, and offering comforting words to us, the bereaved. But my mind was stuck on the fact that Mama had discussed dying with a stranger; why, I wondered, was that new knowledge so devastating to me? All I could later recall of Reverend Stotts's eulogy was his saying how peaceful and calm he felt every time he entered my mother's spacious blue living room.

Toward the end of the service, Rita walked up to the casket and yelled out, "Get up, Mama, get up!" I rose, rushed over, guided my sister back to the seat beside me on the church's front pew, and held her hand in mine.

I wrote the obituary, attempting to capture my mother's life in 375 words. An excerpt:

A SERVICE OF MEMORY CELEBRATING
THE LIFE OF FANNIE M. ROBINSON

Fannie was a beautiful woman with a feisty personality and many interests. She loved to travel to new places, to read voraciously, to buy lovely furnishings and clothing and to hold lively conversations with countless friends and acquaintances. An independent, proud spirit, she marched through life providing others with a stellar example of strength and spiritual will. Mired in the belief that "God helps those who help themselves," Fannie flourished in the face of challenges and used her resourcefulness to create a life of abundance and comfort for her family.... Throughout her life, Fannie was there, giving support to those who asked and those who didn't. These things Fannie did without comment. She believed in doing for others and not discussing what had been done....it is in the lingering, warm midst of that flow of love that we celebrate Fannie's life—a life lived with compassion and lived with dignity.

At her death, I was the same age my mother had been when I was born. *She'd lived half her life when she had me. I may have already lived half of mine.... I'm afraid of dying,* I noted in my journal, then added: *I think I'm faking sanity...I don't know who I am anymore.*

"You're an orphan now," said John, the chair of the English department at my college. I'd just returned to work and was so stunned by that word, *orphan,* that I headed back to my office, closed the door, and sat there staring at nothing. I felt numb. On the wall hung the student newspaper article about me. After the funeral, I'd found the laminated copy in Mama's bedroom, bent and worn from her showing it to everyone. I looked up at that framed story, its headline proclaiming, BARUCH GETS A NEW ENGLISH PROFESSOR—MAKING AN IMPACT IS HIGH ON HER PRIORITY LIST, and it seemed to mock me. *What does it matter how well I do my job?* I thought. *Who would care?* For the first time in my life, I had no one to make proud. I'd lost her, and myself as hers. I wanted to quit.

But Rita wanted to keep Mama's Numbers business aloft. This was difficult, given that she worked full-time as a special-education teacher in a Detroit public high school, so was effectively choosing to manage two careers. But she wanted to honor Mama's last wish and see our nephew, Tony, complete college; revenue from the business allowed him to remain at Clark Atlanta University. And so, each morning before she went to work, and in the afternoons after work, Rita took customers' numbers. In the evenings, she checked the business for hits and paid out winnings. On the weekends, she took more numbers, collected payments, ran customers' tapes, and purchased lottery tickets daily from the corner party store, to thwart a hit's breaking her modest bank. I was no help at all, living in New York, avoiding Detroit, which felt to me like the very capital of loss. Meanwhile, in September of that year, the Michigan lottery set an all-time-high annual sales record of over $1.2 billion.

While Rita processed her grief by stepping in and running our mother's business, "doing what Mama would want," I desperately needed to believe that Mama was still with me, if only in spiritual form. I searched for her presence everywhere and in all kinds of situations. There were other times, though, when clinging to the idea of her with me in spirit was not working. *It hit me hard again,* I wrote in my journal. *She's dead.* I dreamed about her often, and cried often. I dreamed of crying often. Missing her with a vengeance, I found the pain achingly physical; my chest hurt constantly. I did not want to do the work of living without her, and I had epiphanies of guilt. *I could have accommodated her more if I'd accepted her human frailty more,* I wrote. *I feel guilty for taking that trip to St. Thomas, for not spending January at home, for not acknowledging Mama's fear and pain, for not being there for her.*

Meanwhile, my attitude to the outside world was "Fuck everything else. I lost my mother." But I secretly regretted that I was so private, suffering alone, and lonely without someone "who loves me for me," to help me through it. *I haven't had a genuine, heartfelt conversation in a long, long time,* I lamented. *And my friends? Some are wonderful, some haven't bothered. Life goes on.*

Later that fall, I went home and packed up the things I wanted. In the bathroom, atop the long marble counter, sat her mirrored brass dressing room tray, overflowing with skin care products just as she'd left them. She wore very little makeup, but I did find her Charles of the Ritz Feather Touch Face Powder and her Fashion Fair rouge and lipstick. What she loved most were face creams, and she had a wondrous variety. I grabbed them all, the Clarins Toning Lotion, Lancôme Tonique Douceur, Clinique Crystal Clear Cleansing Oil, Neutrogena night cream, the pretty jar of La Prairie Cellular Moisturizer, and tossed them into my travel bag. I made sure to take the Estée Lauder Youth Dew Eau de Parfum, her lifetime fragrance in the classic turquoise bottle, which I spritzed on my bed pillow for weeks; I also grabbed from the tub's rim her giant bottles of Vitabath and Jean Naté After Bath Splash, later using them up on long, teary baths in hot-to-cold water. From the kitchen I took her cookbooks, and from her bedroom the natural healing and Unity books. I didn't take the *Man, Myth and Magic* encyclopedia from the den shelf, or her books by Edgar Cayce or Bertrand Russell, and I later regretted that; just running my eyes across those titles took me back into her world and affirmed anew that who I was came from who she'd been. I got other things, thanks to Rita: the family sofa, Mama's diamond-encrusted watch, some nightgowns, two Hermès scarves (one of which I gave to my cousin Lisa; the other I lost), some pairs of shoes that didn't fit me, linen, her china... but now I wish I'd taken even more, like the Super 8 footage my stepfather shot of Mama over the years. I didn't think to get those home movies from him, and now they're gone.

The loss of her moving image, like the loss of the sound of her voice (which I never recorded), still hurts. What, I ask myself, were the rhythms of her speech, the cadences and inflections? How would I never again hear her distinctive Southern way of speaking, never again hear her pronounce the last name Thompson as "TOMEson," the state Hawaii as "Ha-WHY-YUH" and the word *mature* as "maTOUR"? Never again witness how she moved, how she walked with her chin out, back straight and the slightest switch in her hips? Photos simply don't bring her to life.

That trip to Detroit made me fully realize she was gone. When I returned to New York, I reached a new depth of despair—late-night drinking, falling asleep while meeting with a student, crying and more crying, insomnia, anger, bitchiness, jealousy toward mothered friends. I felt bereft and deformed, as though I'd suffered an amputation of a limb I could still feel but couldn't touch.

"It is a pain that reaches all the way down to your ligaments and bones," writes journalist David Ferguson about losing a mother. "Our mothers were our first firmament, literally, our first homes, the universe from whose substance we were formed."

Frightened by my own sorrow, I entered therapy for the first time. I recently found a laundry list of topics I wanted to bring up in my early sessions: my mood swings and feelings of inadequacy; my guilt; and my deep disappointment at not having accomplished the Big Three before Mama died: a beautiful wedding for her to attend; a grandchild to spoil; and a real success to make her proud. *I need to know where I'm headed emotionally without her,* I scribbled at the bottom of that list. Linda, my therapist, later said I needed to create a new emotional relationship with myself, and others, to compensate for what I no longer had with my mother. I told her I had no idea how to do that, and Linda said, "Just look at how great your capacity to love another person is."

My therapist also tried to help me wrestle with my guilt. I couldn't understand how I had failed the person I loved more than anyone on earth. Yet my mother wanted to protect me, and for a long time that meant protecting me from the truth of her condition. In *617 Crawford,* Mama wrote in Rose's voice: *She knew all along she was going to die. Why didn't she tell me?...There was a sealed letter for me. A week passed before I could bring myself to open the letter. She started off by saying I am sorry for not telling you. I had known for some time.* And in a different color ink, clearly the last lines added to the story, lines I believe she composed toward the end, Mama wrote: *To tell you would only have made matters worse.*

But at the same time, my mother expected me to do right by her when it was evident just how sick she was. *I will always stay with you and see after you,* says Rose in Mama's story. *You haven't been too well lately.*

This I must face: I was all too willing to remain in denial about a frightening truth I refused to accept. And my mother's protectiveness made that easy. With others handling her care, my denial blossomed. As the youngest, I essentially got to act like the spoiled child I was. And it cost me then and now.

While I worked through my depression, for nine months Rita managed to juggle the business alongside her teaching, before doing both became increasingly untenable. Finally, in January of 1993, she announced that she was giving it all up, and officially closed the Numbers business that Mama had launched thirty-five years before. *If you should ever decide to close the place do so, and if you want to continue to run it, do that too,* Minnie tells Rose. Later, Minnie dies three weeks after Rose's twenty-first birthday, which turns out to be "on the ninth of May." (*Minnie kept her promise. She stayed through my first year at Vanderbilt. She got everything in order.*) Mama's grandson, Tony, turned twenty-one that summer and finished his last three semesters of college with help from us, his aunts.

Suffocating from my grief, I no longer wanted to be part of the Fort Greene, Brooklyn, neighborhood where I'd lived for five years; I sought a fresh start where no one knew me, where no one would know what I'd lost, and set out to do the improbable—find a Manhattan apartment quickly. I did just that, signing a lease on the first anniversary of my mother's death. The date, 5/29, was a 7, and I remain convinced that Mama gifted me that West Fourteenth Street one-bedroom triplex, still caring for me from the spirit world.

May 29, 1993—1st-Year anniversary
  In one year, it's all different. Without her....
  I see this layer of my life peeling off: That huge part of me that was a daughter before all else...not wanting to be a fool for any man (she'd never approve) and depending on her love (all encompassing) as the litmus test for or the substitute for others' love. My needs were lessened because I had her. All of them: emotional, financial and even spiritual.

Now she's gone.

And I'm being forced to grow up, to really handle my own shit, to be more than a pseudo-independent woman. I'm truly "out here on my own."

It's as though she died so I could live.

Uncharacteristically, once in my new Manhattan space, I left my computer inside its box. For two years I'd been writing as if running out of time, spending hours and hours each day frenetically working on both the novel and the screenplay, determined to make my mother proud, on autopilot even after she died. Now I couldn't bring myself to unpack the computer. For the first time in years, I couldn't write. And without the will or ability to dive back into "the work," I felt as though I'd suffered yet another devastating loss. *I'm just this mixture of heartbreak, failure and grief,* I wrote.

Meanwhile, Michael Terrell still had big hopes for Broadstreet, dreams he'd nurtured since he'd bought the house from my mother in 1988. He'd created blueprints with an architect, renderings that brought to life his plans, which included turning the third-floor attic into a master bedroom with a walk-in closet, en suite bathroom, and small study area. "That was going to be my little penthouse up there," he tells me. "I was just gonna make it a grand and beautiful place to live." And he was going to put period-style railings and woodwork back into the house, so it could have as many original details as possible; he'd done the research and found places where he could buy handcrafted 1920s-style materials.

"I designated a room for Mikey"—his son—"and all the

little things I was going to do to make this little room special," he says. "All my fantasies kicked in."

The house was so well built, with lath and plaster where drywall or Sheetrock might be, that it had withstood the 1986 fire. And its frame was only singed in a few spots. "It looked terrible, but it was mainly superficial damage," recalls Michael. He gutted the house and began rewiring. He set up his tools and worktable in the living room and often slept in the basement. But vandals kicked in his door, ripped out the new circuit-breaker panel, stole some of his tools, damaged the work he'd done. Still determined, Michael boarded up everything and tried to work quickly enough so he could occupy the house and protect it. My mother had had security doors installed, but thieves ripped out those doors. "I said, 'My God, would these people leave me alone?'" says Michael.

This time, he made the house like a fortress, blocking all the windows and all other points of entry, and began working on the renovations yet again. But progress was slow and many months went by—my mother died in the interim—and then Rita rang him one afternoon and said, "Mike, the fire department called to tell us that Broadstreet is on fire."

When he got to the house, "It was practically burnt to the ground," he says. "I stood on that sidewalk in front of the house, and I just cried." He pauses, unable to speak for several seconds. "I still had planned to make that my home."

Defeated, and knowing he would only want to rebuild a house of the same caliber, a daunting prospect he simply couldn't afford, and now facing a huge property tax bill, Michael let the City of Detroit take Broadstreet. On June

19, 1994, the house my mother had bought thirty-three years before "on contract" from Mr. Prince, the white man she remained grateful to for not "doing her dirty," was razed by the city. Its lot was divided between the two homeowners on either side; each expanded her front yard, and together they erected a chain link fence across the divide.

I avoided going home for most of that summer, even though I had no reason *not* to—I certainly wasn't writing. Finally I made myself get on an airplane. In Detroit for several days, I waited until the last possible moment before I got into my rental car and drove to Livernois Avenue, made a left at Buena Vista, turned right onto Broadstreet Avenue, and pulled up to what once was 12836. As the car idled, I stared in disbelief at the gaping hole where our family home used to be.

After some minutes, I pulled away from the sight of that vacant, ghostly space existing between two proud-looking homes, its nakedness exposing the backside of another, random house. I drove straight to the airport. Memories of our lives on Broadstreet pushed up against one another: the whole family crowded into the kitchen's leather banquette, talking over each other as we grab hot, buttery biscuits before Mama can even set them on the table...me and Daddy watching TV together in the den, him laughing so hard at Flip Wilson's Geraldine impersonation (*What you see is what you get, sucker!*) that tears spring from his eyes...Mama in the basement, doing laundry and talking on the phone, me right beside her with my Suzy Homemaker washer, dolls' clothes churning inside...and later, when I've moved back to Broadstreet at twenty-three, in the living room with Dianne and Anthony, album covers spread across the carpet, stereo atop a TV tray, speakers blaring, the three of us dancing together to "Billie Jean."

I thought of how we'd all returned to that house again and again over the years, in different familial constellations, to receive its succor. But I didn't cry. On a wintry night months before, I'd gone out alone to see a friend perform. I'd felt my mother's presence, felt her spirit all over me the entire day; that evening, I met the man I would marry. He was waiting for me back in New York.

Four years went by, and I returned to Detroit, to show a film I'd made about a young woman's relationship with her mother. After an emotional screening at the Opera House, as I helped Mama's dear friend Lula climb onto the bus that would take her home, she turned to me and said, "I told Fannie one day while we were sitting on Broadstreet's front porch, just talking, that you would go on to do great things. She said to me, 'I know she will. I'm not worried about my baby at all.'"

As the doors closed behind her, I waved at Lula and watched as the bus slowly pulled off, made its way down the street. Then I cried.

Epilogue

Folks still play the Numbers in Detroit, and still use the state's lottery for their winning combinations. To this day, when I visit Aunt Florence, she wants to know my flight number, my rental car's license plate number, and my hotel room number. And I want her to hit on one of those numbers; I want to be her good-luck-charm niece.

Older blacks like my aunt see playing the Numbers as a communal gesture, and a way to patronize the bookies they trust, rather than give their money to the state. I've spoken with a few of those aging Detroiters who still "take Lottery"; they use their proceeds to supplement modest pensions, pay large heating bills, and help grown children survive Detroit's battered economy. I admire them; they keep the tradition alive.

Writing this book gave me the chance to relive those sweet years when I was surrounded by the world of the Numbers and its magical rituals of luck, when *What'd you dream last night?* was a daily mantra and my mother's customers celebrated my achievements. In the process, I've come to see that a certain type of black person, the kind I grew up around, has disappeared from public consciousness: working-class, blue-collar African-Americans who raised families in stable homes and crafted lives of worth in spite of limited education and access. I'm thinking of the women in my mother's life, no longer with us, like Miss Lucille and Lula and Miss Carter and Pearl Massey. Some made a way out of no way through the Numbers, others through small businesses, others as caregivers, and still others through steady jobs in the plants or with the post office, or for the city. They were all honest, hardworking women.

Fannie was the one on a mission. It didn't matter to my mother that the Founding Fathers weren't thinking about the likes of her when they declared America's citizens entitled to, among other things, the pursuit of happiness. She believed in her right to that pursuit and she understood that wealth was the key to attainment; she was happier when money was flowing, because it gave her the life she wanted and the liberty to share it freely.

Thanks to my mother, who went after her American dream one dollar at a time, I now have my own solid piece of that dream: I inherited property Mama bought with money made through the Numbers. Selling that property provided the down payment for a co-op my husband and I purchased in Park Slope, Brooklyn, which we later sold to buy a brownstone. With a family home my children will inherit—my own version of Broadstreet—I am acutely aware that this privilege is un-

288

available to most African-Americans, who are five times less likely to inherit wealth than white Americans. (All of my white friends in New York received cash gifts from their parents to buy their first homes.) Without help from family, it's no wonder that the home ownership rate among blacks is barely more than half that of whites.

What has it meant to finally reveal this secret I've carried in my belly for over half a century? I've spoken with dozens of people who've known me most of my life, and when I confess that Mama was a number runner, I often get a stunned reaction.

"I'm like blown away," says my friend since fourth grade, Diane. But then a memory returns to her: "You know, somebody said that to me when I was an adult. They said that the gray house on Seven Mile was a Numbers house, and I said, 'No, no, no.' I dismissed it." She thinks about it now. "Actually, I'm not surprised that your mother was running an enterprise, because she had all those innate characteristics.... I knew your mother was in charge. I just didn't know in charge of what."

Other friends had already figured it out and kept the secret of knowing from *me*. "You want me to talk about that?" asks Elliott, my high school buddy. When I assure him it's fine, he says, "Okay. One time at your house I heard all these adding machines, this tick, tick, tick, tock—you know, this noise coming from the basement, and there was a lot of action going on down there. And that's when I put two and two together, and I said, 'Oh....'"

Once he knew, he says, "It didn't cause any kind of fear

or trepidation or anything like that. It just was what it was. I mean, people do what they have to do to in order to survive and get through this life, right? And she was doing what she was doing, at that time."

For those who knew us, our family secret (as far as it was a secret at all) didn't possess the potency I gave it. People admired my mother not so much for what she did as for the kind of woman she was.

And yet I don't want this point to get lost: My mother launched a Numbers operation out of necessity, but despite its constant challenges, she *enjoyed* running her own business. Self-employment allowed her a coveted life of rugged individualism, as they say. By contributing to this thriving underground economy, my mother was able to live out Booker T. Washington's dream of Negroes' self-reliance, and as such she moved through the world as a head-held-high, race-proud black woman.

A friend of mine once argued with me over what she saw as a simple fact that mothers envy their daughters, oft-times showing jealousy when their daughters are smarter or prettier or have more options in life than they did. This was a foreign concept to me, and I told her so; she interpreted my response as denial. But the truth is that my mother didn't succumb to envy because she wasn't a frustrated careerist or intellectual or artist who subjugated her dreams for her husband and children. Of course she didn't get the chance to do all that she would've liked, nor were enough opportunities available to her. But my mother *did* live a life that she created for herself, not the one handed to her. She had her own agency; and that allowed her to go farther and achieve more than any of her sisters. Compared to them, she soared. And she wanted her own daughters to soar higher.

Now that I've come clean about my mother, I'm relieved. But also, I'm a little sad. I am no longer the keeper of her secret. I have given that up, lost that special status in exchange for sharing her story. I believe it was worth it; and I'd like to believe she'd approve of my choice, she'd agree that sometimes some good *does* come from running your mouth.

Every day except Sunday, I walk a block from my Bed-Stuy, Brooklyn, home to Mechy's, the corner bodega, to play the New York Daily Numbers lottery. (Yes, it's actually called Numbers.) I stand in line behind men and women who work unglamorous but vital jobs or live on fixed incomes or who might hustle to make ends meet, people harshly judged, seen as wasting their money on lottery tickets. These are people like those of my youth, people I grew up around and got to know as my mother's customers, and even though my life is likely more privileged, I have a deep, visceral connection to them. Emotionally, they are more my tribe than friends who are teachers and lawyers and writers. As we wait in line together, we discuss our hunches, the dreams we had, the numbers missed, the ones caught.

I have many special numbers that I could play when it's my turn. One of them is 410. That's my mother and stepfather's anniversary, April tenth; it's also my husband's birthday, *and* it's the address of my mother's family home, the house her father purchased in 1919. The number 410 plays for *good luck* in *The Three Wise Men Dream Book*. I could also play 516, both the day that lotteries became legal in

Michigan, May sixteenth, and my own wedding day. I could play 719, which is the day, July nineteenth, in 1968 when so many Detroiters, including Mama, hit big on Mama's pet number, 788, that it almost broke major bankers. It's also my mother's beloved grandson, Tony's, birthday. I could of course play 788, which changed my mother's life and therefore my own. Whenever I see that particular combination out in the world, I'm convinced my mother is sending me a message of some sort—*stay focused, be careful, enjoy life.* Too, I could play a certain four-digit, the combinations of 1121 that I found scribbled on that piece of paper in my mother's purse, most likely the final numbers she played. Those numbers she wrote down twenty-five years ago resonate like a future foretold, as my own family home's zip code is 11221. (And my husband's name, Rob, plays for 121 in *The Red Devil Dream Book.*)

When it's my turn, I might play one of those numbers. I *always* play two others: the first is 675, which is my home address, as I know the symbolism of playing your address. Also, 675 plays for *Fannie* in *The Red Devil.*

As for the other number: I haven't yet found a dream book that lists what *happiness* plays for, but I do know that *joy* plays for 313, which fittingly is also Detroit's area code. And so each day, six days a week, I also play 313, a fancy, because of my hometown and my mother's pursuit of happiness there, and the joy she gave me as her daughter. I play each straight and boxed for a dollar. In the past couple of years I've hit fifteen times for small money on some combination of either 313 or 675.

"You have always been lucky," Mama reminded me more

than once. She would say this as a verbal talisman for me to carry forward in the world. Whenever I hit, it's an exclamation point at the end of what my mother told me was true. But having a hit isn't the point. Playing the Numbers is my homage to Fannie Drumwright Davis Robinson, for gambling on a way of life and winning.

Acknowledgments

This book has been a nine-year odyssey. Along the way my children grew into teenagers and into an understanding that their mother was writing about her own mother. The time I spent away, often in Detroit interviewing family and friends, they accepted with maturity and grace. Both knew how important this was to me, telling their grandmother's story. My gratitude to Tyler and Abbie is immense.

This memoir exists at all because of the support and generosity of my aunt, Florence Jones, who spent tireless hours talking to me about her beloved big sister, Fannie. I am endlessly indebted to her. I'm equally indebted to my uncle, John Drumwright, a man in his nineties with a vigorous memory who also shared with me invaluable anecdotes about his favorite sister.

Rob, my first, my last, my everything, shifted universes so

I could have the space and time to write about his mother-in-law, who sadly he never met—but whom he speaks of with such fond admiration, as if he had.

I'm especially thankful for my nephew Anthony Davis II (Tony), who is in every way that matters my brother, and whose vivid account of life with Grandma provided insights that enhanced my own understanding.

I have deep appreciation for my extended family of loved ones who shared their remembrances of my mother, each with an open heart: my cousins Jewell Jones, Lisa Robinson, Elaine Franklin, Ava Christian, William Pierce, Robert Cantrell II (Junior), Alvin Cantrell (Buddy), June Drumwright, and Gene Curtis Jones; my late uncle Gene Jones; my sister-in-law Renita Plummer; and the late Alvin Cantrell II, my cousin's son, who at a dinner one evening in Nashville regaled me with funny tales of how Aunt Fannie spoiled him during his summers in Detroit.

I also thank personal and family friends who willingly shared their memories of her with me: Diane Fuselier-Thompson, Stephanie James, Elliott Ware, Linda Fegins, Jill Armenteros, Vatrize Brazoban, Michael Terrell, and Eric Beamon.

I am ever grateful to Vanessa Mobley, my brilliant editor, for her incisive yet sensitive editorial guidance. Because she understood my vision for this memoir—indeed, because she understood my mother—she helped me to tell the story I wanted to tell, yet better than I would have. The influence of her warm intelligence is all over this book. My wonderful and talented agent, Anjali Singh, advised me well through a rigorous proposal process, was tireless in her pursuit of the right home for this project, and has been my unwavering advocate and protector from day one. Ayesha Pande Literary has established an impressive roster of authors that reflects true diversity and inclusion. Reagan Arthur, Publisher of Little, Brown & Company, is a visionary, and I'm glad that she took a chance on me. My mother always said I was lucky, and I am, to be wrapped in the professional embrace of such smart and savvy women.

I owe much to Louise Meriwether, whose seminal novel *Daddy Was a Number Runner* inspired this book long before I understood that it would, and whose unflagging support and friendship has inspired me throughout recent years. I am honored by the words she wrote in my childhood copy of her book: *"My Daddy, Your Momma, were Number Runners and we are soul sisters."*

Tayari Jones graciously stepped in at a crucial moment with astute insights, guiding me down a better storytelling path. Karen Thomas listened patiently as I voiced my fears about revealing too much, offering steady doses of reassurance. Linda Villarosa effusively cheered me on along the way. Eisa Ulen and Tonya Hegamin each read early pages and gave helpful feedback. Denyce Holgate is, bar none, the best first reader of a book an author could ask for.

A special thank you to the gifted scholar Felicia Bridget George, who in 2013 miraculously found me, revealing that she was writing a dissertation on Detroit Numbers. She devoted a chapter to my mother, and in return generously gave me a plethora of documents, photos, and articles; these original materials made it possible for me to add an historical depth and context to this story that it would've otherwise lacked;

Dr. George also gave me a timely pep talk that helped me be brave on the page.

While writing this book, I was nurtured by two stays at the lovely Virginia Center for Creative Arts (VCCA), where I did early, crucial readings from my work-in-progress. I have also received generous support from Baruch College's Weissman School of Arts and Sciences, as well as PSC-CUNY's Research Award Program.

Given the plethora of published work I relied upon for context, I'm reminded anew of the important and too-often underappreciated role that scholars and thinkers and journalists play in our society. The same can be said for civil servants: Clerks at Detroit's Assessor's Office and Office of Register of Deeds patiently helped me retrieve vital documents that aided my research. Also, like gifts from the Universe dropping into my lap, many folks shared with me helpful articles and books and, best of all, personal anecdotes about the Numbers. Lots of encouragement from lots of people came my way. Transcript Divas came to the rescue.

I appreciate the entire team at Little Brown, especially Elizabeth Garriga and Ashley Marudas. Michael Noon, my production editor, deftly guided the manuscript towards its life as a bound book. My copyeditor, Barbara Perris, saved me from major errors in accuracy and navigated through a sea of numbers in need of stylebook conformity. And the design team produced a beautiful-looking book.

I'm sorry that my mother's closest friend, Lula Mae Isom, didn't live to see this book in print. She loved my mother with a mighty love, and in wondrous foresight shared treasured photographs and memorabilia with me, wanting *only* Fannie's baby to have them.

Most of all, I'm sustained by the memory of those so dear to me who loved Mama and whom Mama loved and whose presence lives on throughout these pages: John Thomas Davis, Deborah Jeanne Davis, Selena Dianne Davis, Anthony Ray Davis, Rita Renee Davis, and Burtran A. Robinson.

Life eternal.

Sources

PART I: HITSVILLE, USA

Chapter One

Sugrue, Thomas. *The Origins of the Urban Crisis: Race and Inequality in Postwar Detroit*. Princeton: Princeton University Press, 1996

Coates, Ta-Nehisi. "The Case For Reparations." *The Atlantic*, June 2014.

Satter, Beryl. *Family Properties: How the Struggle over Race and Real Estate Transformed Chicago and Urban America*. New York: Picador, 2009.

Mooney, Richard E. "Temporary Cut in Interest Sought by Administration; Kennedy Pushing Cut In Interest." *New York Times*, March 5, 1961.

PeripheryCenter.org. "Redlining: Race and Inequality in America." January 27, 2015.

Davis, Bridgett. "Broadstreet, Detroit, Michigan." *VENUE international literary magazine*, Volume 4. G&B Arts Intl.,1999.

Chapter Two

Sugrue, J. Thomas. *The Origins of the Urban Crisis: Race and Inequality in Postwar Detroit*. Princeton: Princeton University Press, 1996

White, Shane, Stephen Garton, Stephen Robertson, and Graham White. *Playing the Numbers: Gambling in Harlem Between the Wars*. Cambridge: Harvard University Press, 2010.

Gutman, Herbert G. *The Black Family in Slavery and Freedom 1750-1925*. New York: Vintage Books, 1976.

Wilkerson, Isabel. *The Warmth of Other Suns*. New York: Random House, 2010.

Wolcott, Victoria W. "Mediums, Messages and Lucky Numbers: African-American Female Spiritualists and Numbers Runners in Interwar Detroit."

The Geography of Identity ed. Yaeger, Patricia. Ann Arbor: The University of Michigan Press, 1996.

"Poor Man's Gambling: The Deadly Policy Shops and Its 'Coon Row' Gig." *Detroit Free Press,* Jan. 4, 1887.

"Policy Playing Continues." *Detroit Free Press*, March 30, 1903.

"'Policy Game' May Come Back: Colored Population of Detroit Is Interested in Resumption of Cheap Lottery." *Detroit Free Press,* July 5, 1908.

"Two Negro Gambling Houses Are Raided." *Detroit Free Press,* August 22, 1915.

Early, Gerald. *Speech and Power,* Volume 2. Hopewell: The Ecco Press, 1993.

Lewan, Todd and Barclay Delores. "Torn From the Land: A 3-Part Series." Associated Press, December 2001.

"Death Notes Charge Police Bribery: Mother Kills Girl and Self." *Detroit News,* August 7, 1939.

George, Felicia. *Numbers and Neighborhoods: Seeking and Selling the American Dream in Detroit One Bet at a Time.* PhD dissertation, Department of Anthropology, Wayne State University, 2015.

Ancestry.com: 1910 Census and 1930 Census.

Photograph of Grace McKinley walking her daughter Linda Gail McKinley to Fehr Elementary School, September 9, 1957. *Nashville Public Library, Special Collections.*

Beito, David T. and Linda Royster Beito. "The Grim and Overlooked Anniversary of the Murder of the Rev. George W. Lee, Civil Rights Activist." *History News Network.org,* May 9, 2005.

"5 Million a Year Numbers Ring in Ford Plant Found." *Washington Post,* July 3, 1948.

"More Ford Firings Loom in Gambling." *Los Angeles Times,* September 23, 1947.

"Plant Rackets." *New York Times,* December 14, 1951.

Arnesen, Eric. "'Red Summer: The Summer of 1919 and the Awakening of Black America' by Cameron McWhirter." *Chicago Tribune,* November 18, 2011

Carlisle, John M. "Chancy Games People Play." *Detroit News,* May 12, 1970.

Moore, Antonio. "The 5 Largest Landowners Own More Land Than All of Black America Combined." *HuffingtonPost.com,* October 28, 2015.

Smith, Douglas. "Anti-Lynching Law of 1928." *Encyclopedia Virginia.* Virginia Foundation for the Humanities, June 12, 2012.

"The Lynching of Emmett Till." *Black American OURStory,* black-ourstory.tumblr.com, April 6, 2015.

Wilson, August. *Fences.* New York: Samuel French, Inc., 86th edition, paperback, 2010.

"The Negro Woman: The Long Thrust Toward Economic Equality." *Ebony Magazine,* August 1966.

Chapter Three

White, Shane, Stephen Garton, Stephen Robertson, and Graham White. *Playing the Numbers: Gambling in Harlem Between the Wars.* Cambridge: Harvard University Press, 2010.

Jones, William P. *The March on Washington.* New York: W.W. Norton & Company, 2013.

Sugrue, Thomas. *The Origins of the Urban Crisis: Race and Inequality in Postwar Detroit.* Princeton: Princeton University Press, 1996

Smith, Suzanne E. *Dancing in the Street: Motown and the Cultural Politics of Detroit.* Cambridge: Harvard University Press, 1999.

George, Felicia. *Numbers and Neighborhoods: Seeking and Selling the American Dream in Detroit One Bet at a Time.* PhD dissertation, Department of Anthropology, Wayne State University, 2015.

Jefferson, Margo. *Negroland.* New York: Pantheon Books, 2015.

"41 Seized in Detroit's Largest Gambling Raid." *Los Angeles Times,* November 11, 1962.

"T-Men Hit Gotham Hotel Like Raging Football Team." *Michigan Chronicle,* November 17, 1962.

"Police Will Continue Drive Against Numbers Operators." *Michigan Chronicle,* November 24, 1962.

Remnick, David. "The Outsized Life of Muhammad Ali." *The New Yorker,* June 4, 2016.

DisasterCenter.com—Michigan Population and Number of Crimes 1960–2015.

Al, Hilton. *The Women.* New York: Farrar, Straus and Giroux, 1996.

"Stokely Carmichael Speaks on Black Power in Detroit, July 30, 1966." *Pan African News Wire,* June 15, 2006.

Calamur, Krishnadev. "Muhammad Ali and Vietnam." *The Atlantic,* June 4, 2016.

Baldwin, James. "Down at the Cross: Letter from a Region in My Mind." *The Fire Next Time.* New York: Dell Publishing Co., Inc. 1963.

Reuss, Alejandro. "That '70s Crisis." *Dollars & Sense,* November 9, 2009.

Carter, D. Swanson. *Numbers Gambling: The Negro's Illegal Response to Status Discrimination in American Society.* Master of Arts thesis, Department of Sociology, Wayne State University, 1970.

Chapter Four

Sugrue, J. Thomas. *The Origins of the Urban Crisis: Race and Inequality in Postwar Detroit.* Princeton: Princeton University Press, 1996

Smith, Suzanne E. *Dancing in the Street: Motown and the Cultural Politics of Detroit.* Cambridge: Harvard University Press, 1999.

History Channel, History.com, *Vietnam War Timeline.*
"Fountainebleau, Herald Agree On Dismissal." *Miami Herald,* April 21, 1968.

PART II: HEY, YOU NEVER KNOW

Chapter Five

George, Felicia. *Numbers and Neighborhoods: Seeking and Selling the American Dream in Detroit One Bet at a Time.* PhD dissertation, Department of Anthropology, Wayne State University, 2015.

Shafton, Anthony. *Dream-Singers: The African American Way with Dreams.* New York: John Wiley & Sons, 2002.

Wolcott, Victoria W. "Mediums, Messages and Lucky Numbers: African-American Female Spiritualists and Numbers Runners in Interwar Detroit." *The Geography of Identity* ed. Yaeger, Patricia. Ann Arbor: The University of Michigan Press, 1996.

White, Shane, Stephen Garton, Stephen Robertson, and Graham White. *Playing the Numbers: Gambling in Harlem Between the Wars.* Cambridge: Harvard University Press, 2010.

Ricke, Tom. "Numbers Runners Sell Dreams." *Detroit Free Press,* March 3, 1972.

Simmons, Zena. "Detroit's Flamboyant Prophet Jones." *Detroit News,* September 12, 1997.

Zonite, Professor. *The Original Lucky Three Wise Men Dream Book.* Annapolis: Eagle Book Supply Inc., 1972 edition.

The Lucky Red Devil Dream Book, Annapolis: Britt's Industries. 1981 Edition.

Carlton, Gustav G. *Number Gambling: A Study of a Culture Complex.* PhD dissertation, Department of Anthropology, University of Michigan, 1940.

Gibson, Walter B. and Litzka R. Gibson. *The Complete Illustrated Book of the Psychic Sciences.* New York: Pocket Books, 4th printing, 1969.

Chapter Six

George, Felicia. *Numbers and Neighborhoods: Seeking and Selling the American Dream in Detroit One Bet at a Time.* PhD dissertation, Department of Anthropology, Wayne State University, 2015.

Smith, Suzanne E. *Dancing in the Street: Motown and the Cultural Politics of Detroit.* Cambridge: Harvard University Press, 1999.

Adcock, Larry and Ralph Nelson. "58 Arrested as Betting Ring is Smashed by FBI in Detroit." *Detroit Free Press,* May 12, 1970.

Sources

Shanahan, Edward. "Wiretaps Credited in Numbers Raids." *Detroit Free Press*, May 12, 1970.

Carlisle, John H. "FBI Seizes 58 in Record Betting Roundup." *Detroit News*, May 12, 1970.

Carlisle, John H. "FBI Lists Names in Bets Raid." *Detroit News*, May 12, 1970.

Davis, Bridgett. "Write from the Start: My Mother, Fannie Mae Robinson." *Bold as Love Magazine*, May 12, 2013.

Helms, Matt. "Detroit Businesswoman Was Devoted to the City." *Detroit Free Press*, July 22, 1997.

Ricke, Tom. "Numbers Runners Sell Dreams." *Detroit Free Press*, March 5, 1972.

Ricke, Tom. "Numbers' Golden Era Fades." *Detroit Free Press*, March 6, 1972.

Ricke, Tom. "Numbers Today: A Tough Job." *Detroit Free Press*, March 7, 1972.

Carlisle, John M. "Chancy Games People Play." *Detroit News*, May 12, 1970.

"Bankers, Not Runners Real Culprits, Says Detroit Judge Crockett." *Jet Magazine*, May 4, 1972.

"New Jersey Lottery Goes Daily; Numbers Racket Is the Target." Associated Press, November 24, 1972.

Dewey, James. "Voters OK State Lottery." *Detroit Free Press*, May 16, 1972.

Vaz, Matthew. "'We Intend To Run It'": Racial Politics, Illegal Gambling, and the Rise of Government Lotteries in the United States, 1960–1985." *The Journal of American History*, June 2014.

Michigan's Official Website, Michigan.Gov/lottery. *Michigan Lottery Through the Years.*

Schuster, Gary F. "State's 1st Lottery Drawing Set for Nov. 24 at Cobo Arena." *Detroit News*, October 27, 1972.

Schuster, Gary F. "1st Winning Lottery Numbers." *Detroit News*, November 24, 1972.

Annual State Lottery Report 1973, State of Michigan Bureau of State Lottery.

"Favorite People Present at Bridgett's Sweet 16 Party." *Michigan Chronicle*, June 5, 1976.

Chapter Seven

Smith, Suzanne E. *Dancing in the Street: Motown and the Cultural Politics of Detroit*. Cambridge: Harvard University Press, 1999.

Morrison, Toni. *Conversations with Toni Morrison*, editor, Danille Taylor-Guthrie, Jackson: University Press of Mississippi, 1994.

George, Felicia. *Numbers and Neighborhoods: Seeking and Selling the American Dream in Detroit One Bet at a Time*. PhD dissertation, Department of Anthropology, Wayne State University, 2015.

Bro, Harmon H. *Edgar Cayce on Dreams*. New York: Warner Books, 1968.

Baker, Jean-Claude and Chris Chase. *Josephine: The Hungry Heart.* New York: Random House, 1993.

Hertz, Daniel. "You've Probably Never Heard of One of the Worst Supreme Court Decisions." *Washington Post,* July 24, 2014.

Young, Coleman and Lonnie Wheeler. *Hard Stuff: The Autobiography of Coleman Young.* New York: Viking, 1994.

1973 Annual Report, State of Michigan Bureau of State Lottery.

Photograph of Hermus Millsap, Michigan's first million-dollar lottery winner, February 22, 1973. *UPI.*

Photograph of Christeen Ferizis, Michigan's second million-dollar lottery winner, April 6, 1973. *UPI.*

1977 Annual Report, State of Michigan Bureau of State Lottery.

Ad for Michigan Daily 3 Lottery, *Detroit Free Press,* June 9, 1977.

Watson, Susan. "If You Dream of Winning, They've Got Your Number." *Detroit Free Press,* June 12, 1977.

PART III: LIVING TAKES GUTS

Chapter Eight

1977 Annual Report, State of Michigan Bureau of State Lottery.

DisasterCenter.com—Michigan Population and Number of Crimes 1960–2015.

Stahl, Kenneth. *The Great Rebellion: A Socio-economic Analysis of the Detroit Riot.* Livonia: Stahl, 2009.

National Institutes of Health, *Research Portfolio Online Reporting Tools (RePORT), Research Timelines: Hypertension (High Blood Pressure),* Fact Sheet.

Jangi, Sushrut, Dr. "Medicine Has a Long History of Failing Black People: Let's Change That." *Perspective Magazine,* November 2, 2016.

Chapter Nine

George, Felicia. *Numbers and Neighborhoods: Seeking and Selling the American Dream in Detroit One Bet at a Time.* PhD dissertation, Department of Anthropology, Wayne State University, 2015.

1978 Annual Report, State of Michigan Bureau of State Lottery.

Schultz, David Andrew. *Property, Power, and American Democracy.* New Brunswick: Transaction Publishers, 1992.

"State Welfare Cases Increase By 40,000." *Detroit Free Press,* November 20, 1980.

Sources

DisasterCenter.com – Michigan Population and Number of Crimes 1960-2015
"Detroit Mayor's Bid for Casinos on Island In River No Sure Bet." *Associated Press,* July 28, 1988.

Woutat, Donald and William Vance. "Chrysler Swings US Aid Deal." *Detroit Free Press,* May 11, 1980.

Burnstein, Scott. "The Drug Wars Part I." *The Gangster Report,* July 2014.

Michigan's Official Website, Michigan.Gov/lottery. *Michigan Lottery Through The Years.*

Rubenstein, Nathan. "The Daily Dream Machine." *Detroit News Magazine,* May 27, 1979.

Brodersen, Elizabeth (publications editor). *Words on Plays: Lackwanna Blues.* American Conservatory Theater, 2002.

Stroot, Bradley. "Devils Night: On the Rebellious History of Halloween." *Mask Magazine,* Maskmag.org, The Asylum Issue, October 2015.

Flanigan, Brian. "21 Locations Hit by Cops in Numbers Raid." *Detroit Free Press,* November 10, 1982.

Russell, Kim. "What Percentage of Lottery Money Goes to Michigan Schools?" *WXYZ.com,* February 12, 2016.

Chapter Ten

Butterworth, Eric. *The Universe Is Calling: Opening to the Divine Through Prayer.* New York: HarperCollins, 1994.

Ferguson, David. "We Don't 'Lose' Our Mothers—The Reality Is More Violent Than That." *The Guardian,* March 3, 2016.

Robinson, Fannie D. *617 Crawford,* novelette, unpublished.

EPILOGUE

Coy, Peter. "The Big Reason Whites Are Richer Than Blacks in America." *Bloomberg Businessweek,* February 8, 2017.

About the Author

Bridgett M. Davis is also the author of two novels, *Into the Go-Slow* and *Shifting Through Neutral*. She is writer/director of the award-winning feature film *Naked Acts* and a creative writing professor at Baruch College, where she's director of the Sidney Harman Writer-in-Residence Program. Her essays have appeared in the *Washington Post, The Millions, Salon,* and *O, The Oprah Magazine*. A graduate of Spelman College and Columbia University's Graduate School of Journalism, she lives in Brooklyn with her family. Visit her website at bridgettdavis.com.